BATTLE IN THE BALTIC

By the same author

Southern Thunder: The Royal Navy and the Scandinavian Trade in World War One

Bayly's War: The Battle for the Western Approaches in the First World War

Securing the Narrow Sea: The Dover Patrol, 1914–1918

Blockade: Cruiser Warfare and the Starvation of Germany in World War One

Formidable: A true story of disaster and courage

The Coward? The Rise and Fall of the Silver King

The Scapegoat: The life and tragedy of a fighting admiral and Churchill's role in his death

BATTLE
IN THE
BALTIC

The Royal Navy and the Fight to Save Estonia & Latvia 1918–20

STEVE R DUNN

Seaforth
PUBLISHING

Dedication

For Joseph and Eve: may they grow up without fear.

First published in Great Britain in 2020 by
Seaforth Publishing,
A division of Pen & Sword Books Ltd,
47 Church Street,
Barnsley S70 2AS

www.seaforthpublishing.com

British Library Cataloguing in Publication Data
A catalogue record for this book is available from the British Library

ISBN 978 1 5267 4273 5 (HARDBACK)
ISBN 978 1 5267 4274 2 (EPUB)
ISBN 978 1 5267 4275 9 (KINDLE)

Pen & Sword Books Limited incorporates the imprints of Atlas, Archaeology, Aviation, Discovery, Family History, Fiction, History, Maritime, Military, Military Classics, Politics, Select, Transport, True Crime, Air World, Frontline Publishing, Leo Cooper, Remember When, Seaforth Publishing, The Praetorian Press, Wharncliffe Local History, Wharncliffe Transport, Wharncliffe True Crime and White Owl.

Typeset and designed by Mousemat Design Limited
Printed and bound in Great Britain by TJ International Ltd, Padstow

CONTENTS

Appendices

List of Illustrations

Plate section between pages 96 & 97

Maps

Plates

Aft turret on the *Oleg*, 1905. (AUTHOR'S COLLECTION)

A Russian *Orfei*-class destroyer. (AUTHOR'S COLLECTION)

British squadron in Kaporia Bay in October 1919. (AUTHOR'S COLLECTION)

A copy of a painting by Cecil King (1881–1942) of Libau Harbour in February 1919. (AUTHOR'S COLLECTION)

A restored CMB on the River Thames. (PHOTO: DR V A MICHELL)

A close-up view of the torpedo launching trough aboard the CMB. (PHOTO: DR V A MICHELL)

The French armoured cruiser *Montcalm* pictured in 1902. (AUTHOR'S COLLECTION)

The crew of *CMB-4* that sank the *Oleg*. (AUTHOR'S COLLECTION)

Admiral Rosslyn Wemyss. (LIBRARY OF CONGRESS)

Admiral Walter Cowan. (© NATIONAL PORTRAIT GALLERY)

Johan Laidoner, commander of the Estonian Army. (AUTHOR'S COLLECTION)

Konstantin Päts, Estonian political leader. (AUTHOR'S COLLECTION)

K rlis Ulmanis, first Prime Minister of independent Latvia. (LIBRARY OF CONGRESS)

David Lloyd George. (AUTHOR'S COLLECTION)

The Estonian Army High Command in 1920. (AUTHOR'S COLLECTION)

General Gustav Adolf Joachim Rüdiger Graf von der Goltz. (AUTHOR'S COLLECTION)

Baron Mannerheim, Regent of Finland (seated) with his aides. (AUTHOR'S COLLECTION)

An old postcard of Dunbeath Castle, home to Rear Admiral Alexander-Sinclair. (AUTHOR'S COLLECTION)

An old postcard of Wemyss Castle, ancestral home of Admiral Rosslyn Wemyss. (AUTHOR'S COLLECTION)

Memorial to four RN admirals, Alexander-Sinclair, Cowan, Fremantle and Thesiger, erected in Tallinn by a grateful Estonian nation. (PHOTO: ERNEST BONDARENKO)

Inside of the Church of the Holy Spirit, Tallinn, showing the memorial plaque to the Royal Navy. (PHOTO: ERNEST BONDARENKO)

Memorial plaque to the Royal Navy sailors who died in the Baltic Campaign, Church of the Holy Spirit, Tallinn. (PHOTO: ERNEST BONDARENKO)

The interior of the Church of the Holy Spirit, Tallinn. (PHOTO: ERNEST BONDARENKO)

Cowan's rear admiral's flag, hanging in St Peter's Church, Kineton. (AUTHOR'S COLLECTION)

Admiral Sir Walter Cowan's tombstone at the New Cemetery, Kineton. (AUTHOR'S COLLECTION)

A Sopwith Camel 2F.1 such as was flown from HMS *Vindictive*. (AUTHOR'S COLLECTION)

'Fighting, rightly understood, is the business, the real highest, honestest business of every son of man. Everyone who is worth his salt has his enemies, who must be beaten, be they evil thoughts and habits in himself, or spiritual wickedness in high places, or Russians, or Border-ruffians, or Bill, Tom, or Harry, who will not let him live his life in quiet till he has thrashed them.'

Thomas Hughes, Tom Brown's Schooldays (1857).

'I hope that you will not have the Litany in my flagship; but if you insist will you please omit the petition where we ask to be delivered from battle, murder and sudden death. Hang it! I've never been trained for anything else.'

Rear Admiral Sir Walter Cowan to the Chaplain of HMS *Hood* in 1921.[*]

'Russia is rapidly being reduced by the Bolsheviks to an animal form of barbarism … civilisation is being completely extinguished over gigantic areas, while the Bolsheviks hop and caper like troops of ferocious baboons amid the ruins of cities and the corpses of their victims.'

Winston S Churchill, speech 24 November 1918.[‡]

'We believe that if Germany, far from making the slightest effort to carry out the peace treaty, has always tried to escape her obligations, it is because until now she has not been convinced of her defeat … We are convinced that Germany, as a nation, resigns herself to keep her pledged word only under the impact of necessity.'

Raymond Poincaré, prime minister of France, writing to his
ambassador in London, December 1922.[§]

---

[*] Quoted in Bennett, *Cowan's War*, p 54.
[‡] As cited by Gilbert, *The Stricken World*, p 227.
[§] Quoted in Norwich, *France*, p 319.

Preface

The First World War ended on 11 November 1918: except it didn't. For in Russia and its former territories, now struggling to be independent entities, the forces set loose by the Great War continued to be in conflict, a war – or more properly a set of wars – which would not end until 1921.

In the Baltic States – Estonia and Latvia in particular – the German army carried on fighting the Bolsheviks of Russia (at the demand of the Allies). German proxies battled to fulfil Teutonic dreams of a Reich-dominated eastern German border, as articulated in the German statement of war aims made in 1914 and reiterated in 1917.* In Russia, Finland and the Baltic States, White Russian forces, loyal to the monarchist cause and seeking a Tsarist restoration and the return of the Russian Empire's lost territories, warred against the newly-formed Red Army of the Bolsheviks' Trotsky and Lenin. The Bolshevik regime itself fought against its internal enemies, parties of the left and centre which were still attempting to bring about some democratic version of Russian government, with brutal repression and murder. Meanwhile the Red Army attacked to the west to recover the rich lands which it had lost when Lenin took Russia out of the World War. And British, French, American and Japanese military missions were all committed to action within Russia, supporting the White Russian armies and their disparate leaders.

---

* These included 'Poland and the Baltic group, annexed from Russia, would be under German sovereignty for "all time"' (Tuchman, *The Guns of August*, p 315). These aims were reaffirmed on 17–18 May 1917 by Germany and Austria-Hungary.

Each of these warring parties had different aims; the Japanese, who had landed at Vladivostok as early as April 1918, ultimately sought mineral wealth and territorial gain;[*] some, like the Americans, were unsure why they were there at all – they had landed on Russia's east coast as a reaction to the Japanese incursion. The Germans, or at least some of them, dreamed of a Baltic empire. The French and British, the latter country driven on by Winston Churchill against the almost complete indifference or opposition of his Cabinet colleagues, wished to crush the – as he saw it – dangerous disease of Bolshevism. The Balts wanted their independence and to be left alone to enjoy it, as did the Finns. Lenin and Trotsky sought *revanche* and a revolution that they could export to the world to bring about the downfall of the existing order of capitalism – and, of course, power for themselves.

Allied forces fought with the White Russians against the Reds in Archangel, Murmansk, Siberia, Baku and numerous other places. But it was in the Baltic that all of the interested parties, and their conflicting priorities, came together to prevent or support the formation of the neutral, independent states of Estonia and Latvia.

Into this maelstrom of conflicting loyalty, objectives and nationalist fervour was plunged the Royal Navy. Tired and weary after four hard years of war, the navy, its ships, men and commanders, were despatched in ever-increasing numbers to try to hold the ring in the Baltic Sea and its littorals. Its objectives were never clearly defined and its role constantly evolved in the face of changing events. Support from the British Parliament and people was lukewarm at best, and commanders were often left to 'make it up as they went along'. For thirteen long months, men who had expected demobilisation and a joyous return to 'a land fit for heroes'[§] were instead condemned to a cold and risky life in the confines of the Baltic Sea.

Unsurprisingly, there were complaints and eventually mutiny. But there was also considerable bravery and élan, actions at sea,

---

[*] Although to be fair, in March 1918 Japan had been requested by the ambassadors in Tokyo from Britain, France and Italy to 'take the necessary steps to safeguard Allied interests in Siberia' (*Daily Mail*, 5 March 1919). Lloyd George telegraphed President Wilson of the USA to urge him to encourage the Japanese to intervene on 17 March 1918 (Roskill, *Hankey Man of Secrets* vol 1, p 510). The primary motivation was to prevent German access to Siberia's mineral wealth.
[§] Lloyd George election campaign speech, Wolverhampton, 24 November 1918; 'What is our task? To make Britain a fit country for heroes to live in.'

three Victoria Crosses won in battle against the Bolsheviks, decisive naval gunnery support for land-based conflicts and tragic losses of ships and life. And the Royal Navy's protection for the fledgling states of Estonia and Latvia went far beyond the military. There was also humanitarian lifesaving and succour and shelter for legitimate politicians. And when a final peace was declared in early 1920, one Estonian politician noted that 'the Allied fleet rendered irreplaceable help to the fighters for freedom'.

This book is the story of the Royal Navy and its vessels, officers and sailors in the Baltic Sea between December 1918 and January 1920. It is a little-known and seldom-told tale and one which reflects small credit on the politicians who tried to deny it, or even on Britain's later colossus of war Winston Churchill who, almost alone and for deeply held personal reasons, drove the Russian campaigns on in the face of his fellow minsters' apathy or obstructionism and caused the deaths of British sailors to continue well beyond the limits of the Great War. Nonetheless it is a story which deserves its moment in the sun, as does the courage, tenacity and sheer bloody-mindedness of the British sailor and his achievements in the cold and icy Baltic Sea. That, at least, is the author's intention in the telling of this narrative; not a dry recital of facts but an account of men and their places in history.

A Note on Language and Geography
Place names in both Estonia (especially) and Latvia are often palimpsests, where over the centuries, different ruling cultures have left their linguistic mark – be they German, Russian, Polish or those used by the indigenous peoples.

In Estonia, for example, the capital and main port of Reval was referred to as such by the Royal Navy. But in fact it had changed its name to Tallinna (replacing the previously used official Germanic name of Reval) in early 1918, when Estonia became independent. In the early 1920s the official spelling of the city's name was again changed from Tallinna to Tallinn. Furthermore, the local languages themselves are difficult for Western readers: Estonian is related only to Finnish and Hungarian; and Latvian is the nearest surviving language to Sanskrit. The convention adopted in this book therefore, for ease of reading, is to use the names by which towns and cities were known to the Royal Navy at the time of the events chronicled. At the first mention, the modern name will be given in brackets, thus – Reval (Tallinn). A summary of these names is given after the Appendices.

The Bolsheviks (a name which simply meant 'majority' originally) officially announced their name change to the 'Russian Communistic Party' in March 1918. Contemporary Western speakers and writers used Bolshevik, Communist, Reds, Russians and Soviet interchangeably; this book will follow their example.

The Baltic Sea is a sea of the Atlantic Ocean, enclosed by Scandinavia, Finland, the Baltic countries, and the North and Central European Plain. The northern part of the Baltic Sea is known as the Gulf of Bothnia, of which the northernmost part is the Bay of Bothnia. The more rounded southern basin of the gulf is called the Bothnian Sea and immediately to the south of it lies the Sea of Åland. The Gulf of Finland connects the Baltic Sea with Saint Petersburg. The Gulf of Riga lies between the Latvian capital city of Riga and the Estonian island now known as Saaremaa.

On its northern coasts the Baltic is fringed with pine forests, fjords of red granite, pebble beaches and a myriad of small islands. The southern coast has a gentler aspect with a green shore lined with white sandy beaches, dunes, marshes and low mud cliffs. Long stretches have shoals and sand spits, outlying shallow lagoons, which are a constant hazard to navigation. In this flat marshy country, the rivers Neva and Dvina run into the sea (along with the Vistula and Oder which have less relevance to this story). The rivers dump their fresh water into the Baltic so that the prevailing current is outwards and for that reason it is difficult for salt water to enter and there are no tides at Riga, Stockholm or the mouth of the Neva; and the lack of salt brings the ice.

In winter the Baltic Sea is iced up for up to 45 per cent of its surface area. The ice area might typically include the Gulf of Bothnia, the Gulf of Finland, the Gulf of Riga, the archipelago west of Estonia, the Stockholm archipelago, and the Archipelago Sea south-west of Finland. The remainder of the Baltic will not freeze during a normal winter. The ice reaches its maximum extent in February or March; typical ice thickness in the northernmost areas in the Bothnian Bay, the northern basin of the Gulf of Bothnia, is about 28in. Freezing commences around the middle of November and is widespread by January or February at the latest.

Entry to the Baltic is gained via the eastern part of the North Sea, where it becomes a sort of corridor heading for the Baltic Sea, known as the Skagerrak. Then, east of a line that starts at the top of Jutland and runs north to the Swedish–Norwegian border, it becomes the Kattegat.

The Belts are the three channels connecting the Baltic Sea to the North Sea at the southern end of the Kattegat.

For consistency, the 24-hour clock is used throughout; where quotations used post/ante meridian, these have been converted. Ships' times are generally given as per the log book.

The Structure of this Book
The early chapters of this volume deal with the political, military and social situations in Russia and the Baltic States immediately preceding the arrival of Royal Navy forces and examine the reasons for them.

The book then chronicles the Royal Navy's deployment and actions in the Baltic, its leadership, victories, losses and achievements, together with the political considerations which dictated the navy's role.

Finally, the concluding section critically examines the successes and failures of the campaign, and its participants, and goes on to consider both the future careers of some of the key players in the story in the aftermath of the operations and how the Baltic nations remember and celebrate the Royal Navy's support and sacrifice.

The story is told in chronological order, but a strict chronology is sacrificed when it is logical to finish one aspect of the tale before commencing another. There is thus some, hopefully forgivable, temporal overlap.

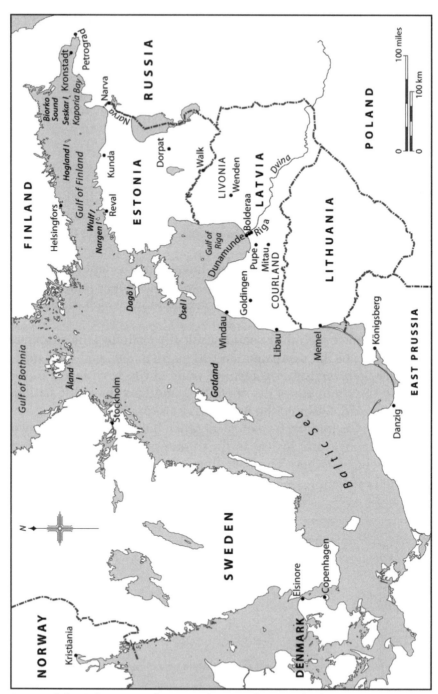

A map of the Baltic Sea and surroundings, indicating the key towns and ports mentioned in the text. (PETER WILKINSON)

CHAPTER 1

The Decline of the Russian Empire, 1904–1917

In the aftermath of the First World War, many new nations, or proto-nations, were called into being, primarily from the ruins of the German, Austro-Hungarian and Turkish empires. But in the Baltic, the emergence of Finland, Lithuania, Latvia and Estonia as separate polities was fathered by the collapse of the Romanov dynasty and the subsequent Treaty of Brest-Litovsk, and threatened by the rise of Bolshevism and German post-war ambitions in the East. And in the case of Estonia and Latvia, if the ruination of Russia was the father of independence, then the Royal Navy was their guardian and guarantor during the harsh thirteen months that immediately followed the end of worldwide hostilities.

In order to properly understand the forces, political and military, which acted both for and against these countries' nationhood, and which the navy had to contend with, it is necessary to start this story with a brief review of the Russian revolution of 1917 and the treaty with Germany which followed it, bringing a temporary respite to the fighting in the East.

In 1914, Russia was the largest autocratic empire in the world; from the Siberian wastes to the Baltic Sea, it bestraddled the Occident and the Orient like a colossus. But it was a giant with a rotten core, a decaying *sequoiadendron giganteum*, ruled by an increasingly out-of-touch Tsar, Nicholas II, and containing the festering sores of revolution, both on the political left and on the right. Russia may have had the largest population and army of all the combatants in the First World War, but the masses were largely uneducated peasants and the army both strategically backward and poorly equipped, especially in the areas of artillery and communications.

A map of the Gulf of Finland, with an insert showing the Russian Kronstadt base and its protective forts. (PETER WILKINSON)

There was a notional parliament, the Duma, but in reality all decisions were concentrated in the hands of the Tsar, weak, uxorious, shy, religious and increasingly unloved by the people he claimed to rule. This had not always been the case; Nicholas II came to the throne in 1894 after the assassination of his father with the peasantry thinking him still the 'Great Father' and the landowning nobility prepared to tolerate Tsarism if it continued to uphold their privileges. But support for him ebbed away amongst the on-going tragedies and repression of his reign; and if one event can be said to have represented the turning point in the nation's opinion of their Tsar was the Russo-Japanese War of 1904–5.

The war was largely Tsar Nicholas's doing: he was an 'easterner', looking to the large and unexploited lands in Russia's eastern provinces and seeing the potential for vast wealth and benefit from the exploitation of them. But to make this a reality, one of the *desiderata* was a warm-water port on the Pacific coast to act as a base for the Russian navy and for the increase of maritime trade and access to the Pacific markets.

The Russian mainland port of Vladivostok was operational only during the summer, due to winter ice, whereas Port Arthur, a naval base in Liaodong Province which was leased to Russia by China, was operational all year. Japan feared Russian encroachment on its own plans to create a sphere of influence in Korea and Manchuria. Seeing Russia as a rival, Japan offered to acknowledge Russian dominance in Manchuria in exchange for recognition of Korea as being within the Japanese sphere. Russia demurred and demanded that Korea north of the 39th Parallel be established as a neutral buffer zone between the two countries. After negotiations broke down in 1904, the Japanese Navy opened hostilities by launching a surprise attack on the Russian Far East Fleet based at Port Arthur and without a declaration of war; the Russian fleet was neutralised and later largely destroyed by artillery fire in the siege that followed.

In the resulting war, the Russian Far East and Baltic Fleets were destroyed, the latter at the Battle of Tsushima on 27–28 May 1905 where the Russian armada was annihilated, losing eight battleships and numerous smaller vessels, while sustaining 4,380 men dead and another 5,917 sailors captured, including two admirals. The Japanese lost only three torpedo boats and 116 sailors. And on land Russia's armies were repeatedly bested, concluding with the Battle of Mukden, where they suffered almost 90,000 casualties.

At home in Russia, public opinion was firmly against the war and revolution was in the air. The Imperial Russian government was rocked by an uprising from the political left and the population was against any further escalation of the war. Tsar Nicholas elected to negotiate peace with Japan, so he and his ministers could concentrate on the internal dissent set loose by the disastrous war, and a peace treaty was eventually signed under the auspices of US President Theodore Roosevelt on 5 September 1905 at the Portsmouth Naval Shipyard on Seavey's Island, Kittery, Maine.

It was a humiliation for Nicholas. Russia had been defeated on land and at sea by the supposedly racially inferior 'yellow men' so despised by most Russians (and by many in other Western countries). As the historian Dominic Lieven has put it 'no-one with inside knowledge of the Russian government could doubt that the emperor was primarily responsible for Russia's debacle in East Asia and his reputation never recovered'.[1] Not since the Crimean War had Russia suffered such a defeat and at least then, Russians told themselves, they had been beaten by the great European powers, not by a single Asiatic enemy. All sections of society were united, at least temporarily, in the view that change was necessary and here were sown the seeds of eventual revolution. It was the beginning of the end for the Romanov dynasty.

Revolution forced Nicholas to cede various powers to the Duma and appoint ministers more in favour with the masses, but over time he was able to take back his autocratic control and appoint to power men who were compliant with his wishes or simply too incompetent to oppose him. He began to rebuild his navy with expensive dreadnoughts – a navy being the toy box of choice for all monarchs in the early twentieth century – but at a cost which denuded the army of equipment and the people of food. Russia, humiliated repeatedly by Austria-Hungary over the latter's annexations of Bosnia-Herzegovina in the years after the Russo-Japanese war, and militarily still trying desperately to rebuild her armies after that disaster, was eventually pushed too far over the Austrian desire for revenge on, and the destruction of, Serbia, using the assassination of Archduke Franz Ferdinand as a *casus belli*. On 31 July 1914 Russia mobilised for war – and the world mobilised with her.

The Baltic Russian Empire

Russia 'owned' the Baltic Sea. Finland was an Imperial Duchy whose Grand Duke was the Tsar. St Petersburg (Petrograd from 1914) was both the seat of government and the site of the Baltic Fleet's base, on and around the island fortress of Kronstadt, at the head of the Gulf of Finland – although ice-locked in winter, necessitating the fleet to move to Helsingfors (Helsinki) as winter quarters. The eastern Baltic coast was dominated by the Russian estates of Estonia, Livonia and Courland, the latter two of which comprise in some part modern Latvia.

German influence was strong in the region. It dated back to the late twelfth century when, frustrated in the Holy Land, German crusading orders decided instead to subdue the pagan tribes of the eastern Baltic. This Teutonic Order of Knights prospered and in 1346 purchased the lands which became Estonia and Latvia from the Danes.

When these regions were absorbed into the Russian Empire in 1721, Tsar Peter the Great confirmed the privileged position of the Baltic Germans, as did his successors up to the time of Alexander III and his late nineteenth-century policy of Russification in his western lands. From 1845 to 1876, the Baltic governorates of Estonia, Livonia, and Courland were administratively subordinated to a common Governor-General.

In Courland in 1863, the Russian authorities issued laws to enable Latvians, who formed the bulk of the population, to acquire the farms which they held from their Germanic owners, and special banks were founded to help them. Some tenants were successful in acquiring their farms but the great majority of the population remained landless, and lived as hired labourers, dominated by German elites.

In both Latvia and Estonia, the German influence extended to language, culture and particularly land holding and wealth. The population of Riga, for example, was 280,000 in 1897, of whom 22 per cent were German speakers and 45 per cent Latvian.[2] In the whole of Livonia,* the German 'nobility' represented but 2 per cent of the population but owned between 60 and 74 per cent of the land.[3] Ruling as proxies for the Tsar and enforcing their control through their ownership of vast agricultural estates (*Ritterschaften*),

---

* A term for a medieval region, brought back into use to describe the province of Tsarist Russia which approximately encompassed (until 1918) Estonia, Livonia and Courland.

these German Barons effectively ran the country as a quasi-German colony under the suzerainty of Russia.

In 1905, when Russia rose in revolt during and after the Russo-Japanese War, Estonian peasants revolted against their German masters and 184 manors were burned to the ground with eighty-two Baltic German landowners killed.[4] There was widespread anarchy through the winter of 1905–6. In January 1906, the British consul in Riga asked for the intervention of the Royal Navy and the landing of parties of Marines to protect British lives and property from the Latvian revolutionaries, who he described as 'very prone to violence, armed to the teeth and enjoying mass support'.[5] The British government did not respond but Kaiser Wilhelm II of Germany promised Professor Theodore Schuman, a leading spokesman for the Baltic German 'Barons' in Berlin's corridors of power, that if the Russian monarchy fell, 'Germany would not abandon the Balts'.[6] With Baltic nationalist forces on the rise, the position of the Baltic Germans came under pressure; they reacted by entrenching themselves in their privileges and opposing all attempts at change. Repressive governance became the norm.

And when the German army marched into the region in 1915, following Russia's great retreat after the Second Battle of the Masurian Lakes, Courland came under control of the German Eastern Front army headed by *Oberbefehlshaber der gesamten Deutschen Streitkräfte im Osten* (Supreme Commander of All German Forces in the East), Paul von Hindenburg and General Erich Ludendorff. The previous Russian authorities of the Courland Governorate were permanently exiled to Dorpat (Tartu) and Courland District was made one of three districts of the region, which was known as *Ober Ost*.

With dominion on land assured, German naval forces also controlled the Baltic Sea. They were assisted by the Danes and Swedes who, under German pressure, mined the key entrance and exit channels. The Russian Baltic fleet was largely confined to its Kronstadt base. As one historian noted 'the Baltic battleships achieved nothing ... on the other hand the army's shortage of heavy artillery ... contributed to its failure in the field against the Germans'.[7]

The Russian Revolution

Russian losses in the field became unbearable. Nicholas had placed himself at the army's head in September 1915; but he was no field commander and his lack of ability only made matters worse. Total losses for the spring and summer of 1915 amounted to 1,400,000 killed or wounded, while 976,000 had been taken prisoner. The Brusilov Offensive of June to September 1916 was the Russian Empire's apogee of arms during the war but it also cost one million casualties and broke the Russian army.

By early 1917, Russia was on the verge of complete collapse. The army had taken 15 million men from the farms and hence food prices had soared. An egg cost four times what it had in 1914, butter five times as much. And her armed forces had been crippled for months by horrific casualties, which when coupled with high rates of desertion and endemic indiscipline, rendered them almost nugatory as fighting units.

On 23 February 1917, a combination of very severe cold weather and acute food shortages in Petrograd caused people to start to break shop windows to get bread and other necessities. In the streets, red banners appeared and the crowds chanted 'Down with the war! Down with the Tsar'. Troops, even the elite and previously loyal Guards and Cossack units, proved unwilling to put down the protest and joined the rioters. Order broke down and members of the Duma and the Petrograd workers Soviet formed a Provisional Government to try to restore calm. They issued a demand that Nicholas must abdicate. Far from Petrograd, and isolated from his advisors, his military commanders advised Nicholas that he no longer commanded the support of the army and should abdicate as Tsar. On 15 March he did so and Prince Lvov, described as 'an other-worldly Tolstoyian dreamer'[8] and thus an unlikely leader in any situation far less in the middle of revolution, formed a government.

Anxious to ferment further trouble in Russia and try to take her out of the war altogether, Germany arranged for the Bolshevik leader Vladimir Lenin to be shipped by special train from Switzerland to Petrograd's Finland Station. In July he made a bid for power and failed, leading to temporary exile. Governments came and went and a further revolution, this time from the political right, was abandoned without a shot being fired. Following this failure, in September the Petrograd Soviet established a Military Revolutionary Committee, composed mainly of Bolsheviks and with Leon Trotsky as its chairman, to coordinate the defence of the capital against German attack, but also to prevent counter-revolution by forces of liberal or right wing/monarchist leanings. Lenin, in hiding in

Finland, returned to Petrograd under cover, urging a new revolution; and the Soviets in Petrograd and Moscow became dominated by the extremist left.

On 7 November 1917, and after further political manoeuvring, Lenin led his Bolshevik revolutionaries in a revolt against the ineffective Provisional Government. This 'October Revolution'* finally replaced Russia's short-lived provisional parliamentary government with an administration based on soviets, local councils elected by bodies of workers and peasants and dominated by the Bolsheviks (see Appendix 1 for a more detailed chronology).

One immediate consequence of the Bolshevik seizure of power was that Russia was plunged into a civil war. As the *Daily Telegraph* of 14 December reported 'Civil War is now no longer a probability but a fact'. A loose confederation of anti-Bolshevik forces joined together against the Bolshevik government,§ including landowners, republicans, conservatives, middle-class citizens, reactionaries, pro-monarchists, liberals and ex-army generals and became known as the 'Whites', fighting against the Bolshevik Red Army. Additionally, Lenin and his supporters found themselves at loggerheads with non-Bolshevik socialists and democratic reformers, in league only as a result of their shared opposition to Bolshevik rule. The Bolsheviks attacked this faction with terror tactics and murder, forcing them too into the White alliance.

The White armies were led by three former Tsarist officers, Generals Yudenitch and Denikin and Admiral Kolchak, the notional leader. Of most interest to the Baltic story was General Nikolai Nikolayevich Yudenitch, who would eventually (in 1919) lead the White army operating against the Bolsheviks in the Baltic Sea area and in north-west Russia.

Progressively, the Whites were supported by the Allies in an attempt to keep Russia in the war. For Britain and her allies, the collapse of Russia into Bolshevism presented a huge headache. There were some 600,000 tons of munitions and military equipment together with 650,000 tons of coal at Archangel alone which had been sent to Russia by the United States, Britain and France and were presently in danger of falling into either German or Bolshevik

* Russia was still using the Julian calendar at the time, so period references show the date as 25 October, and the event is known to Russians as the October Revolution.
§ The word 'Communist' was not incorporated into their self-description until March 1918, when the party was named 'Communist Party of Bolsheviks' or 'Russian Communistic Party'.

hands. Furthermore, it was feared that the vast agricultural and natural resources of Russia now accessible to Germany would render the Allied 'starvation blockade' ineffective. Germany could now establish a submarine base on Russia's northern coast. And finally there was a widespread belief that Bolsheviks were German agents and that therefore, a strike against the Bolsheviks was a strike against Germany. Winston Churchill, Minister for Munitions at the time, later noted that 'in such circumstances, it would have been criminal negligence to make no effort to reconstruct an anti-German front in the East, and so to deny the vast resources of Russia in food and fuel to the Central Powers'.[9]

So troops and supplies were sent to Russia by Britain, Japan, France and the United States to assist and advise those Russians willing to continue the war against Germany and the Bolsheviks. And to protect the arms dumps, of course. Cost was seemingly no object; on 14 December 1917 the British War Cabinet decided to give the Whites money as long as they continued to resist the Central Powers.[*]

Meanwhile, in the Baltic region, the Germans launched a major offensive on the Eastern Front. On 1 September, 8th Army troops under General Oscar von Hutier mounted an operation to cross the River Dvina (Daugava) and take the port of Riga. They achieved stunning success. By the 3rd, Riga was in German hands and the Russians had sustained 25,000 casualties compared to just 4,000 for Germany. At the same time, an amphibious assault, Operation 'Albion', invaded the West Estonian archipelago landing at Ösel Island (Saarenmaa) and taking the entire island group. Nineteen troop ships and twenty-one supply vessels were screened by destroyers, cruisers and battleships while minesweepers worked in front of them. The success of this operation allowed the Germans to outflank the Russians, threatening Petrograd with bombardment and invasion. Such success irked ex-First Sea Lord 'Jacky' Fisher, now Lord Fisher, whose own pet plan had always been for the Royal Navy to stage a landing of the army on Germany's Baltic coast. Writing to Winston Churchill on 9 September he noted that headlines in the newspapers such as 'Landing the German Army

---

[*] 'Any sum of money, required for the purpose of maintaining alive in South-East Russia the resistance to the Central Powers, considered necessary by the War Office, in consultation with the Foreign Office, should be furnished; the money to be paid in instalments so long as the recipients continued the struggle' (CAB/23/4, NA).

South of Reval' and 'German Fleet Assist Land Operations in the Baltic' had much upset him. It moved him to tell Churchill that 'we are five times stronger at sea than our enemies and here is a small fleet that we could gobble up in minutes playing the great vital sea part of landing an army in the enemy's rear and probably capturing the Russian capital by sea'. Hell hath no fury like an admiral whose favourite plan has been enacted by his foe.

The drive to dominate the Baltic coast was a particular enthusiasm of Erich Ludendorff, by now effectively co-dictator of Germany with von Hindenburg, who saw two great benefits in this strategy; firstly, as a base for a drive on Petrograd in 1918; and secondly, solidarity with the Baltic Barons and the opportunity to create a German enclave and buffer in the East. Indeed, since the winter of 1915–16 the German army had occupied present-day Lithuania, western Latvia, and north-eastern Poland, an area almost the size of France, and Ludendorff had shown himself to be strongly in favour of Germanization of these newly acquired territories and of offering land to German settlers. He foresaw Courland and Lithuania turned into border states ruled by a German military governor answerable to the Kaiser and proposed huge annexations and colonisation in Eastern Europe once victory was achieved. Unsurprisingly, these ideas were welcomed by the Baltic Barons.

The German advance was received with trepidation in Britain. Prime Minister Lloyd George thought that if the Germans controlled Courland and Lithuania then 'two great empires would emerge from the war', whilst Lord Milner* declared to the War Cabinet of 24 September that he could foresee Germany 'coming out of the war more powerful than she had entered it and another war in ten years' time'.[10] The October Revolution of 1917 also gave the Finns the opportunity to seek independence and self-determination. On 15 November 1917, the Bolsheviks had declared a general right of self-determination 'for the Peoples of Russia' including the right of complete secession. On the same day the Finnish Parliament issued a declaration by which it took power in Finland. The non-socialists in the Finnish parliament proposed that parliament itself declare Finland's independence, which was voted through on 6 December 1917 and approved by the Soviets a little later. Both

---

* Alfred Milner, 1st Viscount Milner, a member of the War Cabinet since December 1916 and who would become Secretary of State for War in April 1918.

Germany and Sweden (on 4 January 1918) also recognised Finland's new independent status.* The declaration, known as the 'Rights of the Nations of Russia' had encompassed Lithuania, Latvia and Estonia, but as these proto-states were under the German heel this was hardly a consideration.

The autocratic Russian empire was over. The people of the Baltic States were largely under German domination. On the other side of the Baltic, Finland was in turmoil. Rival armies were beginning to rampage across the old Russian empire. The global war was still in progress; and nobody knew what was going to happen next.

---

* Finland descended into a civil war in January 1918, between pro- and anti-Bolshevik factions, Red and White, the former supported by the Bolsheviks and the latter by Germany.

CHAPTER 2

The Treaty of Brest-Litovsk and its Consequences, 1917–1918

Lenin and his Bolsheviks desperately needed a cessation of the war with Germany. It had been a key part of their 'manifesto' before the assumption of power; additionally, the Russian army was in chaos and had effectively stopped fighting and Lenin's overwhelming priority was to cement his authority and see off the multitude of internal enemies that the Bolsheviks now found themselves contending with. A newspaper reporter based in Petrograd described the situation;

> The Bolsheviks are the *de facto* rulers of Petrograd and Moscow and, to a certain extent, of an ill-defined territory in the neighbourhood of those cities. The *Rada* rules the Ukraine, again with incompletely defined frontiers. The Cossacks control the Northern Caucasus and an independent coalition composed of the local Nationalist and Moderate Socialist parties rules Transcaucasia. The Ural territory is largely controlled by the local Cossacks, who have in the Tartars semi-rivals and semi-allies. An independent government is slowly taking root in Siberia ... Finland has declared its independence with great emphasis.[1]

As the historian Orlando Figes put it 'a separate peace with Germany would give the Bolsheviks the breathing space they needed to consolidate their power base, restore the economy and build up their own revolutionary army'.[2] Accordingly, on 8 November 1917 (one day after his coup), Lenin signed the Decree on Peace, which was approved by the Second Congress of the Soviet of Workers', Soldiers' and Peasants' Deputies. The Decree called upon 'all the belligerent nations and their governments to start immediate negotiations for peace' and proposed an immediate withdrawal of Russia from the war. Leon Trotsky was appointed Commissar of Foreign Affairs and was tasked with overseeing the process. By 15 December an armistice between Soviet Russia and the Central Powers (Germany, Austria-Hungary and Bulgaria) was concluded and negotiations commenced in the town of Brest-Litovsk* on the 22nd.

The Bolshevik negotiating position was 'no annexations or indemnities'. They were soon disabused of this rather naïve objective, for Germany and Austria-Hungary planned to annex slices of Polish territory and then set up a rump Polish state with what remained, while the Baltic provinces were to become client states ruled by German princes. They were concerned to create barrier states against any future Russian expansion. Distressed and without a fall-back position, the Bolsheviks decided to play for time, hoping that their quondam allies would agree to join the negotiations or that the Western European proletariat would revolt. Trotsky himself now took control of the process and looked to prolong the negotiations.

This book will not detail the tortuous process of the forging of an agreement but summary of how things unfolded is important for the narrative to come. Trotsky's tactics progressively infuriated the German delegation. The Germans fell out amongst themselves as to whether or not they should seek annexations of large tracts of western Russia. Ludendorff continued to press for the Baltic States and declared himself willing to hand over Austrian Galicia to the Russians (without, one assumes, telling the Austrians) so long as Germany could get them. The Ukrainians declared independence from Soviet Russia and in January 1918 the Bolsheviks invaded to prevent it. The Ukrainian *Rada* (parliament) sent a deputation to Brest-Litovsk to ask Germany for assistance. This led to Germany agreeing a separate peace with Ukraine on 27 January and 9 February (the 'Bread Peace') in which Ukraine agreed to supply Germany and Austria-Hungary with an annual one million tons of badly-needed wheat and other foodstuffs in return for recognition of the newly declared Ukrainian People's Republic (UNR).

---

* The town had been captured by the German army in 1915. It lies in modern-day Belarus at the confluence of the Bug and Mukhavets Rivers.

Furthermore, frustrated by Trotsky's Fabian tactics, Germany withdrew from the peace conference and resumed hostilities against Russia. On 16 February the German delegation notified Soviet Russia that the war would resume in two days. Fifty-three divisions advanced against the near-empty Russian trenches and, meeting little or no opposition, they made significant inroads into Russia's western territories. German troops kept advancing until 23 February when Germany presented new terms, ones which now included the withdrawal of all Russian troops from the Ukraine and Finland.

Panicked, Lenin insisted that Russia sign a treaty, any treaty. In the teeth of opposition from Trotsky, Lenin told the Central Committee that they must sign the peace in order to save the world revolution. A continuation of the war would destroy both him and his party. The treaty was finally signed on 3 March; Trotsky resigned his position in protest.

The terms of the Treaty of Brest-Litovsk were extremely onerous on Soviet Russia. She was forced to 'cede Ukraine as an independent country in principle and a German satellite in practice'.[3] The eight provinces of the Ukraine were massively important to Russia. In 1914 they had produced 33 per cent of its wheat, 80 per cent of its sugar, 70 per cent of its coal, 68 per cent of its cast iron and 50 per cent of its steel. Additionally, Russia was stripped of Courland, Riga, the Estonian Islands,[*] Lithuania, the Caucasus and Bessarabia, losing one-third of her population. She was also made to renounce all claims to Finland. The territory of the Kingdom of Poland was not mentioned in the treaty, because Russian Poland had been a personal fief of the Tsar and not part of the Empire, but it nonetheless became a German/Austrian 'possession'. As soldier and historian Major General Clifford Kinvig has written, 'the Treaty of Brest-Litovsk represents one of the most savage settlements ever imposed by one state on another'.[4] Russia was out of the war; but at a huge price.

Further Consequences

The demarche allowed Germany to begin the process of shifting men from the Eastern Front to that in the West, boosting the manpower available for a major offensive against Britain and France in early 1918. This process had actually started even before the

---

[*] Soviet Russia renounced its sovereignty over the rest of Estonia in a separate accord on 27 August.

Armistice had been signed. On 14 December 1917, the British War Cabinet heard from Major General Sir George Mark Watson Macdonogh, Director of Military Intelligence, that the Military Attaché in Petrograd, General Alfred William Fortescue Knox, had 'reported that the Germans were moving the greater part of their heavy artillery from the Eastern front to the West'.[5]

But there were other immediate geographic and naval consequences resultant upon the signing of the treaty. On 12 March the Soviets transferred the government to Moscow, to keep it safely away from the now perilous border.* There was possibly another reason too. After the signing of the treaty, Germany began to release Russian prisoners of war, although they held back the more able-bodied as labourers given the depletion of Germany's manpower resources by the needs of the army. Under the auspices of Red Cross societies, a few thousand invalids daily were released to return to Russia; thus did the so-called Spanish Flu enter the country, although it had already been reported in Odessa. Influenza joined typhus as a joint epidemic swept through Russia; and a doctor in Petrograd wrote that the diseases 'follow Lenin's communism like the shadow follows the passer-by'.[6]

The treaty required the Soviets to evacuate their naval base at Helsingfors (where the Baltic Fleet was overwintering) in March 1918 or have the ships interned by newly independent Finland. Despite the Gulf of Finland being frozen over, the fleet sailed for Kronstadt on 12 March in what became known as the 'Ice Voyage'. Led by the new battleship *Sevastopol* (twelve 12in guns) and her sisters *Gangut*, *Petropavlovsk* and *Poltava*, they completed the crossing in five days. These ships, so expensively built (at the Tsar's insistence) to defend the Baltic against the Germans, had not fired a shot during the war and their crews had joined a general mutiny on 16 February 1917 after they received word of the February Revolution in Petrograd. Now they sheltered impotently behind the guns and minefields of the Kronstadt forts.

As for the Baltic States, they were a German fiefdom. Latvia had suffered terribly during the war, not least from its Russian overlords. By May 1915 the war had enveloped most of Latvia, with Libau (Liepāja) being taken on 7 May. In the face of the German success,

---

* The day before the peace treaty was signed, German planes dropped bombs on Petrograd. Lenin was convinced that the Germans intended to take the city and remove the Bolsheviks.

the Russian Supreme Command ordered the whole population of Courland evacuated on 29 June and conducted a scorched earth policy, burning crops and housing as they retreated; around 500,000 refugees fled to the east. This was followed in July by the evacuation of all productive materials from Riga, with 30,000 railway wagons loaded with machines and equipment from local factories taken away and the population reduced by some 50 per cent.

A public proclamation by Latvian State Duma members led to the formation of volunteer Latvian Riflemen units and from 1915 to 1917 these Riflemen fought in the Russian army against the Germans in defensive positions along the Daugava River. In December 1916 and January 1917, they suffered heavy casualties in the month-long 'Christmas Battles' and in September they strove to prevent the Germans taking Riga,[*] fighting on the defensive at the Battle of Jugla. After hours of German bombardment, the Russians fled and columns of Germans marched into Riga. German submarines entered the Gulf and shelled the villages of the littoral. Riga had fallen and Germany finally gained complete control of the entire Courland/Latvian region.

Now the Treaty of Brest-Litovsk supervened to give the Courland and Livonian Governorates to the Germans, who quickly established a regime of occupation which lasted until the Armistice. During this time Germans tried to create a new state, the United Baltic Duchy, in perpetual union with the Crown of Prussia, a project much favoured by the Baltic Barons. German royalty bickered over who should rule the new Baltic States. The Kaiser himself coveted Courland; and indeed, on 5 November the Germans proclaimed the United Baltic Duchy, to be ruled by Duke Adolf Friedrich of Mecklenburg. This project (just like the similar Kingdom of Lithuania) collapsed together with the German Empire at the Armistice. The Duke of Urach had wanted to be King of Lithuania; he had been offered the throne as King Mindaugas II on 13 July 1918 but was never crowned; the Austrian Archduke Wilhelm Franz von Hapsburg (aka Vasil the Embroidered) schemed for the throne of Ukraine and the Kaiser's brother-in-law, Prince Friedrich Karl of Hesse, had designs on Finland (and was asked by the Finnish nationalists to accept the throne in October 1918).

After the occupation of Riga in September 1917, the Germans had

---

[*] Controlled by a Bolshevik-dominated Soviet.

also entered parts of Estonia. But the Baltic Germans' estates and fortunes throughout the region had been threatened by both the revolutionary provisional governments in Petrograd and, after the October Revolution, by the Bolsheviks. The Baltic Barons appealed for help and protection which eventually led to German troops fully occupying both Latvian and Estonian territory in February 1918.

Before then the nationalist movement in Estonia had seized the brief opportunity afforded by the ceasefire of 15 December 1917 to declare a republic. At the head of the Estonian independence movement was Konstantin Päts. In 1917, Päts had led the Provincial Government of the Autonomous Governorate of Estonia but had been forced to go into hiding after the October Revolution. On 19 February 1918, Päts became one of the three members of the Estonian Salvation Committee that issued the Estonian Declaration of Independence on 24 February. It was the first time that Estonia had been an independent nation for 700 years.

This brief flicker of nationalism was soon snuffed out by the arrival of German troops and Päts was imprisoned during the second half of the German occupation; he did not return to his position and power until 20 November 1918. Despite this subjection, the Estonian Provincial Assembly had sent envoys abroad and they were able to exploit Allied fears of Germany and of the spread of Bolshevism to gain some diplomatic recognition of their proto-republic from Britain, France and Italy in May 1918.[*] And in October, Britain accorded the Latvian Provisional National Council the same dignity. Henceforth, the future status of the Baltic provinces was 'transformed into an international issue to be decided at the peace conference at the end of the war, rather than just an internal Russian matter'.[7]

The German occupation was anything but benign. According to British Foreign Secretary A J Balfour 'announcing themselves as liberators, they [the Germans] divided up the whole region by frontiers, which deliberately violated national sentiment; they imposed commercial treaties with the most cynical indifference to the interests of anyone but themselves; and they compelled the use of German in schools where no German child was in the habit of attending'.[8]

[*] Great Britain (3 May), France (13 May) and Italy (29 May) recognised *de facto* the Estonians and their representative body (the *Diet*), but not the new state. A temporary Estonian embassy was established in London.

The flame of Baltic independence had momentarily fluttered before it was extinguished; but the Reich itself was soon to die. The moment was close, but not yet nigh, for Phoenix to rise once more from the ashes of empire.

Armistice and Anarchy

The Global War ended with the Armistice on 11 November 1918, at 1100: but not in the Baltic States. Lenin had declared that 'the Baltic must become a Soviet sea'[9] and a spirit of *revanche* was alive in him and his comrades. Russia wanted her territories back for reasons of both economic need and of self-defence.

Two days after the Armistice, the Red Army, now under the overall command of Trotsky,* advanced on the western borderlands of the former Tsar's empire. They met little resistance.

Article XII of the Armistice Terms had laid down that the Germans were to withdraw from the territory which previously formed part of the Russian Empire 'as soon as the Allies shall think the moment suitable, having regard to the internal situation in those territories', and Article XIV of those terms adumbrated that 'German troops were to cease at once all requisitioning and seizures and all other coercive measures with, a view to obtaining supplies intended for Germany … in Russia'.

The Germans did not comply with those terms; they began to withdraw from the Baltic States systematically and seemingly in cooperation with the Bolsheviks. According to contemporary British reports 'this withdrawal was carried out systematically, the evacuation of towns being made to coincide with entry of the Bolshevik troops and, as has been proved, by direct agreement with the latter. At the same time, advance arms, supplies and rolling stock were left by the Germans for use by the Bolsheviks. In addition to assisting the Bolsheviks in this manner, everything was done by the Germans to hinder the organisation and execution of measures for the defence on the part of the newly-formed local governments.'[10] Stocks and arms were removed or destroyed; supplies of food and clothing were confiscated; railway rolling stock was seized and conveyed to Germany; Estonian merchant vessels were appropriated; and telegraphic communications were disrupted.

On the day of the Armistice, an Estonian Provisional Government

---

* He was appointed People's Commissar for Military Affairs on 14 March 1918.

(the *Maapäev*) was formed with Konstantin Päts again at its head. But the local Estonian armed forces were unprepared for the Bolshevik advance; Narva was taken on 29 November and by 10 January 1919 the Red Army was within 45 miles of Reval. In Latvia, the head of the Latvian Farmers' Union, the American-educated (and educator) Kārlis Ulmanis,[*] became one of the principal founders of the Latvian National Council[§] (*Tautas Padome*), which proclaimed Latvia's independence from Russia on November 18, 1918 with Ulmanis as the first Prime Minister. But the Red Army's advance was made easier in Latvia for there were many Bolshevik sympathisers in the area[†] (Lenin's personal bodyguard was Latvian). Riga was taken on 3 January and Ulmanis's government was forced to fall back on Libau whilst Bolshevik troops occupied most of the former Livonia.

Lenin lost no time in establishing Bolshevik-sponsored *soi-disant* governments in both countries; in Latvia, the 'Latvian Soviet Republic' and in Estonia a much smaller organisation, 'The Commune of the Working People', with its headquarters at Narva. Both swiftly began to enact Bolshevik doctrine, 'including the expropriation and nationalisation of property and land in the hands of the middle classes, while suppressing the population with brutal force'.[11]

The Allies watched the Russian advance with deep misgivings. As they had no forces in the region they exercised their rights under the Armistice to ask the German government to halt its withdrawal of forces from the region and act to stop the Bolshevik advance (under Article XII of the Armistice, see Appendix 2). And the German Baltic Baron element now felt themselves severely threatened; they had effectively ruled Latvia through their *Ritterschaften* council since the revolution. But now the Ulmanis government was in charge, although seemingly existing in parallel with the Bolshevik-backed Soviets. And marching for the Bolsheviks against Latvia were Latvians, the Latvian Rifle Regiment, battle-hardened men who had 'saved' the revolution when in July 1918 they prevented socialist revolutionaries in Moscow from toppling Lenin's dictatorship. They saw themselves as the true liberators of Latvia and mistrusted Ulmanis's government as being too close to the Germans, both Baltic and otherwise.

---

[*] Ulmanis was a quondam member of the faculty at the University of Nebraska.
[§] Which comprised all political parties in Latvia except the Bolsheviks.
[†] In the elections to the Russian Constituent Assembly in November 1917, 72 per cent of the Latvian vote was for the Bolsheviks.

Desperate for military support against the Red Army, on 29 December, immediately before the fall of Riga and with Allied agreement, Ulmanis called for the formation of a self-defence force, the *Baltische Landeswehr*. This was to be composed of volunteers from the Germanic-Balt families, remnants of the German Eighth Army and new recruits from Germany. These latter sought their fortune and escape from the turmoil and unemployment in their own country and were attracted in part by the Baltic Baron-dominated government's offer of land to those from Germany who would join them – an offer which satisfied both the Germanic Balts desire to maintain a strong German identity in the area with the need for more manpower for the fighting. Named the 'Iron Division', the force eventually comprised some 16,000 men. Over time the men began to liken themselves to freebooters or pirates, giving themselves the name of *Freikorps*.

Estonian nationalists likewise moved to re-assert their authority. Johan Laidoner was a former Imperial Russian Army officer. Following the October Revolution, he commanded the Estonian national units of the Russian army, based in Petrograd. On 30 November, Laidoner left Russia and arrived in Tallinn on 8 December. The provisional government, with Päts to the fore, immediately appointed him Chief of Staff and then, on 23 December, Commander-in-Chief of the Estonian Armed Forces. Eventually, he had around 13,000 men to call upon, mainly from the Estonian national regiment which remained loyal to the Estonian Provincial Assembly although nominally fighting with Red forces against the Germans.

And so throughout the region forces moved to confront each other. Communists who wanted to take back the lands lost at Brest-Litovsk. Nationalists who wanted to achieve the independence which the treaty terms (and Lenin's declaration of 15 November 1917) had briefly promised them. Latvians intent on fighting other Latvians. A German-backed and manned vagabond army, which sought land, booty and strong Germanic influence and control in the territory. And coming up on the rails were the anti-Bolshevik White armies, seeking to rescue Mother Russia from the Soviets, restore a monarchy and return the Baltic States to a new Russian Empire.

It was a recipe for disaster. The Devil himself could not have brewed a more confusing stew. And the Royal Navy would be plunged into the middle of it.

CHAPTER 3
Baltic Bound, November – December 1918

On 13 November 1918, a sub-committee of the British War Cabinet met at the Foreign Office under the chairmanship of Foreign Secretary Arthur James Balfour. Their agenda was to discuss the appropriate British response to the situation in Russia and its borders. Over four years of war had impoverished Britain and stretched its resources to the utmost. Everybody wanted to get back to peacetime conditions as soon as possible and work to rebuild the economy. But affairs in Russia, and the threat to Europe implicit in the Bolshevik war of *revanche*, could not be ignored.

Opening the meeting, Balfour noted that

the British Government cannot embark on an anti-Bolshevik crusade in Russia. It was natural that our advisers on the spot should take a contrary line, as they were obsessed with the external and visible violence of Bolshevism. On the other hand, the people of this country would not consent to such a crusade. Secondly, it is necessary that support should be afforded to the border states of Western Russia from the Baltic to the Black Sea. These States should be recognised, and support should follow on recognition.[1]

Lord Alfred Milner, Secretary of State for War, agreed with the chair in principle but added that 'anything which could be done to protect the Baltic States should be done, but British troops could not be despatched to these regions'.[2]

But Lord Robert Cecil, cousin to Balfour and Parliamentary Assistant Secretary of State for Foreign Affairs, averred that whilst he was in substantial agreement with what had been said by both

Balfour and Lord Milner, he was not prepared to go so far as to say that we should protect the Border States against Bolshevik attack. If help was to be provided to the Baltics then he was 'in favour of the creation of a Baltic Block', failing which, he thought, 'we should supply arms to any local authorities which might prove themselves capable of exercising control'.[3] In this he was consciously referencing the widely-held view, particularly favoured by the French government, that the Baltic States should be used to form a *cordon sanitaire* against the virus of Bolshevism. This appeared to be have been French policy since November 1918 when Prime Minister Georges Clemenceau instructed his General Staff that 'the main line of the plan of action that should be adopted is not only to continue the struggle against the Central Powers but to encircle Bolshevism and bring about its downfall'.[4*]

The matter was again discussed at the War Cabinet the following day. The diffidence towards committing substantial resources towards a programme in the Baltic, and in Russia generally, is again seen in some of the comments made. Prime Minister David Lloyd George noted that 'with regard to Esthonia [*sic*], he took the view that the sooner the peasants got on to the land there the better, as peasants in possession of the land would constitute a strong anti-Bolshevik nucleus. The German landowners had been a curse to the country and had been used by the German Government as an alien garrison.'[5] Cecil again stated his opposition to interfering in the Baltics, adding that he 'doubted very much whether it was part of our duty to protect Esthonia [*sic*] and the Baltic States against Russian Bolshevism'.[6] And Milner reiterated his view that 'under no circumstances could we send troops'.[7§]

But eventually the War Cabinet agreed a ten-point plan developed by the sub-committee the previous day. Point eight stated that Britain should 'supply the Baltic States with military material, if, and when, they have governments ready to receive and utilise such material'.

---

[*] France had a particular interest in restoring the Tsarist regime. Russia's pre-war debt to France was 25 billion francs, to which could be added half as much again in war loans which was unlikely to be repaid by the Bolsheviks. Additionally, France had made substantial investments in Russian banking, coal, oil and railways.

[§] Although Britain had sent troops to occupy Archangel on 2 August 1918, in order to protect the large ammunition dumps there. The government's policy towards support of White Russian forces, as opposed to the Baltic States, was defined on 30 November thus; 'to remain in occupation in Murmansk and Archangel ... to continue the Siberian expedition ... to occupy the Baku-Batum railway; to give General Denikin ... all possible help in the way of military material' (ADM 137/1733, NA).

Thus Britain had committed itself to some, non-land based, form of support. In what shape would it come?

Der Tag

The *Kaiserliche Marine* had long dreamed of the day it would meet and defeat the Royal Navy in a fleet action. Throughout the war, its officers drank toasts to *Der Tag*, 'The Day', when that would happen. Finally, only part of their wish came true. They would meet, but not fight, the British fleet. Under the terms of the Armistice, the German navy was to be interned in neutral ports. But as no neutral nation was willing to take the German fleet on these terms, it was agreed that the surface ships (there were separate arrangements for the U-boats) would sail into the Firth of Forth to be interned. Commander-in-Chief of the Grand Fleet, Admiral David Beatty, had long desired some humiliation for his foe and was annoyed that his recommendation for a formal surrender of the fleet had been omitted from the final Armistice terms. As he wrote to First Sea Lord Rosslyn 'Rosy' Wemyss on the day after the peace, he thought it appropriate that 'the sea power of Germany is surrendered under the eyes of the fleet it dared not encounter, and in the harbours of the power that swept them from the sea'.[8]

Shortly after midnight on 21 November, the 'C'-class cruiser HMS *Cardiff*, wearing the flag of Rear Admiral Edwyn Alexander-Sinclair, commanding the 6th Light Cruiser Squadron (LCS), stole quietly out of the Forth of Forth to meet the German battle fleet and lead it to a pre-arranged rendezvous with Admiral Beatty and the Grand Fleet, code named Operation 'ZZ'. Later that morning, *Cardiff* met and led the German High Seas Fleet – fourteen capital ships, seven light cruisers and forty-nine destroyers – towards the coast of Scotland. They were greeted by the entire Grand Fleet, some 192 ships in total, which formed into two flanking lines of escort. Led by HMS *Cardiff* and her admiral the Germans sailed to internment and a formal ceremony of submission at Rosyth. There Beatty signalled 'the German flag will be hauled down at sunset today and will not be hoisted again without permission'.

Cardiff and her sisters in 6LCS had endured a long and arduous war. The officers and men aboard were immensely proud of being chosen to lead the High Seas Fleet to captivity; but they were also looking forward to ten days post-war shore leave, rest and – in many cases – demobilisation.* This aspiration was to be dashed as a result of the War Cabinet meeting seven days earlier. Engine Room Artificer (ERA) Harry Boyd of HMS *Windsor* had been expecting leave but instead 'we got orders to complete with three weeks' stores and prepare for "special service"'.[9] And as Stoker Petty Officer Fred Smith put it 'our dreams of leave were fading fast'.[10]

Orders – or Not

On 20 November an Estonian delegation had visited the Foreign Office to plead for arms, troops and ships. Their entreaty was considered by the War Cabinet in the light of the discussion already held on 13 and 14 November (*vide supra*) and it was finally decided to send a cruiser squadron and a destroyer flotilla to the Baltic 'to help strengthen the populations of that part of the world against Bolshevism and to assist British interests in the Baltic'.[11] The ships would also carry a cargo of arms and ammunition.

Now the rush to mount an operation started. The navy required assistance from Denmark before it could contemplate the mission to the Baltic, for it needed a base en route. There was also the problem of mines; some 60,000 were thought to have been laid in the Baltic Sea and its approaches.

The navy had asked as to the positions of the Danish and German minefields (to some extent the same thing as the Germans had forced the Danes to mine their own waters in the early days of the war). The British *Chargé d'Affaires*, Lord Kilmarnock (Victor Alexander Sereld Hay, 21st Earl of Erroll and 4th Baron Kilmarnock), informed London that the Danes would lift their own mines and German mines in Danish territorial waters, but that 'no steps will be taken to sweep other German minefields until a request has been received, preferably from the German Government'. On 21 November Kilmarnock further informed London that the Germans had asked the Danes to take responsibility for watching their minefields, but not to remove them. The Danes knew little about the positions of German mines in the Great Belt fields.[12]

Secondly, the Royal Navy needed a secure base away from the putative war zone where it could refuel and re-equip. Copenhagen would be perfect. On 21 November, the Foreign Office asked Kilmarnock to make clear to the Danes that 'we are anxious to send

---

* In fact, the 'commence demobilisation' order was not given by the Admiralty until mid-January 1919.

British naval forces to the Baltic. The terms of the Armistice with Germany gives us full right and liberty to do so. The Admiralty would like these forces to visit and be based on Copenhagen. Will you enquire whether this would be agreeable to the Danish Government which we trust may prove the case?'[13]

Opinion was divided in Denmark. Some thought that the presence of a fleet which would be seen as opposing the Bolsheviks could lead to an adverse reaction; it also possibly compromised the neutral status which Denmark had tried to protect throughout the war. But the King was happy, as he saw the force as a protection against Bolshevism. On 23 November, the Danish Government gave the required permission. Ove Rode, the Minister for Interior Affairs, noted in his diary: 'the English Government has asked if the Royal Navy could visit Copenhagen and use it as a basis for visits in the Baltic Sea. They want to show the flag in the Baltic countries and Finland. Scavenius [the Danish Foreign Minister 1913–20, Erik Scavenius] had answered that they were welcome, but had underlined that our difficult supply situation made it necessary that the force brought everything it needed'.[14] And so the Royal Navy had its base.

When Rear Admiral Alexander-Sinclair returned from his starring role in the internment of the German Fleet he was greeted with sailing orders for the Baltic directing him to proceed the following day (the 22nd) to Libau and Reval. His actual operational orders were not issued until two days later, perhaps indicating the rush with which the whole programme was being arranged. Dated 24 November, these instructed him to 'show the flag and support British policy as circumstances may dictate'.[15] He was also empowered to use the military weapons loaded on his ships to arm the national forces of the Baltic States as he saw fit. To make sure that he didn't deviate from a line satisfactory to the Foreign Office, he was (in a faint echo of Soviet practice with their Political Commissars on board warships) given a Foreign Office political adviser, Vivian Henry Courthope Bosanquet, previously British Consul in Riga.

In fact, Alexander-Sinclair and his ships did not leave until the 26th. His orders were extremely vague, the sort which might get a man hanged or made a hero, or hamstring an indecisive commander. At the 28 November War Cabinet, Rear Admiral Sidney Robert Fremantle, Deputy Chief of the Naval Staff and deputising for First

Sea Lord Rosslyn Wemyss, asked 'the Imperial War Cabinet for the instructions which they wished given to the squadron which was being sent to the Baltic'.[16] He went on to add that 'the Admiralty wished to be informed of the government's policy, particularly in relation to the Bolsheviks, as to whether or not naval support was to be given to the Esthonians [*sic*] in resisting the Bolsheviks. Further, if Germans were co-operating with the Esthonians in opposing the Bolsheviks, were we to assist the Germans?'[17] In other words, what were what we might now call Alexander-Sinclair's 'Rules of Engagement'. But the best the War Cabinet could offer was to 'adjourn the consideration of this subject until the Secretary of State for Foreign Affairs could be present'.

Persistently, Fremantle then sought clarification directly and asked Foreign Secretary Balfour whether Britain was at war with the Bolsheviks. In response Balfour stated that he could give no juridically satisfactory answer but that 'we must treat Bolsheviks attacking our friends as hostile'.[18] The Admiralty then signalled Alexander-Sinclair that 'a Bolshevik man-of-war operating off the coast of the Baltic provinces must be assumed to be doing so with hostile intent and should be treated accordingly'[19] which, as historian Stephen Roskill noted, 'perhaps went further than the Foreign Secretary had intended'.[20] The admiral was also advised that 'the British government has definitely decided against any military commitment in Esthonia [*sic*] and any assistance you may think to give should be limited to the supply of arms, and the moral support given by the presence of the British Flag'.[21]

Actually, Wemyss was concerned about sending light forces to potentially face heavier opposition. He was 'not anxious to meet heavy Bolshevik naval forces with light cruisers and destroyers' especially given that no-one really understood what the mission was. He had 'no objection to meeting them with light forces if his orders were to attack but that if he was to bluff them into not fighting, he would prefer to have a prepondering force of capital ships'.[22] But Wemyss viewed this as impossible as big ships could not get through the narrow entrance to the Sound and the Great and Little Belts were not swept clear of mines: and then there was the cost to consider.

The conflicting pressures already acting on government departments can be seen in a letter received by First Lord of the Admiralty Eric Geddes on 23 November, one day before Alexander-

Sinclair received his orders. Chancellor of the Exchequer Andrew Bonar Law wrote to state that he was 'most anxious that the cutting down of unnecessary war expenditure should take place at once'.[23] And the day before, Geddes himself had recommended to the Admiralty Board that 'as a purely temporary measure … a twenty per cent cut on manpower on the pre-war numbers'[24] should be adopted as a goal. On the one hand making immediate economies was necessary; on the other, there were still military and naval commitments which were deemed vital to the national interest and must be met.

Alexander-Sinclair

Who was the man to whom the Admiralty had entrusted this difficult and ill-defined mission?

Edwyn Sinclair Alexander-Sinclair CB, MVO, 12th Laird of Freswick and Dunbeath, had joined the navy in January 1879, aged thirteen. His career followed the usual progression of the pre-war navy with service as flag lieutenant to three admirals, then attainment of the ranks of commander in 1901 and captain four years later.

He was a keen huntsman and polo player, as were most of his peer group. Whilst posted to Malta in the 1890s, an old polo team sheet shows him playing alongside 'Kit' Cradock, 'Rosy' Wemyss and David Beatty (the latter two future First Sea Lords) together with Lewis Bayly, Hedworth Lampton (later Meux), Mark Kerr and Hugh Evan-Thomas – all of whom were to hold high flag rank. The friendships formed here lasted for years. Rear Admiral Sir Christopher Cradock, who died on 1 November 1914 at the Battle of Coronel, left Alexander-Sinclair a gold hunter watch in his will.[25]

On 8 February 1915, Alexander-Sinclair was appointed Commodore, Second Class, Commanding the First Light Cruiser Squadron, and hoisted his broad pendant in HMS *Galatea* on 16 February. He commanded 1LCS at the Battle of Jutland, one of three squadrons screening the Battlecruiser Fleet commanded by Beatty, where his ships gained the distinction of firing the first shots of the battle: at 1428 on 31 May 1916, HMS *Galatea* and *Phaeton* opened fire on German destroyers investigating a neutral steamer.

Advancement to rear admiral followed in April 1917, aged fifty-one, and on 11 July he was appointed Rear Admiral Commanding 6th Light Cruiser Squadron, with his flag in *Cardiff*. He was still in this post at the Armistice.

His ancestral homes were Freswick Castle[*] and Dunbeath Castle, both in Caithness, at the extreme north-east corner of Scotland, and which he had inherited from his uncle. He was married, with a son and a daughter, and comfortably wealthy. The naval historian Arthur Marder thought Alexander-Sinclair 'a first-class sea officer' but 'not gifted with much brain and [he] was never expected to … reach the highest posts'.[26] Now, his quondam polo partner and – since January – First Sea Lord, Admiral Rosslyn Wemyss, sent him and his ships to the Baltic. He sailed from Rosyth with the five ships of 6LCS, nine destroyers, seven minesweepers and two minelayers to a new zone of conflict, with very different challenges to anything he had faced before.

Alexander-Sinclair's force was comprised the five 'C'-class cruisers of the 6LCS; *Cardiff*, *Caradoc*, *Ceres*, *Cassandra* and *Calypso*. These were modern vessels launched and completed during the war. Although of different sub-classes they were all broadly similar, good but cramped sea-boats capable of 28.5–30 knots, armed with five 6in, two 3in and two 2pdr guns together with eight 21in torpedo tubes and carrying a crew of between 350 and 450 men, depending on type.

In company were nine 'V & W' class destroyers from the 13th Destroyer Flotilla. This was a class of sixty-seven vessels, all completed in the latter years of the war. Typically, they carried four 4in guns and one 3in together with two 21in torpedo tubes at a maximum speed of 34 knots, with a crew of 134. HMS *Valkyrie*, *Windsor*, *Wolfhound*, *Woolston*, *Wessex*, *Vendetta*, *Westminster*, *Verulam* and *Wakeful* were the chosen ships. Four Royal Fleet Auxiliary (RFA) vessels sailed with them, carrying supplies. RFA *Bacchus* (for stores and distilling fresh water), *Slavol*, *Belgol* and *Prestol* (tankers carrying fuel oil).

Mines were a constant danger in the North Sea and the Baltic, during the war and for many months to come after its conclusion. Consequently Alexander-Sinclair's miniature fleet also comprised seven minesweepers from the 3rd Fleet Sweeping Flotilla. Based at Granton, on the Forth River, these were 'Town'-class ships, coal burning (which would prove to be a fatal flaw), armed with one 4in and one 12pdr and capable of about 16 knots.

There were also two minelayers, *Princess Margaret*, a Dumbarton-

* In reality more of a Peel Tower or Broch rather than a castle.

built 5,934grt ex-Canadian Pacific Railway passenger liner taken up for service as a minelayer in December 1914[*] and *Angora*, a merchant ship completed in 1911 which was converted for use as a minelayer in 1915. These were to sail separately from Rosyth and join the flagship at Copenhagen, departing on 30 November. They also served to carry the cargo of weapons destined for the Baltic nationalist forces,[§] the loading of which was the cause of their delay.

Finally, Captain Bertram Sackville Thesiger of *Calypso* was appointed second in command of the force. He was the grandson of Frederic Thesiger, 1st Baron Chelmsford, twice Lord Chancellor in Lord Derby's administrations, brother to the actor Ernest and cousin to Wilfred Patrick Thesiger, the explorer. He was also no slouch. During March to June 1913 he had attended the Royal Naval War College as a captain where he was placed second out of nine captains in order of merit and was rated 'first class'. His instructors commented 'V[ery] G[ood] I[ndeed)]. Has done and worked well.'[27]

Destination Libau

Acting Paymaster Sub Lieutenant Stuart Francis Stapleton was enjoying two weeks leave when, after only seven days, he received an urgent telegram ordering him to join HMS *Caradoc* at Rosyth. There he found preparations in hand for the Baltic. Sheepskin coats were issued and the wardroom mess-men embarked ten days' supply of potatoes and several live chickens. The ship also welcomed an official photographer; pictures of some of their activities were later published in the *Daily Mirror* amongst other newspapers.

Caradoc departed Rosyth at 2100 on the 26th. The sea was rough and the ship rolled considerably but by the 28th all was calm. At 1515 the squadron passed the transport ship *Russe*, returning home carrying British prisoners of war. All ships 'cleared lower deck' and 'manned ship' to cheer the transport as she came alongside.

The rushed nature of the planning for the passage showed immediately. The first port of call was Copenhagen on 29 November, where Alexander-Sinclair intended to refuel. For the oil-burning

---

[*] She was considered to be the best minelayer in service owing to her great radius of action (1,500 miles at full speed), shallow draught and oil-burning machinery. However, she had only a single drop point for her mines, she presented a big target with her high freeboard and could not embark mines directly onto her rails aft, required special low-freeboard barges to bring them alongside (Annual Report of the Torpedo School, Mining Appendix, 1917–18, p 12).

[§] Which comprised of 6,500 rifles, 200 machine guns and two field guns.

BATTLE IN THE BALTIC

cruisers and destroyers this was not a problem – the RFA tankers had sufficient supplies. But the minesweepers needed coal – and the collier *Tregarth* which was meant to have met them there had failed to arrive, having been run ashore; and there was no coal to be had in Copenhagen either.

On the 30th, *Caradoc* was despatched to find and assist the grounded collier, travelling to Elsinore (Helsingør) at her full speed of 27 knots. Two sloops had already tried to tow her off, unsuccessfully, but the light cruiser managed to re-float the collier in a very short space of time; but it was already too late.

Given the ever-present danger of mines, the sensible thing to have done would be to wait, for the minesweepers could go no further. In a better-planned operation, the coal might have been prepositioned. But now Alexander-Sinclair received a pressing message from Päts, relayed to him by the British Ambassador in Denmark, to the effect that 'it is urgently requested that a fleet of the Allied powers appear in Reval at the earliest possible moment, to prevent anarchy and the inevitable massacre'.[28] This entreaty left him very little choice if his mission was to succeed. And so, forty-eight hours after their arrival in Denmark, the little armada sailed without the minesweepers.* They sailed in line ahead, the cruisers in the van with paravanes§ deployed, each ship following in the wake of the one in front; and trusted to luck. When *Caradoc* returned to Copenhagen, she found the squadron already departed and orders for them to remain as W/T link ship.

The squadron proceeded in bitterly cold weather, without the benefit of reliable charts and with little knowledge of the many minefields that had been laid during the duration of the conflict. Harry Boyd noted that 'a sharp lookout was kept for mines, our only enemy now we knew where to find the Hun'.[29]

Most of the ships reached Libau on 1 December, but Lady Luck

---

* This proved an expedient decision for the second collier sent was mined in the North Sea and sank, and the third did not arrive until January.

§ Developed during the war to destroy naval mines, paravanes were strung out and streamed alongside the towing ship, normally from the bow. The wings of the paravane would force the device away from the towing ship, placing a lateral tension on the towing wire. If the tow cable snagged the cable anchoring a mine, it would either cut it or the mine would slide down the paravane towing wire to cable cutters which would sever the mine tether, allowing the mine to float to the surface for destruction by gunfire. If the anchor cable would not part, the mine and the paravane would come together and the mine would explode against the paravane. The cable would then be retrieved and a replacement paravane fitted.

did not attend them; whilst entering the harbour just before 1500, HMS *Calypso* struck a 'submerged obstruction', sustaining damage to her propellers. That evening, all ships used searchlights through the hours of darkness to illuminate the harbour surroundings and kept a full watch with some gun crews closed up. Radio messages were regularly received from Reval throughout the night, asking for the British ships' assistance. On *Cassandra*, Chief Petty Officer John Fleming thought that 'the whole atmosphere was creepy and we were glad when we sailed'.[30] Harry Boyd merely thought that Libau was 'very forlorn and desolate spot and bitterly cold'.[31]

Calypso sent divers down the following morning to examine her damage. It proved to be a dockyard job. Alexander-Sinclair ordered her home and she weighed and sailed for Copenhagen that afternoon, in company with RFA *Slavol*. The fighting force had been reduced by one.

The following two days were spent receiving official deputations from Libau. The mayor came on board and begged Alexander-Sinclair to stay and protect the town; he also requested that the papers and money from the town hall be taken on board for safety. He told the admiral that the 'surrounding countryside was infested with Bolsheviks waiting for the German occupiers to leave'[32] and that the poorer classes were in sympathy with them and would rise against the moneyed class. The Germans, he said, were oppressing the population and robbing the town of money and food, leaving worthless IOUs.

Finally the remaining ships of 6LCS joined up, with *Caradoc* eventually arriving on the fourth. She had suffered her own grounding scare leaving Copenhagen harbour; sounds of grating on the ship's bottom lasted for a minute but later inspection showed no harm had been done.

Alexander-Sinclair forbade any shore leave but did make a general signal stating that there was no harm in shooting ducks on the breakwater. However, this was a short-lived diversion for no sooner had *Caradoc* completed her mooring than, at 1410, the admiral ordered his squadron to depart for the Estonian capital.

CHAPTER 4

To The Rescue, December 1918

On leaving Libau, HMS *Cardiff* took the lead with the other cruisers following in line ahead, streaming their paravanes, while the nine destroyers brought up the rear, arranged in two divisions. By 1530 they had worked up to 15 knots but were unable to hold that speed through the night. Orders were given to sink on sight any enemy craft and gun crews were closed up, torpedo men ready for action, the ships alert and prepared for any Bolshevik intervention.

The Germans, through whose old minefields they were now traversing, had provided a guide to the safe channel. However, Alexander-Sinclair, presumably a little spooked by the pleas for his urgent arrival, was steering about eight miles west of the recommended route, trying to save time by taking a more direct passage. And in the absence of the minesweepers, trusting to luck and paravanes proved to be an inappropriate strategy.

At 0050 on the 5th, the squadron was to the north-west of Ösel Island (Saarenmaa) when the night was suddenly rent by a blinding flash and the loud roar of an explosion. The concussion was felt on board *Cardiff* and on *Ceres* 'the ship shuddered, the deck plates lifted and we suddenly listed as the steering went over'.[1]

The cruiser second in line, HMS *Cassandra*, had hit a mine which had exploded beneath her engine room; it broke the ship's back, flooded two boiler rooms and left her dead in the water, without power. Only the prompt reaction of the officer of the watch in the following vessel, *Ceres*, stopped a collision adding to the problem. It seemed that a tethered mine had been caught by the starboard paravane which failed to cut the mooring cable, instead dragging the mine into the ship.

Cassandra's commander, Captain Edward Coverley Kennedy,

had now to assess if his ship was capable of being saved or towed. The other cruisers and destroyers surrounded her and illuminated the stricken ship with their searchlights, while *Caradoc*'s engineer officer was sent across to assist in the assessment. But five minutes after the explosion the deck was awash; after that she continued to gradually sink. There was no possibility of saving the vessel. Kennedy gave the order for the lower decks to be cleared and the hands fallen in.

The other ships of the squadron went to launch their boats. But there was a problem; 'all ships were frantically trying to free up the lifeboats which were frozen to their davits. Axes and hammers were used to try to free the falls.'[2]

Chief Petty Officer ERA John Fleming Foster of *Cassandra* had been in his bunk, worrying about a feed pump he had been working on in the boiler room, when the explosion occurred. 'All around me men were tumbling from their hammocks,' he recalled, 'and pushing without panic for the ladders which led to the upper deck where we were assembled in shivering groups and waited as the ship slowly settled.'[3] The problem for the admiral was how to safely get the survivors off. There were some 450 men on board and the icing was preventing the use of the small boats of his force.

Two destroyers and their skilful commanders rose to the occasion. First HMS *Westminster* took position on the weather side of the sinking ship and lifted fourteen men off. But the heavy swell repeatedly threw the little ship against the stronger plating of the cruiser and inflicted serious damage. Her captain, Lieutenant Commander Francis George Glossop, had to back away.

But on the lee side, Commander Charles Gordon Ramsey had better fortune; twice he took *Vendetta* alongside and in total transferred 440 men onto his small vessel. Only one man, 22-year-old Able Seaman Arthur Shrapnell, was lost when he slipped and fell into the water between the ships.

Meanwhile, CPO Foster had been feeling the cold. Against orders, he went back to his mess where, to his surprise, he found an ERA called Percy dressing himself in front of a mirror. Foster put his civvies on and bolted back up the ladder. 'When I reached the deck my heart almost stopped. *Cassandra* was very low in the water and a destroyer was standing off with most of the crew. I was one of about twenty-four left on deck.'[4] He felt rather forlorn. Captain Kennedy was still on the ship though. When *Vendetta* made a further surge towards the sinking cruiser, 'we jumped and eager hands grabbed us'.[5]

Kennedy, the Engineer Commander, and two ERAs were still on board *Cassandra. Ceres* had finally manged to get a boat in the water. Worried that his colleague would take too literally the adage that a captain goes down with his ship, Captain Henry Gerald Elliot Lane of *Ceres* sent an officer and two men in it to bring off Kennedy and the others and told them to ensure *Cassandra's* captain returned with them, whatever his protests. As the boat came over, Kennedy came down from his bridge, wading through waist-deep water and shouting into various compartments as he did so. *Ceres'* men clambered on board their stricken sister and forcibly grabbed Captain Kennedy; he struggled but was overpowered and brought across to *Ceres*. There he insisted on staying on deck, gazing at the *Cassandra*. CPO Stoker Fred 'Smudge' Smith remembered that Kennedy had 'tears rolling down his cheeks as she sank' and that he 'stood to attention and saluted'* as she slipped beneath the waves.[6]

Cassandra sank by the bow within an hour of the mining, her stern in the air until she broke in two. It seemed very fast to Lieutenant Selby of *Ceres*. 'I never imagined one of those ships would have gone down in an hour,'[7] he noted in his diary. Apart from Shrapnell, a further ten men had died in the explosion, all of them trapped in the boiler room, the one where Foster had been working hours previously. Men who had thought that the war was over and their lives were safe: men who probably didn't understand why they were in the Baltic at all. 'There but for the Grace of God' thought Foster.[8] They had yet to see action but the force was now two cruisers down. It had not been an auspicious start.

Worried about the danger from mines, and in the absence of his sweepers, Alexander-Sinclair decided to take his ships back to Copenhagen. But now they fell foul of an older enemy than a mine; the squadron became enveloped in thick fog, so dense that the navigators lost their bearings and on the 6th Alexander-Sinclair ordered that all ships should anchor and await the fog clearing. Whilst so becalmed, 100 survivors were transferred from *Vendetta* to *Caradoc* and a further nine officers and 128 men were taken on

---

* Kennedy would lose his life in the next war, in command of the armed merchant cruiser HMS *Rawalpindi,* when on 23 November 1939 he met and fought the German battlecruisers *Scharnhorst* and *Gneisenau*. His ship was sunk and 238 men died. Captain Kennedy was the father of naval officer, broadcaster and author Ludovic Kennedy.

board *Calypso*. Stuart Stapleton noted that 'they had very little clothes on but as soon as they came on board they were mostly kitted up'.[9]

Finally, the ships were able to put in to Copenhagen in the early morning of the seventh. During the dog watches all the remaining survivors of *Cassandra* joined *Calypso* and she then sailed for home and repairs at Rosyth, whilst *Princess Margaret* and *Angora* arrived from England.

Moreover, *Westminster*'s condition meant that she too had to return to Britain, as did another destroyer, *Verulam*, damaged in a collision in the fog. From Rosyth, *Cassandra*'s survivors were sent to Devonport by train. There, on 20 February 1919, CPO John Foster was demobilised. He had been in the navy since 14 July 1914 when, as a RNVR member doing his annual two weeks' training, he and many others were held in their ships – and not allowed to return home – by the 'stand the fleet fast' signal which kept the navy at full complement ahead of the war.

Alexander-Sinclair was full of praise for his destroyer commanders, writing that 'Commander C G Ramsey of *Vendetta* and Lieutenant Commander F G Glossop of *Westminster*, particularly the former, appear to have handled their boats in a very seamanlike manner and their general conduct in the circumstances is much to be commended', adding that 'the behaviour of Lieutenant Hervey of *Cassandra* in continuing to carry out his duties after his arm had been broken is most praiseworthy'.[10] Four seamen from *Cassandra* received the Meritorious Conduct Medal for their actions during the rescue, Leading Seaman Arthur Green, Able Seaman Henry John Long, ERA Allen Waring and ERA Alfred Campbell Rundle, all of whom were notified of their honour at RN Barracks Devonport the following February.

But the court of enquiry into the loss was dissatisfied with the admiral's decision-making. They judged that 'no reason is given for the squadron not following the route on the map'; and that 'it would appear that the squadron tried to gain time by cutting the corner at [map reference] P12. Squadron was delayed by bad weather and [Alexander-Sinclair] appeared to think that the risk of leaving the track was justified.'[11] Moreover, the paravanes did not work at less than 10 knots and 13 knots should have been the minimum speed maintained; the squadron had dropped below this rate owing to the weather conditions at night.

When the report reached the Admiralty, Their Lordships took a fairly dim view of things, commenting that the 'primary cause of the loss was the departure from the authorised channel' and that 'Rear Admiral Commanding 6th Light Cruiser Squadron was responsible for this'. Furthermore, they judged that 'The Rear Admiral erred; such a departure would only appear to be justified by urgent necessity. The mere possibility of a late arrival at a rendezvous does not appear to be sufficient cause.'[12] Nor did they consider that the weather was bad enough (force 3–4 winds) to run at speeds at which the paravanes might not work properly. All in all, it was not a great 'report card'.

Reval

On 8 December, Alexander-Sinclair left Copenhagen once more. As well as his flagship, he had *Caradoc* and the remaining seven destroyers in company, together with the two minelayers and their cargo of military aid. *Ceres* was left behind to act as communications ship. They arrived at Libau during the night of the following day and anchored up until the 11th when, at 2150, all his ships set course for Reval.

The situation in Estonia was desperate. Between 28–30 November a Red Army formation under the overall control of a Latvian native, Colonel Jukums Vācietis,[*] and supported by the Russian Baltic Fleet operating from its base at Kronstadt, had staged an amphibious landing against the town of Narva.

The Seventh Red Army had attacked with 7,000 infantry, twenty-two field guns, 111 machine guns, an armoured train, two armoured vehicles, two aircraft, and the cruiser *Oleg* with two destroyers. Narva was defended only by men of the Estonian Defence League (a type of Home Guard and consisting partly of secondary-school students) and *Infanterie-Regiment* Nr 405 of the German Army. The Red Army captured the town on 29 November, and the Germans withdrew westwards in a mutinous condition. They just wanted to go home.

At the same time, Russian forces in the south of Estonia opened a second front at Lake Peipus. The 2nd Novgorod Division, comprising 7,000 infantry, twelve field guns, fifty machine guns, two armoured trains and three armoured vehicles, eventually took the towns of Walk (Valga) and Dorpat (Tartu)[§]. In both regions, the

[*] The first commander-in-chief of the Red Army; he was replaced on 3 July 1919.
[§] Walk on 18 December, Tartu on the 24th.

Soviet occupiers immediately set about butchering anyone who they thought a 'class enemy'.

Alexander-Sinclair and his ships arrived in Reval at 1440 on the 12th. The Red Army was now only forty miles east of Reval. The townspeople appeared very glad to see them; vessels in harbour 'dressed ship' to greet the British squadron. At 1630 a desperate Konstantin Päts came aboard *Cardiff* to plead for support from the admiral. Amongst his shopping list of wants was that Estonia become a British protectorate, a military mission should train his army and that a Royal Navy fleet should remain in Estonian waters and, moreover, provide the nascent Estonian navy with two destroyers. None of these wishes were in Alexander-Sinclair's gift. But he did what he could; the following day arms and munitions were offloaded from the two minelayers and sailors were sent ashore to train Estonian soldiers in their use.

As previously noted, the admiral's orders were at best vague. Although he had not been told that he could not engage an enemy, he wasn't told that he could either. But admirals have often interpreted their orders loosely. And Alexander-Sinclair knew that if Reval fell, so would Estonia. The Nelsonian tradition was still strong; Rear Admiral Edwyn Sinclair Alexander-Sinclair knew what he should do.

At 0553 on 14 December, *Cardiff*, *Caradoc* and five destroyers (*Windsor*, *Wolfhound*, *Wessex*, *Woolston* and *Wakeful*) proceeded to sea from Reval, sailing eastwards at 22 knots. At 0740 Action Stations was sounded and the guns cleared away. Harry Boyd could see 'a few factories and a railway with forest in the background at the top of a ridge, four miles range'.[13] Ammunition was readied, guns' crews closed up, expectation mounted. At 1115 the flotilla stopped and opened fire on the estimated positions of the Bolshevik forces. At first they concentrated their fire on and around the railway, but at 1205 switched target to the bridge across the River Narva in the Bolshevik rear.

The history of naval gunfire against shore positions is chequered. Nelson believed that it was futile for ships to engage fortresses and the disaster of the Dardanelles in 1915 would seem to prove his point. But in 1914 Horace Hood and the Dover Patrol had done sterling work in the English Channel shoring up the Belgian and French left wings with shellfire from the sea. Writing on behalf of General French, Colonel Tom Bridges noted that Hood's 'action undoubtedly saved the Belgian left flank and, in my opinion, had a decisive effect on the final success of the defenders'.[14]

Artillery had been of critical importance on the Western Front throughout the war and the 6in guns carried by the cruisers compared favourably with the most common calibres used on land. But they were designed to shoot long distances at flat trajectories, not necessarily useful in a land war. However, in this instance 'British naval gunfire against shore targets has seldom been more effective'.[15] The bridge was totally destroyed and the Bolshevik army cut off from their line of supply to Petrograd. Alexander-Sinclair took his force back to Reval and anchored at 0600. His prompt action had ensured that the Bolsheviks could not nor would not advance further towards the Estonian capital; the Royal Navy had saved the immediate situation and allowed the Estonian army time to organise.

By way of reprisal, the Bolsheviks tortured 200 Estonian prisoners, 'cutting off their ears and blinding them [before] turning them out in the snow'.[16]

The Fall of Riga

As noted above, Soviet Russia had invaded Latvia at the beginning of December and rapidly conquered almost all the territory, with the exception of a small area around Libau and in Riga. A Latvian Socialist Soviet Republic was proclaimed on 17 December 1918 with the full backing of the Bolshevik government of Soviet Russia. The legitimate Latvian government of Kārlis Ulmanis was confined to Riga where their writ ran little further than the perimeter of the city.

Alexander-Sinclair felt that he needed to return to Latvia to offer support to Ulmanis. This would, of course, reduce his forces in Estonia which were the most vulnerable to a Soviet naval attack. He knew that the Baltic Fleet, weakened by mutiny, Bolshevism and lack of fuel had nonetheless some powerful units. Would they sally out to attack Royal Navy forces at Reval? Should he take all his ships to Libau and Riga or leave some to maintain a presence and deterrent? In the end, and in the face of Päts' determined pleading, he decided he could not leave the Estonians unsupported.

On 17 December, *Cardiff* weighed anchor and in company with *Ceres*, five destroyers and *Princess Margaret* set course for Libau. *Caradoc* left with them for Copenhagen. His remaining ships stayed at Reval. Captain Thesiger was to be Senior Naval Officer (SNO) at Reval, although he and *Calypso* would not arrive back from repair at Rosyth until 21 December.

Alexander-Sinclair arrived at Riga, via Libau, on the 17th but then returned to Denmark, leaving Captain Harry Hesketh Smyth* of the *Princess Margaret* as senior officer. *Wolfhound*, *Wakeful* and *Windsor* had accompanied the admiral. Access to the city was via a seven-mile channel up the River Dvina and on arrival *Windsor* went up it and moored opposite St Saviour's, the 'English church'.

Bosanquet had travelled with Alexander-Sinclair and now went ashore to assess the situation. He reported back to Smyth that the German troops in situ, who were supposed to be resisting the Red Army, were in fact falling back and intending to quit Latvia all together, leaving their stores and weapons to fall into Bolshevik hands. This was in direct contravention of the Allied requirements under Article XII of the Armistice terms (see Appendix 2). Smyth and Bosanquet remonstrated that the Germans should comply and resume an offensive stance, a request which was greeted with indifference. The commanding general merely laughed and stated that 'he could not command or rely on his troops, who wanted to go home'.[17] But all night on the 23rd, German troops were marching to their troopships with 'wagon load after wagon load of goods, fodder and fuel'.[18] Harry Boyd saw 'twenty-five trucks of sheepskins go past in half an hour'.[19] To Boyd it seemed that the German Balts 'are trying, under the supervision of the Huns, to establish a government against the will of the people who want an elected one but cannot get the different parties to unite for that purpose'.[20]

Without the German troops the defence of Riga rested on around 700 *Baltische Landeswehr*, clearly an inadequate force. *Ceres'* captain of Marines, Craig (and *Cardiff*'s who had been transferred to *Princess Margaret*) tried to organise companies of Latvian volunteers but this was a drop in the ocean compared to the forces ranged against them. They nonetheless equipped them with 5,000 rifles, carried from Britain in *Princess Margaret*.

On Christmas Day, a volunteer party of 1,000 men was assembled for church parade at the English Church. They marched there with

---

* Smyth was a minelaying specialist who had undertaken a special minelaying course at *Vernon* before taking command of the old cruiser *Amphitrite*, which had been converted into a minelayer. During his command of that ship he was awarded the CMG (Gazetted 1 October 1917) for 'services in minelaying operations'. He took command of *Princess Margaret* on 3 January 1918.

drums and fifes playing and thousands of the local inhabitants gathered outside to watch and cheer them. It was yet another festive season away from home for many men. Would they have been pleased to know that on Christmas Eve the Dean of King's College, Cambridge, Eric Milner-White,[*] had prepared and delivered a new order of service, based on one first given at Truro cathedral in 1880? He called it 'Nine Lessons and Carols' and wrote a special bidding prayer for it which encouraged the congregation to remember in their prayers those 'on another shore'; as the Baltic certainly was.

However, Christmas dinner was a less than cheerful affair. Harry Boyd's mess had salt pork, beans, spuds and (as they had saved some raisins) a 'dough'.[§] 'One or two of the men had more rum than was good for them and they started to moan and telling their family history and troubles. What with no mail and that to cheer us up we were just as disgusted.'[21] And on Boxing Day, 'things were dreary, with no leave [and] no exercise.'[22] Some of *Wolfhound*'s crew broke ship and returned at midnight when they were fired on by the sentries. They spent the night in the steerage flat under armed guard for their moment of enjoyment.

On the 27th and 28th, *Ceres* had landed armed parties to march through the town in an attempt to give reassurance and maintain order. They commandeered four motor-lorries, fitted them with 12pdrs and Lewis guns, and drove them around the town as a visible armed presence.

By the 28th it was clear to Smyth and Bosanquet that the situation was dire. The Red Army was only 25 miles distant and a communist rising in support of them was expected hourly. Smyth decided to embark some 392 Allied and neutral refugees on board his ship, which included 169 women and 80 children. To make room for them, arms and ammunition intended for Reval were offloaded onto *Windsor*. The following day two Latvian regiments, which had retired into the city, mutinied and declared for the Bolsheviks. They made small-arms target practice against the British ships through the night. In the morning, Ulmanis called on them to surrender, an invitation that they declined. Smyth then ordered *Ceres* to open fire

---

[*] Milner-White had served as an army chaplain during the war on the Western Front and in the Italian Campaign. He had been appointed senior chaplain to the 7th Infantry Division and was Mentioned in Despatches in December 1917 and awarded the DSO in the 1918 New Year Honours List.
[§] A duff, cf plum duff.

on the troops' barracks. Five 6in guns were trained towards the barracks and 'at 0700 exactly we fired a salvo which sounded like an earthquake in the cold, silent morning air. After three or four salvos a white flag fluttered and so they surrendered and were disarmed.'[23] All through the night *Ceres* burned her searchlights and kept number four and five guns closed up.

Petty Officer Stoker Fred 'Smudge' Smith was one of those detailed for duty ashore. Returning to his ship he saw what appeared to be a bundle of rags, mostly covered in snow. But when he looked more closely he found it was an old woman, near death and unconscious. He and his mates revived her and discovered that she was an Englishwoman, a Mrs Hill, thrown out of her home by the Bolsheviks and with her family scattered to the four winds. Smith carried her to *Princess Margaret* but was told that there were no more cabins available. 'Are there any Germans in them?', he demanded. Receiving an affirmative, he told the petty officer in charge to kick one out. A German *soi-disant* 'countess' was evicted; and Mrs Hill received a bed and medical care – and survived to reach Britain.[24]

By 1 January 1919 it was apparent to Smyth that Riga must fall soon. He decided to embark the members of Ulmanis's government*, who would surely have been murdered when the Bolsheviks took control. Alexander-Sinclair arrived the following day with *Cardiff* and the destroyers *Valkyrie* and *Woolston*. After consultation with Smyth and Bosanquet, he gave the order to evacuate. *Valkyrie* and her captain, Commander Geoffrey Mackworth, led the British forces down the River Dvina, now mostly frozen over, to the sea and hence to Libau where the official government of Latvia tried to re-establish itself. Riga fell on the 3rd, amid rioting, looting and mayhem.

---

* Ulmanis himself, together with his Ministers of Finance and Agriculture.

CHAPTER 5
'Destroy At All Costs', December 1918

Thirty-five-year-old Johan Laidoner had been appointed Commander-in-Chief of the Estonian Armed Forces on 23 December 1918. From the time of his arrival two weeks beforehand, he had set to work with a will, using the breathing space that Alexander-Sinclair's attack had brought him to organise his forces and plan a counter Bolshevik campaign. By the day of his promotion to CinC he could boast a force of 600 officers and 11,000 volunteers.

December 23rd was also the day Laidoner began the fight back. Escorted by HMS *Calypso* and the destroyer *Wakeful*, he landed 200 men at Kunda, in the Bolshevik rear; they caused panic, destroyed supplies and severed communications before retreating, all the time covered by gunfire from the Royal Navy. By 1900, the ships were safely back in Reval harbour, without any interference from the Red navy.

This assault, and the previous destruction of the railway and bridge by *Cardiff* and *Caradoc,* occurring as they did so close to the Baltic Fleet's base at Kronstadt, infuriated Trotsky. He ordered the immediate annihilation of the vessels at Reval, stating 'they must be destroyed at all costs'.[1] Kronstadt was a formidable fortress, a major source of protection for the Soviet fleet. In 1919 it was probably the best protected fleet base in the world. Built initially by Peter the Great, and developed over the succeeding centuries, it lay on the southern side of Kotlin Island. To the west of the base there were minefields stretching to the shore, with only one swept channel. Closer in, the northern channel around the island was spanned by a line of forts linking Kotlin to the mainland. These forts had a chain of submerged breakwaters between them. The main, southern, approach and the River Neva also had several sea forts. On the high

58

ground overlooking the narrow neck of the bay were large fortified gun batteries mounting heavy artillery, including the 12in guns of the major fortress of Krasnaya Gorka. The Tolbukhin lighthouse commanded a view of all approaches to the island. And behind these impressive defences lurked the Baltic Fleet.

Numerically the fleet was strong and significantly overmatched Alexander-Sinclair's forces. There were three battleships, *Andrei Pervozvanni* of 1910, a pre-dreadnought armed with four 12in and fourteen 8in guns; and the dreadnoughts *Petropavlovsk* and *Sevastopol*, sister-ships armed with twelve 12in guns, and already met in the 'Ice Voyage'. In addition, there were two cruisers, *Oleg* of 1903, twelve 6in and twelve 12pdrs, *Aurora*, eight 6in, and *Pamiat Azova,* launched in 1888 but now in use as a depot ship. Another cruiser, *Gromoboi*, was laid up there. Of smaller vessels there were eight destroyers, five modern submarines and an old minelayer. The guns of the battleships and the cruisers were a significant threat to the ships of the 6LCS and their consorts.

The Imperial Russian Navy had long been deficient in training, however, and the situation had worsened since the revolution. The crews at Kronstadt had joined the October Revolution with enthusiasm,[*] some officers had been murdered and most others had fled or been imprisoned. The ships were largely controlled by Soviets of sailors and discipline was practically non-existent. As a fighting force, they were possibly less formidable than first appeared.

This was in part demonstrated by their intelligence-gathering work. The Russians believed that two battleships had covered Laidoner's landing on 23 December; and, despite reconnaissance by three submarines in November and December, they understood the British ships at Reval to number four battleships and up to 'fifty or sixty vessels'.[2]

The task of fulfilling Trotsky's wish for the destruction of the British forces was allotted to Member of the Revolutionary War Soviet (the *Revvoeyensovet*) of the Red Navy at Kronstadt, Deputy Commander of the Seventh Army and Commissar of the Baltic Fleet, 26-year-old Fyodor Fyodorovich Raskolnikov, previously a midshipman (*michman*) in the Tsar's navy.

---

[*] Indeed, a blank shot from *Aurora*'s forecastle gun signalled the start of the assault on the Winter Palace, which was to be the beginning of the October Revolution. Her commander, Captain Mikhail Nikolsky, was murdered by his crew.

His plan was for a task force comprising the battleship *Andrei Pervozvanni*, cruiser *Oleg* and destroyers *Spartak*, *Avtrovil* and *Azard* to undertake the operation. The destroyers, under Raskolnikov's direct control, would enter the Reval roads and bombard the port, bringing to action any ships therein. If superior forces were encountered, they were to retire on *Oleg* with the battleship further back as heavy support. The action was slated for Christmas Day.

At the appointed hour, only *Spartak* and *Andrei Pervozvanni* left port, the others being either away or out on patrol. When they all finally rendezvoused, *Azard* was found to be out of fuel and *Avtrovil* delayed by an engine breakdown. The operation was put back until the 26th.

Accordingly, at 0700 on St Stephen's Day, Raskolnikov, aboard *Spartak*, declared his intention to start the attack; but first he stopped to fire on Wulf (Aegna) and Nargen (Naissaar) Islands (both of which lie across the entrance to Reval harbour and had been fortified in the nineteenth century), ostensibly to see if they were occupied and armed; he then captured a small Finnish steamer which was sent to Kronstadt under a prize crew. These delays were to prove his undoing.

Meanwhile, at Reval, the local authorities had decided to hold a noontime banquet for the Royal Navy officers and crews to thank them for their support. Ladies were to be provided 'for hire' as dancing partners. But the preparations for the festivities were interrupted by the sound of gunfire – the attack on the defensive islands – and then by the unpleasant noise of shells dropping in the harbour. Urgently, the 'recall' signal was given; sirens blared continuously and British sailors ran for the quayside and their ships. Thesiger had held his command at two hours' notice for sailing and soon the first vessel left the harbour. It was the destroyer HMS *Vendetta*; as she passed *Caradoc* the cruiser's crew cheered her on. Shortly afterwards *Vortigern* followed her and then *Wakeful*, which had lived up to its name. *Calypso* and Thesiger were immediately behind and *Caradoc* weighed and went to full speed at 1205, by which time *Vendetta* had already opened fire.

When Raskolnikov saw the smoke of the three destroyers leaving port he immediately turned *Spartak* away, heading for Kronstadt, perhaps intending to hide in the Finnish Skerries or find protection under the guns of *Oleg*.

Wakeful opened fire on *Spartak* at around 1220 and Wulf Island was passed fifteen minutes later. There was chaos on board the Russian ship. Shells were falling around them, a blast damaged the charthouse and bridge, charts were lost, and the engines proved unreliable. Then with a sudden bang she ran aground on the Divel shoal and stranded. Raskolnikov despatched a final signal to his base; 'All is lost. I am chased by English'.[3] At 1245, *Spartak* ran up the white flag.

Thesiger put a boarding party on board. She was leaking badly, with her propellers and rudder torn off. The ship was filthy and the crew generally happy to be prisoners.[*] *Vendetta* towed her back to port. Once anchored, *Spartak* was still filling with water so the crew were instructed to raise steam for the pumps; they decided to hold a ship's Soviet meeting to decide if they should. Armed Royal Marines convinced them of the necessity. As for the Soviet Navy's commissar and mission commander, Raskolnikov was discovered hiding under twelve sacks of potatoes and taken prisoner.[§] It was rumoured that he had on his person photographs of himself 'torturing and murdering the old aristocracy'.[4]

Around 1700 the British ships landed their 'entertainment parties' and the banquet, delayed but nonetheless mightily enjoyed, took place.

*   *   *

When Thesiger returned from the festivities, he had an interpreter tell him what information the papers captured with *Spartak* revealed. This informed him that *Oleg* was at Hogland (an island in the Gulf of Finland about 112 miles west of Petrograd) with orders to bombard Reval. This gave him the usual problem; the squadron's orders, vague as they were, did not directly give permission to attack enemy ships. But he also found in the captured papers a transcript of a message from Trotsky saying the British ships should be sunk. This seemed to Thesiger to be a sufficient *casus belli* and he gave orders for an immediate departure.

At 0050 on the 27th *Calypso* weighed anchor and, in company

---

[*] This euphoria probably didn't last. The Estonians 'pleaded to have them as they wanted their boots' (31 December 1918, ADM 116/1772, NA) and executed forty-four of them on Wulf Island the following February.
[§] He was taken to England and held in Brixton Prison.

with *Caradoc* and *Wakeful*, set out to find the enemy. Around 0500, Thesiger observed a destroyer passing on the reverse course; it did not see the British ships and Thesiger resisted pleas to open fire, for he thought that in the dark the destroyer may well be able to mount a torpedo attack unobserved. But he did order *Vendetta* and *Vortigern* to depart Reval and find her.

Hogland was a disappointment; there was no sign of the Red cruiser. Thesiger set up a patrol line, *Caradoc* to the north, *Calypso* south and *Wakeful* in the middle and in that formation began to cruise back to Reval; if the destroyer sighted earlier turned around she would run into his line of advance.

The plan worked. The Soviet destroyer, which was the *Avtroil*, seeking *Spartak*, ran into *Vendetta* instead, fled from her and came across *Vortigern*. She then turned east for Kronstadt and met *Wakeful*, went north and ran into *Caradoc* and finally south where she was intercepted by *Calypso*. Thesiger had previously ordered that he wanted to capture the Russian vessel; *Caradoc* had fired on her at 1135 and *Calypso* at 1150; ten minutes later, now surrounded by five Royal Navy ships, the Soviet destroyer hoisted a white flag. A prize crew took her back to Reval.

The Estonian navy to that point had comprised one vessel, an ex-Russian gunboat *Bobr*, now the *Lembit*, capable of only 12 knots and armed with two 4.7in guns and four 11pdrs. Päts had pleaded with Alexander-Sinclair for two Royal Navy destroyers, a request refused by the admiral. But Thesiger was now able to oblige him. He presented the two captured Russian destroyers to Johan Pitka, a former merchant seaman and owner of a small chandler's shop in Reval. In the 1914–18 war his son had been sent to Siberia for subversive activities amongst the British and Imperial Russian sailors in the Baltic but the family now seemed unconcerned about the past. Pitka had been appointed the Estonian naval commander-in-chief. At a stroke he gained two modern, fast ships and an actual navy to command; he named the new recruits *Wambola* (ex-*Spartak*) and *Lennuk* (ex-*Avtroil*).

But the Gulf was freezing over; Reval would soon be ice-bound, as would Petrograd, locking the Soviet fleet harmlessly in the base. In Reval, the next two days were spent refuelling and embarking refugees; Britons, Danes and the wife and family of the British consul, together with some prisoners of war and Raskolnikov.

Meanwhile *Cardiff* docked at Reval, inbound from Copenhagen, with Alexander-Sinclair and a further consignment of arms for the Estonian arsenal; 1,960 rifles and 1,380,000 rounds of ammunition. There also arrived some 200 Finnish soldiers on board an icebreaker, the first of an expected force of 2,000.

Back in London, Fremantle was concerned for the safety of the Baltic ships. At the 31 December 1918 War Cabinet meeting the minutes noted that:

> Admiral Fremantle wished to know whether the Imperial War Cabinet wished to withdraw the 6th Light Cruiser Squadron, or to face intervention on a larger scale. There was a danger of our being drawn into operations from which it would be difficult to disentangle ourselves. A decision would have to be come to quickly, as the ships would have to leave Riga before the middle of January if they were not to be ice-bound there. From the Admiralty point of view, it was certainly desirable to get the ships away from the whole of that area, both because of the damage they would suffer from the ice, and because of the danger that the ice would obliterate the navigation marks through the minefields. In this connection he mentioned that the port of Libau, further south, was ice-free, and, as there was no Bolshevik trouble there, as at Riga and Reval, there was not the same danger of entanglement if a ship stayed there. He wished to add, however, that it was probable that if we withdrew the ships from Riga the local Bolsheviks would massacre all their political opponents.[5]

Eventually, the Cabinet decided that 'the Admiralty should instruct the Admiral in Command of the 6th Light Cruiser Squadron to withdraw his ships from Riga and Reval, owing to the danger of their being shut in by the ice, but that one ship might be left at Libau ready to be withdrawn at short notice'.[6]

Thesiger thought that they should give one last piece of assistance before leaving. Firstly, on 3 January he took two cruisers and two destroyers to transport refugees to Helsingfors and bring Finnish troops back. *Caradoc* embarked 100 troops and landed them in Reval on the 4th. The ice was already too thick for the destroyers to complete the journey. Indeed, an icebreaker had to be used to take the British ships in and out of Helsingfors port, the ice being 6in thick in places. Stuart Stapleton found it 'rather funny to see men walking on the ice about 50 yards from the ships, as we were proceeding up harbour'.[7]

Then, after returning to Reval on the 5th, Thesiger took his cruisers and a destroyer on a patrol close to the Russian island of Hogland, expecting the Russians there to report the ships' presence to Kronstadt such that the Russian ships might be deterred from venturing out. Finally, on the way back to Reval, he made a further bombardment of the Bolshevik positions to the east of the city. 'This time we managed to blow up a row of houses and set them on fire, otherwise we don't know what result our fire had,'[8] noted Stapleton. *Caradoc* returned to Reval long enough to pick up more refugees and then set out to join the admiral.

As per his orders, Alexander-Sinclair assembled his ships and departed for home, via Copenhagen and thence to Rosyth, where they arrived between 8 and 10 January 1919. They would not return.

CHAPTER 6

In Search of a Policy, December 1918 – February 1919

Whilst Alexander-Sinclair and his ships had been busy in the Baltic States, there had been momentous change in Britain. Owing to the war, there had not been a general election in Britain since December 1910, when H H Asquith's Liberal Party retained power, due only to the support of the Irish Nationalists. A coalition government was formed in 1915 and Lloyd George's coup of December 1916 ousted Asquith and installed the Welsh Wizard in 10 Downing Street.

Immediately following the Armistice, the government called an election for 14 December 1918. It was the first general election to be held under the 1918 Representation of the People Act which enfranchised all men over the age of twenty-one, and those women over the age of thirty who met a property qualification.

Lloyd George's accession to the Premiership had split the Liberal Party. But he was popular in the country as 'The Man Who Won the War' and enjoyed the support of the Conservative/Unionist Party whose leader, Andrew Bonar Law*, had been a key ally in the coalition. He was opposed by the rump of the Liberals, led by Asquith, and the nascent Labour Party. In the election, Lloyd George stood at the head of a Liberal/Conservative coalition.

In order to ensure that the Lloyd George Liberals and Conservative candidates did not 'split the vote' and allow another party to gain traction, the two main parties agreed to a 'coupon'

---

* Bonar Law did not want the premiership as he was in poor health, and after the election accepted the sinecure of Lord Privy Seal but remained Leader of the House of Commons. He stood down due to illness in early 1921 but was briefly prime minister on Lloyd George's defenestration in November 1922, resigning again in May 1923 due to throat cancer.

system. Those candidates for the Liberal Party who had supported Lloyd George's coalition government during the war were issued with a letter of support signed by both Lloyd George and Bonar Law. This was seen as being a mark of approval for those candidates. Asquith, the official leader of the Liberals, referred to the letter as a 'coupon' and the election became known as the Coupon Election. The 'coupon' was given to 159 Coalition Liberal candidates. Where a Conservative stood, no 'Coupon Liberal' challenged him and vice-versa. Thus, there was no possibility of coalition candidates competing with each other. The Asquithian Liberals faced a tough challenge in the face of such tactics and in fact only thirty-three were elected.* Lloyd George retained power on the basis of Conservative support, the coalition candidates of all stripes winning 526 seats.

In forming his new Cabinet, Lloyd George appointed Walter Hume Long (MP for Westminster St George's) as First Lord of the Admiralty, replacing Geddes. And on 9 January 1919 he wrote to Winston Churchill, offering him the post of Secretary of State for War AND Air. In his own hand, Lloyd George annotated the letter 'but, of course, only one salary'.[1] Despite this jocularity, here was set the beginning of a constant headache for the Prime Minister, for Churchill was passionate about the need to oppose the Bolsheviks, and support both White Russia and the Baltic States, in a way which Lloyd George and the rest of Churchill's Cabinet colleagues were not. Their preference was to rebuild the economy and, in Lloyd George's campaigning words, 'to make Britain a fit country for heroes to live in'.[2] This meant spending scarce financial resources on social programmes rather than military and naval commitments. Such ambitions had been laid out in February by Christopher Addison,§ Minister for Reconstruction, viz; 'an adequate housing programme … involving purchases of materials and acquisition of land on a large scale … transfer of agri-cultural land to public authorities for the purposes of small holding, soldiers' settlements, afforestation … the reconstruction of roads and repair of railways … financing by the state of certain essential industries … an extension of unemployment insurance … a strength-ened health service'.[3] But Churchill was ferociously opposed to Bolshevism and all its works and pressed the case hard for military intervention (and the associated costs of course) at every turn.

* Asquith himself lost his East Fife seat. Labour won sixty-three seats and the Irish Republicans seventy-three, which they refused to occupy.
§ Who was not only an MP but a prominent doctor, surgeon and professor of anatomy.

On the stump in his constituency of Dundee in November 1918, Churchill furiously attacked the Reds. 'There is a new form of moral deprivation in the east' he thundered. 'Russia is being rapidly reduced by the Bolsheviks to an animal form of barbarism … civilisation is being completely extinguished over gigantic areas, while the Bolsheviks hop and caper like troops of ferocious baboons amid the ruins of cities and the corpses of their victims.'[4] And he described Russia's decision to exit the Great War as a betrayal of honour, claiming that 'every British and French soldier killed last year was really done to death by Lenin and Trotsky, not in fair war, but by the treacherous desertion of an ally without parallel in the history of the world'.[5] Churchill also saw a rebuilt Germany as a bulwark against the Bolsheviks; 'Kill the Bolshie, Kiss the Hun,' he told his friend Violet Asquith.[6]

During Churchill's tenure as Secretary of State for War and Air his major preoccupation was the Allied intervention in the Russian Civil War. He secured from a divided and loosely organised Cabinet, from which Lloyd George was a frequent absentee in France, an intensification and prolongation of the British involvement which went beyond the wishes of any major group in Parliament or the nation – and in the face of the bitter hostility of the socialist Labour Party and the trade unions.

When he was in Britain, Lloyd George became progressively frustrated by his stormy petrel War Minister. He noted that, on Russia, Churchill had become 'an exceedingly pernicious influence in the Cabinet',[7] adding that 'he wants to conduct a war against the Bolsheviks. That would cause a revolution. Our people would never permit it.'[8] And indeed, certain of the people – or at least those of a left-wing persuasion – would in January 1919 form the 'National Committee for the Hands Off Russia Campaign' in London. Many of the initial members would later be the founders of the Communist Party of Great Britain. As the historian David Somervell has noted, at this stage 'probably all shades of Labour and advanced Liberal opinion sympathised in greater or less degree with the Bolsheviks'.[9] Another time Lloyd George observed of Churchill 'in certain moods he is dangerous. He has Bolshevism on the brain … he is mad for operations in Russia.'[10]

As will be seen, Churchill drove the war in Russia and the Baltic onwards, virtually single-handed.

* * *

At the final War Cabinet meeting of 1918, Lloyd George expressed the view that the present position was highly unsatisfactory. 'We were neither interfering in Russia or evacuating it' he stated. The minutes of the meeting noted him observing that 'the essential thing was to arrive at a definite Allied policy, and he considered that this was the very first thing to which the Allied statesmen should address themselves when they arrived in Paris'.[11] He would much rather the whole problem would go away.

Indeed, Lloyd George's desire to escape from a Russian commitment was demonstrated by his willingness to hold a peace conference with the Bolsheviks. At the beginning of January 1919, he instructed the Foreign Office to send a note to the French proposing that invitations be sent to the Bolsheviks in Moscow, the various White Russian commanders and the Baltic States suggesting a round table meeting to discuss a negotiated peace. It was submitted to hold such a conference at Prinkipo (Büyükada), an island in the Sea of Marmara.

On 5 January the French responded in the negative. Two weeks later the Allied Supreme War Council heard from Joseph Noulens, the former French Ambassador to Russia who made an authorised statement. In it he declared that:

> The Bolshevist power is the enemy of the Entente. It is responsible for the Russian defection from the Entente. It furnished Germany with food during the war. It protested against the terms of the German armistice. These acts show an uncompromising attitude of hostility against the Entente. Tyranny and terror, which are increasing daily, should place the bloody chiefs at Moscow and Petrograd outside the pale of humanity. No society of nations could deal with such a regime, which constitutes a most serious obstacle to a general peace.[12]

Despite this uncompromising stance, US President Wilson, and Lloyd George convinced French Premier Clemenceau that such a conference was a good idea and Wilson sponsored the proposal before the Supreme Council. It was adopted on the 22nd. Unsurprisingly there was a wave of protest from the non-Bolshevik groupings in Russia, and indeed elsewhere; as the *Spectator* magazine noted 'if the representatives of the reputable Russian groups refuse to sit down with the tiger they will have every right on their side'.[13]

Nonetheless the Estonians accepted, stating, *inter alia*, that 'for three months after having organized a regular army, it [Estonia] has been at war with the Russian Soviet communist republic. Therefore, we in no way consider ourselves a part of Russia, although we accept the invitation of the Allied Powers and of the United States … We believe that the participation of the representatives of Estonia and of the communist republic of Russian Soviets is of importance to the future relations between Russia and the Estonian Republic.'[14]

From their temporary home at Libau, the provisional Latvian government accepted too, stating 'we will send three delegates … provided that all armed forces sent or directed by Russia against the Lettish State be withdrawn from Letvia [*sic*], and that all offensive military action cease'.[15]

And it was around the issues of the cessation that the plan finally fell. Firstly, the Bolsheviks havered over the proposed location; then they refused a cease fire, hoping to maximise their territorial gains prior to any truce. By 16 February, the Supreme Council realised it was a dead letter and moved on, formally abandoning the idea on the 27th, and Lloyd George and his government were still stuck with Russia and the Baltic like a fly in amber.[*]

The British War Cabinet did not discuss the situation in Russia again until 12 and 13 February. Here once more, the same divisions of thought which had hamstrung the orders given to Alexander-Sinclair following the November 1918 Cabinets re-surfaced, and Lloyd George's leaning towards non-intervention continued to influence debate.

On the 12th, Churchill had given an impassioned plea for increases in force and for greater intervention in Russia. He noted that 'we were committed in Russia in various directions. We had forces both in the north and in the south of Russia, and in Siberia. The men there were entitled to know what they were fighting for and were entitled to proper support from home. Our enterprises in all these directions were crumbling.'[16] He asserted that 'the

---

[*] There was a further US-sponsored attempt in March, the Bullitt mission, which also proved abortive.

Bolsheviks were getting stronger every day'[17] and that 'there was complete disheartenment everywhere'. With considerable emphasis he stressed his view that 'if we were going to withdraw our troops, it should be done at once. If we were going to intervene, we should send larger forces there.'[18] He himself believed that Britain ought to intervene.

Lloyd George's retort was to ask for a military assessment the following day and the War Cabinet re-convened to discuss the requested paper on the Russian situation, prepared by General Sir Henry Hughes Wilson, Chief of the Imperial General Staff. But Lloyd George immediately attacked it, saying that no decisions were possible because the strategies described therein for supporting the White armies were uncosted.

The paper considered four different alternative policies which, in Wilson's opinion, it was possible to pursue; i) Intervention, ii) Evacuation, iii) Recognition of the Bolsheviks, and iv) Defence of the Embryo States.

Lloyd George once more pounced, stating that 'in regard to the fourth alternative "the defence of the small States", he had stated quite clearly that there was complete agreement among the Allies as to the defence of the small states against the Bolsheviks or anyone else who might attack them'.[19] In other words 'Don't waste my time'. He later also noted that 'that in regard to Estonia he considered that there would be complete agreement amongst the Powers. The League of Nations would have no chance unless they were prepared to defend the small nations.'[20]

Attempting to placate those who were opposed to the sending of British land forces to the conflict zone, Churchill noted that 'there was no doubt that the only chance of making headway against the Bolsheviks was by the use of Russian armies. If Russian armies were not available there was no remedy. Large British and French Armies were not to be thought of.'[21]

But the new First Lord of the Admiralty, Walter Long, took a pessimistic view. He observed that 'we were already committed to the enterprise; we were in a bad position from which we could not escape'.[22] He asked whether a policy of evacuation was not impossible. The Admiralty was facing swingeing budget cuts; it did not want the costs of supporting squadrons in Russian or Baltic Waters if it could be avoided.

Austen Chamberlain, Chancellor of the Exchequer and thus

keenly interested in the costs that might be incurred, argued that Britain should tell the White commanders in mainland Russia that the government would support them with financial and material assistance, and might give them volunteers, but would not commit to a standing army.

Anxious to put the navy's efforts in a good light, Rear Admiral Fremantle declared that the policy Chamberlain recommended had been actually tried in Estonia and Latvia. 'The Admiral in Command [Alexander-Sinclair] was told to confine his assistance to the supply of arms and naval support. In Estonia the policy had been successful. In Latvia at first little had been effected and the Admiral had not felt justified in serving out arms until quite recently, but he desired to point out that the limits of our policy had been very definitely laid down.'[23]

But near the close of the meeting, two statements made by Lloyd George and Churchill showed the intellectual distance between them that was always going to make taking decisions difficult. Lloyd George stated that with regard to the overall position in Russia he 'was not in the least clear that the Russian people did not want something in the nature of Bolshevism. It was true they were tired of it in Petrograd but in the other districts this was not the case.'[24] But Churchill presented a picture based on a broad geopolitical view. Russia was no longer of any use to Britain or France as a counterweight to Germany; the German population would grow at a much faster rate to that of France and in five or six years' time, Germany would have twice as many men available for military service than the French. It appeared to Churchill that the new republic in Germany would model itself on the lines of the Third Republic of France. He did not expect an immediate appeal to arms by the Germans but the future was full of menace. In his view the Germans were going to say at Versailles that they would not sign any more documents or agree to anything further.

In addition to this, Russia would prove a great prize to Germany. If no proper Government in Russia were brought into existence, Russia would automatically fall a prey to Germany, and could be claimed by Germany as the prize she had won in the war. Germany had only to sit tight and there was an immense area open for her forces. The Russian situation must be judged as a part of the great quarrel with

Germany, and unless we were able to go to the support of the Russians there was a possibility of a great combination from Yokohama to Cologne in hostility to France, Britain and America. He regarded a friendly Government in Russia and a strong Poland as the two essentials.[25]

Thus were the Cabinet battle lines drawn: economy, social spending and acceptance of a fait accompli, versus a dystopian view of a future Germany and the role of Russia. Unsurprisingly, the Cabinet came to no decision; the can was kicked down the road with a request that Wilson prepare a new paper, reflecting the points made in the discussion.

Churchill, meantime, hot-footed it over to Paris, with Lloyd George still in London, and spent 14, 15 and 17 February lobbying the Council of Ten[*] to press for full military intervention in Russia. Lloyd George sent "a very hot telegram' totally repudiating the measures for which his ardent Secretary of State was pressing'.[26]

---

[*] The initial body which met to consider peace terms comprising two delegates each from Britain, France, the United States, Italy and Japan.

CHAPTER 7

Possible Saviours, January – February 1919

Rear Admiral Sir Walter Henry Cowan KCB DSO MVO had been designated Alexander-Sinclair's replacement and the two men met briefly at Copenhagen on 5 January 1919, travelling in their different directions. Once moored, *Cardiff*'s crew spent the morning handing over their winter clothing[*] and then departed for Britain, arriving on the 8th. Two days later Cowan was formally gazetted in his new appointment and took up the Baltic crown of thorns.

Cowan was the eldest son of an army officer who received the entirety of his formal education in the navy, never having been to school before he entered the training ship HMS *Britannia* in 1884 at the age of thirteen. From there he joined HMS *Alexandra,* the flagship of the CinC Mediterranean Fleet, HRH the Duke of Edinburgh.

A small and undeveloped boy, he served as a midshipman in the Benin campaign of 1887, before being invalided home, and then as a lieutenant on the East India Station, before being again sent home in 1893 with dysentery. Service once more in the Mediterranean Fleet followed where, like Alexander-Sinclair, he excelled at polo, acquired several ponies and played the sport almost daily.

In June 1898 he was in Egypt as part of a naval squadron attached to Kitchener's forces in the battle against the Mahdi for control of the Sudan. Here he commanded the gunboat *Sultan* and was in company with two other lieutenants who would achieve fame and flag rank – David Beatty[§] and the Honourable Horace Hood. Cowan went on to command the entire Nile gunboat flotilla during the

---

[*] Given that they were going to Rosyth, this may have seemed to some a little premature.
[§] Who had been a fellow midshipman of Cowan on *Alexandra*.

subsequent Fashoda Incident and received the DSO for his overall service in the campaign.

After volunteering for the Boer War (and taking an unauthorised leave of absence to serve as Lord Roberts' ADC), he served in destroyers under Roger Keyes and in 1914, as a post captain, was appointed to command the battleship HMS *Zealandia* and then the battlecruiser HMS *Princess Royal*. In her he fought at Jutland as flag captain to Rear Admiral Osmond Brock.

In June 1917 Cowan was made Commodore of the 1st Light Cruiser Squadron which he led at the Second Battle of Heligoland Bight on 17 November 1917 and ten months later was advanced to the rank of rear admiral, retaining command of the squadron.

Cowan was a small man, barely 5ft 6in tall, and was known throughout the service as 'Titch' Cowan. He loved battle and was famously aggressive. Arthur Marder thought he possessed the offensive spirit[1] but 'was not of the scientific or academic type'.[2] Serving with Cowan in *Zealandia*, Commander Humphry H Smith believed that Cowan was the 'only person on board who thoroughly enjoyed the war' adding 'he was a thoroughbred fire-eater and neither his anxiety to get at the enemy nor his energy ever waned for a second'.[3] At dinner on Armistice night everyone was cheerful bar Cowan; 'Why are you looking so sad?,' someone asked him. 'Nothing left to live for,' he replied. He was, thought Bertram Thesiger, the only person in the room who was sorry that the war was over.[4]

But Cowan was also nervily quick tempered; 'this defect, allied to his determination to enforce his own standards of efficiency, duty and discipline made him a difficult man to serve'.[5] Admiral Roger Keyes liked him; 'I don't think I have ever been quite so taken with anyone as I am with Cowan. He is the gallantest [*sic*] little sportsman I ever met';[6]* and on another occasion Keyes described Cowan as 'an ardent warrior'.[7]§ But others were more circumspect. Commander Andrew Cunningham, who served under him, thought 'hasty he undoubtedly was; but if in haste he unjustly hurt people's feelings or wounded their susceptibilities he was at pains to make amends at the earliest possible moment'.[8]

Now Cowan was to face the greatest challenge of his career; a

---

* Keyes equated officer-like qualities with the ability to ride to hounds well and play decent polo. Cowan met these criteria.
§ In 1903 Cowan succeeded Keyes in command of the Devonport Destroyer Flotilla.

man of action, not a politician. Not a thinker but a doer. And now thrown into a pot-mess of trouble.

His command was a small one; two light cruisers and five 'V & W'-class destroyers. HMS *Caledon*, his flagship was another 'C'-class light cruiser, similar to the ships of Alexander-Sinclair's force, and captained by Commander Henry Steuart Macnaghten Harrison-Wallace. Cowan's second cruiser was a less well armed and rather cramped ship, HMS *Royalist*. She was one of eight *Arethusa*-class light cruisers, launched in 1915, and sporting three 6in, four 4in and two 3in anti-aircraft guns (two, six and one respectively as originally built). The class had been intended as destroyer flotilla leaders. She was commanded by Captain the Honourable Matthew Robert Best DSO, who had been one of four flag captains to Jellicoe on *Iron Duke* at Jutland. Forty years old, he was the third son of Lieutenant Colonel George Best, 5th Baron Wynford.

Cowan's orders gave him a little more clarity than they had his predecessor. Fremantle had briefed him before his departure. He was told that his primary function was to 'show the British flag and support British policy'[9]– a possibly futile task as no one seemed to know what the policy was. He was to maintain the blockade* of Germany. The admiral was further enjoined to prevent the destruction of Estonia and Latvia;§ to have nothing to do with the Germans; and that 'whenever we are in a position to resist Bolshevist attacks from the sea we should unhesitatingly do so'. Additionally, 'a Bolshevik man of war operating off the coast of the Baltic Provinces must be assumed to be doing so with hostile intent and treated accordingly'.[10] For a man of Cowan's aggressive character, such orders were virtually a licence to wage war.

But Cowan was not blind to the difficulties. 'It seemed to me that there was never such a tangle and my brain reeled with it. An unbeaten German army, two kinds of belligerent Russians, Letts, Finns, Estonians [*sic*], Lithuanians; ice, mines – 60,000 of them, Russian

---

* The British naval blockade of 1914–18 was continued after the end of the war and although some help was grudgingly provided with limited food supplies, the German people were kept hungry; part revenge perhaps, part to keep the nation subjugated and part necessity as the French in particular had their own food supply problems to solve first. See S R Dunn, *Blockade* (Barnsley: Seaforth Publishing, 2016). His orders were soon amended in the light of new agreements with the Scandinavian countries of Sweden, Norway and Denmark which allowed them to ship goods to Germany, except for gold, in their own bottoms, and if appropriately licensed.

§ 'To prevent the destruction of the Esthonian [*sic*] and Latvian provinces by eternal aggression, which is only threatened at present by Bolshevik invaders' (ADM 137/1664, NA).

submarines, German small craft, Russian battleships, cruisers and destroyers all only waiting for the ice to melt to ravage the Baltic.'[11]

His first three actions were typical. He asked the Admiralty for permission to go to Reval (despite it being largely iced-in) and shell Bolshevik positions. Permission was firmly denied and he was told to avoid both the Estonian capital and Riga. Next, he requested more ships in the eventuality that both Reval and Libau both fall into Red hands. And he sent Best with *Royalist* and two destroyers to the Libau to assess the Latvian situation.

Best reported that there were 2,000 German troops still in the port but only around a third of them were obeying their commander's orders. The weapons which Alexander-Sinclair had provided had been left in a shed under the care of the harbourmaster; but a German general and a party of German soldiers had raided the store and thrown the majority of the rifles and ammunition into the harbour. Moreover, Prime Minister Ulmanis believed that it would prove impossible to hold Libau as the Bolsheviks were now only 78 miles away and he feared a communist rising in the town. He asked for 10,000 Allied troops to which there was only ever going to be one answer, given the British government's position; no!

In Estonia, things were proceeding rather better. In early January, the Estonian forces were able to halt the Soviet advance, subsequent to the Royal Navy's bombardments, and on 3 January, Laidoner launched a counter offensive supported by the Finnish volunteers (previously transported in part in by 6LCS) and armoured trains. It was this offensive that Thesiger had briefly assisted just before his departure (*vide supra* Chapter 6). Within eleven days, the Estonian forces had advanced 200km eastwards, whilst further forces staged an attack against the Red Army in the south of the country. Both Narva and Dorpat were liberated from Bolshevik oppression.

A grateful government immediately promoted Laidoner to the rank of major general and on the first anniversary of Estonia's original declaration of independence, 24 February, Laidoner was able to state that the Soviet forces had been completely driven out of his country; his men had also captured 6,000 prisoners and forty artillery pieces. It was to prove a temporary triumph but it was the first time a Bolshevik force had been driven eastwards in the whole campaign.

Cowan had arrived in Copenhagen on 31 December 1918. Here he received a warning from the French ambassador that a Bolshevik attempt 'was likely to be made on Allied war vessels at Copenhagen'.[12]

The Danish Admiralty was most helpful, however, and put up barriers along the wharf and 'lent us lighters to interpose between the ships and the jetty',[13] together with an extra allocation of police guards. *Royalist* joined on 5 January and fired a 21-gun salute from her 4in weapons and, after dinner, another thirteen-gun tribute for the Danish port admiral.

There was also a very present danger of spies hanging around on the *Langelinie*. One such was an individual who disguised himself as a Jewish peddler of gold watches who tried to get information out of gullible sailors. Sub Lieutenant de Courcy-Ireland and other officers of HMS *Westcott* tired of this game. 'With the connivance of a friendly Danish policeman, we hired a taxi, pushed the terrified little man into it … and drove fifteen miles to the most sparsely populated area we could find … We then removed his boots and left him to walk home in his socks.'[14]

To Libau

The admiral was clear as to who to blame for the current situation. On 14 January he wrote that 'there is no doubt that the prime cause of this Baltic Provinces debacle is the failure of Germany to comply with Article XII of the Armistice terms'[15]– this without yet having visited the region!

However, given Laidoner's initial success, Cowan decided that his immediate concern should be Latvia, and the perilous position of Libau in particular. On 31 January he paid a flying visit to the country, arriving at Libau and meeting with the deputy Prime Minister, Doctor Walters, as Ulmanis was in Sweden trying to raise a mercenary/volunteer force to come and fight the Bolsheviks. And then on 5 February he returned in *Caledon* and in force.

Firstly, his ships delivered into the port 5,320 rifles and fifty-two Madsen* machine guns with 4.3 million rounds of rifle ammunition and a million rounds for the Madsens, which were unloaded from *Royalist* but stowed on the freighter SS *Saratov*, to keep them safe from the fate the Germans had inflicted on their predecessors. Secondly, he found a fight to get into. The port town of Windau (Ventspils) fell to the Reds on 9 February, which placed them just 40 miles from Libau. Ulmanis asked for a ship to provide artillery support and Cowan was only too delighted to oblige. Fremantle at

---

* A Danish-made light machine gun.

the Admiralty gave the go-ahead and *Caledon* sailed north and anchored off Windau. The Bolsheviks were about to receive a lesson in artillery superiority.

The cruiser's 6in guns fired a shell weighing 100lbs; this was, in the context of a land war, a major piece of ordnance. The standard British Empire field gun of the First World War was the QF 18pdr, which formed the backbone of the Royal Field Artillery during the war and was produced in large numbers. It delivered a shell, as the name suggests, weighing 18.5lbs. The French '75', the iconic gun of the 1914 French army, delivered a 12lb shell, the German 77mm one of 15lbs. The cruiser's gunfire was therefore of substantially greater power than that of the most common artillery weapons of the recently ended war.

Thus, when *Caledon* opened fire, not only did she drive the Bolsheviks into a headlong evacuation of the city, she also destroyed the batteries installed to defend the harbour entrance. It was a textbook operation. This stopped the panic flight of refugees from Libau; and it also seemed the first step in a stabilisation of the situation. The German government was still under pressure from the Allies to abide by the request, previously made under Article XII of the Armistice, to oppose the Red Army; now they decided to do more to comply. They had come to believe that they might get better armistice terms if they sided with the Allies against the Bolsheviks. Accordingly, Germany sent a new commander to the region, ostensibly to ensure that the German army resisted the Russians as had been demanded.

Prussian-born 53-year-old General Gustav Adolf Joachim Rüdiger Graf von der Goltz had been a major general commanding a German infantry division on the Western Front. In March 1918 he was transferred to Finland to aid the 'White' Finns in their brief but savage civil war ('The War of Liberty') against the 'Red' Finns, who were backed by the Russian Bolsheviks. His so-called Baltic Sea Division was instrumental in the success of the Whites and Finland was saved for democracy[*]. On 2 February 1919 he arrived in Latvia, at his government's request, to take command of the Iron Division (*vide supra* Chapter 3).

Both Cowan and Ulmanis welcomed the arrival of the German general, not least because he was to be reinforced with fresh troops from Germany. Goltz immediately began the process of forging the remnants of the German armies, the *Freikorps*, and *Baltische*

Landeswehr into a coherent force. But the admiral and the prime minister might have been less pleased with Goltz's advent if they had known his personal agenda.

Meanwhile, Cowan returned to Copenhagen. On passage he had the opportunity to carry out one hitherto un-actioned part of his orders when *Royalist* intercepted a German blockade runner, SS *Wojan*, and found her carrying contraband goods. He sent her to Rosyth with a prize crew.

Back in Denmark, on 13 February, Cowan had received reinforcements in the guise of the light cruisers *Phaeton* and *Inconstant*, both of the 1st Light Cruiser Squadron, with five 'V & W'-class destroyers. In its wisdom the Admiralty had decided that ships should be relived every six weeks owing to the hardship of the duty; this new force was the relief. Both cruisers were sister-ships to *Royalist*.

Cowan took his flagship and *Phaeton* to Libau so that Captain John Ewen Cameron, second-in-command of 1LCS and commanding *Phaeton*, could get a first-hand briefing on the situation; he was to act as SNO whilst Cowan returned to Britain. During this visit Cowan and Cameron met with Ulmanis and his Defence Minister, who informed him that Goldingen (Kuldīga) had been recaptured and Windau was now occupied by a force of 550 mixed *Baltische Landeswehr* and German *Freikorps*. They also apprised him that the fresh German troops were arriving and that von der Goltz was now able to contemplate an advance on Riga. But the weapons left by Captain Best were still on board the *Saratov*, and Cowan formed the impression that the Germans wanted to prevent them reaching the Latvians. He wondered why.

The admiral finally departed on 21 February, taking *Caledon*, *Royalist* and the destroyers with him. His orders for Cameron included the instructions to visit Libau at no less than ten-day intervals and to hand over 500,000 rounds of ammunition, stowed in

---

*(page 78) This was not altruism. In return for the German assistance, Finnish 'White' politicians travelled to Germany to negotiate a programme for a Greater Finland and a German eastern Baltic. *The Times* newspaper, in a report datelined 'Stockholm 23 May 1918', outlined the programme it believed was under discussion. By May, 'the German Baltic Commander was to take Helsingfors and Petrograd. [The former had in fact already been occupied by German troops.] By June Germany was to have laid the foundation for a Greater Finland, including Petrograd and a new railway … Thus Finland would be bounded on the south-west by a German Estonia, with other Baltic Provinces, and Germany would claim a free harbour on the Arctic Sea in Finland … Such a new Finland would be greater than Norway, Sweden and Denmark put together and thus Germany would become a leading Baltic Power.'

the collier SS *Holywood*, to the Latvians 'by the first convenient opportunity'.[16] Cameron was further urged to maintain the blockade against Germany and to take measures against Bolshevik attempts at sabotage.

Cowan had hoped for action but had only the bombardment of Windau to slake his desire. Accordingly, he pressed upon the Admiralty that, when the ice melted in the spring, he wanted to come straight back to the Baltic in case of naval action by the Russian Baltic Fleet; 'it would be a matter of the greatest satisfaction to me' he told them.[17] His crews were simply pleased to be going home.

At Libau

Captain Cameron, as instructed, returned to Libau on 28 February. He met with Acting Prime Minister Dr Walters and Defence Minister Zālītis. The two Latvians repeated the request for a permanent British naval presence in Libau. Their justification was that they had found letters which implied that the Baltic German leaders planned a coup against the Provisional Government, with support from von der Goltz. The Latvians would be replaced by Baltic Germans who would then appoint a Baltic War Lord as supreme commander. As a prelude to the abortive coup, the Germans had tried to take over the British-donated weapons and ammunition, stored on board the freighter *Saratov*. The Latvian forces had foiled the attempt but to protect the weapons, the freighter was now moved from Libau's inner harbour to the outer one.

Furthermore, the Provisional Government's desire to raise and equip a Latvian army was being stymied at every turn by von der Goltz and the German Governor of Libau. As Cowan himself later put it 'the Letts [Latvians] – under the direction of M Ulmanis, the Acting President – were making every endeavour to raise and equip a sufficient military force, aided by a limited quantity of small arms, machine guns and ammunition supplied by His Majesty's Government, to enable them to undertake the defence of their own country against the Bolsheviks when the time should come for the Germans to withdraw'. It soon became evident, however, that it was 'not the Germans' intention to permit any Lettish [Latvian] force being raised, and constant cases of friction, oppression and disarmament of Lettish Troops began to occur'.[18] Cameron reported the planned coup to the Admiralty and it is possibly this that led the

DNI, Rear Admiral Hugh Francis Paget Sinclair, to express his support for a permanent naval presence at the port.

Captain Cameron also noted the plight of two seamen from *Princess Margaret* who had been left behind when Riga was evacuated in January. They had been taken prisoner by the Bolsheviks, stripped of their boots and greatcoats and were starving and in a very bad way. He arranged with a Major Keenan of the British Mission that a rescue attempt would be staged by some of the major's less formal Latvian contacts; for a fee of course.

On the Prime Minister's return, Cameron then met with Ulmanis who expressed his wish to take over from the Germans the administration of Libau and the recaptured towns of Windau and Goldingen. Cameron again reported back that this request should be supported. The Latvian repeated his plea for heavy weapons and military support.

In concluding his report of the visit, Cameron was moved to state that

> it seems clear that at present the Lettish troops are incapable of driving out the invading Bolshevists and that only the Germans can undertake this operation. However, the result will be that the Germans will become predominant in the country and the great majority of the people are strongly anti-German.
>
> If this state of affairs is not desired by the Allied Governments, it would appear to be absolutely necessary to land a force of sympathetic Allied troops before the Germans can be ordered to withdraw.
>
> A comparatively small but well-equipped British Force would restore confidence and prevent local Bolshevism while at the same time it would greatly encourage the Lettish recruiting and tend to uphold the Lettish Government.

The answer would be as before.[19]

CHAPTER 8

Germany Turns the Screw, March – April 1919

Imperii Germanici Resurget?

Buoyed up by the arrival of fresh German troops (estimated by the British Foreign Office at 13,000 men), von der Goltz had launched an attack against the communist forces on 3 March 1919. He met with immediate success and the Red Army troops were forced to retreat to the east. Goldingen, Windau and Mitau (Jelgava) were swiftly captured.

But Goltz was fighting a different war to that of the previous four years. There were no clearly marked battle lines or even easily identifiable combatants. Ex-German POWs, Russians and Latvians fought on the communist side; Germans, Latvians and White Russians on the other. The Bolsheviks did not have much in the way of uniforms, which led the Germans to believe they were dealing with guerrillas or *francs-tireurs*; they responded with bitter violence, as they had in Belgium in 1914. Rudolf Höss, who in a later war would be notorious as the commandant of Auschwitz, served in Latvia as a volunteer. He wrote that 'the battles in the Baltic States were more brutal and more vicious than anything I had ever experienced before. There was hardly a front line, the enemy was everywhere. Whenever the opposing forces collided, there was a slaughter until no-one was left.'[1]

But Goltz's aim was not just to win a fight against the Bolsheviks; he was bent on conquest. His offensive had captured towns which were largely ethnically German, repelling the Bolsheviks from the coast in the process. He subscribed, as did many on the right back in Germany, to the notion of constructing a new German empire in the east, a ring of colonies to both protect Germany from the Slav threat and give her a better jumping-off point for the war with

Russia that many in the military and beyond believed was inevitable eventually.

Moreover, the left of centre government in Germany, under President Friedrich Ebert, was fully occupied with the peace talks in Paris. Germany itself was a hotbed of communist agitation and the Spartacus League was attempting armed rebellion. Indeed, on 6 January 1919, Karl Liebknecht in Berlin had proclaimed the creation of a German Socialist Republic and red flags flew throughout the city. *Freikorps* groups responded by hunting down the communists and Liebknecht himself was killed just nine days later. *Freikorps* soldiers roamed the streets seeking out Bolsheviks, whilst communists staged riots and killings. The neighbouring cities of Hamburg and Bremen fought a two-day war with each other which resulted in the communists who had taken control of the latter city being driven out.

The army held itself aloof from the government and, indeed, eventually negotiated a compact with Ebert that the government would not interfere with it or attempt army reform. Right wing and militaristic political groups proliferated; some advocating a monarchy, others a military state.[*] Many in the military argued that Germany had been defeated on the Western Front only and that the terms of the Armistice did not apply to the east. As Churchill described them to the War Cabinet,

> the driving power is supplied by the Prussian military party, mainly from patriotic motives. The leaders of this party, men like Generals Ludendorff, Hofman and Lossberg, supported by some of the leading permanent civil officials and certain capitalists, have not given up their hopes of a great German revival in future years. Their motto is *Augen Ost* [Eyes to the East]. They realise that in western Germany there is no hope of territorial or even commercial expansion. The east, on the other hand, provides an unlimited field for German thrift, brains and energy. They have hopes of ultimate territorial gains by means of German settlers, and their immediate object is to help the German Balts to overthrow the Letts [Latvians], and to establish their ascendency in Lithuania and Courland.

---

[*] And indeed, in March 1920, the 'Kapp Putsch' saw a right-wing government, supported by Ludendorff, supplant Ebert – for a week.

Their ulterior aim is the development of Russia by German brains and enterprise.[2]

And as the War Cabinet were later told,

General von der Goltz assumed complete control of the administration, civil as well as military, in the area controlled by the Lettish Government, with the object of depriving that Government, of all authority and discrediting it in the eyes of the population. One of the arbitrary acts of the Germans in this connection was the seizure of local stocks of timber, without the permission of the Government, for the settlement of requisitioning debts. General von der Goltz, moreover, designated his force an German Army of Occupation and, apparently with the enforced concurrence of the Lettish Government, promised the German troops grants of land in Latvia as a reward for their services. In this latter connection, the German intentions are very clearly indicated. Announcements appeared in the German Press ... offering fifty morgen* of land per man to volunteers in the German forces in the Baltic States.[3]

The result of all of these conflicting forces was that the legitimate German government could exercise little direct influence over von der Goltz. He was effectively a free agent. And Goltz was certainly not under the control of the Latvian Provisional Government. Relations between them, not helped by the attempted coup, were 'seriously strained by *Freikorps* violence against Latvian civilians'.[4] By the end of March, with the Red Army on the run and von der Goltz ascendant, the relationship was in tatters.

Libau was a German mini-state; despite its nominal presence there, the Latvian government held no power. It was the German-backed governor and Goltz's soldiers who ruled; and then again in the towns captured in the March offensive. As the general himself said on his arrival in Latvia; 'I alone have supreme command over all the troops and military installations ... the troops at the front, immaterial of nationality, are solely under my command.'[5] He saw himself as no less than the ruler of a new German Grand Duchy.

Goltz harassed any British officers ashore; when Cowan was

---

* A morgen was a unit of measurement used in Old Prussia, the Balkans, Norway and Denmark, and was equal to about two-thirds of an acre.

returning to his ship after a meeting with the British Mission, he was stopped by a sentry who demanded to see his pass to access the quay. Cowan was apoplectic and protested to Goltz in the strongest terms; Goltz merely sent him a pass. He had made the point that on land, Cowan had little or no power. It was the Germans who ruled.

An appreciation, prepared for the US delegation at the Paris Peace Conference by the American diplomat Ulysses S Grant-Smith on 13 April, gives a good summary of the situation in Latvia at this time.

> Germans dominate situation as they are here in force and Lettish Army is insignificant as military factor. Germans now state they are here under Article XII of the Armistice, although they at first claimed to us they were an army of occupation. General von der Goltz commands all forces operating in Courland and is Governor of Libau. In addition he controls police and telegraph and German Military Intelligence Service Bureau of Railroads. Without Germans, [the] country would be quickly submerged by Bolsheviki [*sic*]. This naturally creates [a] most difficult and anomalous situation, as Lettish people historically are anti-German, and this feeling has been reinforced by their experience of German Military Intelligence Service operation during war. Von der Goltz informs us that Germans [are] here under article XII armistice, and also for the international fight against Bolsheviki which threatens western civilization and western culture …
>
> The present *de facto* government of Latvia is extremely weak and represents no mandate from the people of Latvia. It would be overthrown immediately if there were a popular election. It is a self-constituted government by party leaders and men who took things into own hands at Riga and were later driven from that city by Bolsheviki advance. It was recognised by Germans [in] December. Both Balts and Socialists are hostile too and bourgeoisie give only grudging support. At same time it is [the] only organisation we have dealings with and should be supported as *de facto* national government or organisation of Latvia but should not be recognised for present. It should be treated with, however, on all questions concerning food import, blockade, finances, etc. Ulmanis, Prime Minister, and Walters, Minister of Home Affairs, only capable men they have in Cabinet.[6]

While the Peace Conference debated, von der Goltz stopped his advance into Latvia at the important railway junction town of Mitau as a protest over the Allies preventing any further shipment of men to him. Here he established his headquarters. In the absence of any supplies from the British or French, he ordered his men to live off the land. The Latvian citizens, peasants and bourgeois alike, had to compete for their food with two itinerant armies. It resembled Europe in the Thirty Years War, bands of marauders crisscrossing the countryside bringing rapine and plunder in their wake. Starvation stalked the land. In Libau, awaiting Cowan's return, Cameron feared food riots and revolt.

Still Searching

The War Cabinet met in Downing Street on 17 March with Bonar Law in the chair, as Lloyd George was absent in Paris. Two papers had been circulated before the meeting; one from the Admiralty regarding the situation in the Baltic, and the much debated and amended one from Churchill, first tabled in February and greatly altered as a result.

Acting Foreign Secretary Lord Curzon opened the batting. He aimed a shot towards the long grass by stating that it 'was useless for the War Cabinet to take piecemeal decisions with regard to military, naval and financial assistance to Russia until there was a definite Russian policy. At present there was no policy. A policy could not be evolved in London: it must be framed in Paris'[7] – i.e. by the Allies in conclave and the Supreme War Council. Further, Curzon complained that a very sensible 'proposal for a division of responsibility for assisting certain territories had been proposed, namely, Poland to France, the Baltic to Great Britain, and the other border states to other powers. The First Lord [Long] had come to him and asked if the navy could proceed on the basis of this division. He [Lord Curzon] had telegraphed to Paris, with very unsatisfactory results.'[8] One can almost hear the harrumph.

The truth was that the statesman hammering out what would become the Treaty of Versailles had little time for matters in Russia. Forging an agreement amongst the politicians was a problem and in the Supreme War Council, Maréchal Ferdinand Foch, the Allies' chief warlord, was interested only in forcing Germany to abide by the terms of the Armistice.

But Curzon ploughed on. Reflecting on the Baltic States, he noted that Britain was supporting the White Russian forces but their agenda was not Britain's; 'any assistance given to them would be used to revive the old monarchical Russia. They undoubtedly meant to attempt to recover the Border States.' Furthermore, he added, 'while Esthonia [*sic*] was now holding its own, the neighbouring states were only kept from Bolshevism by the aid of German forces … we were refusing to give them help, and at the same time were refusing to send our own troops to oppose the Bolsheviks.'[9]

Churchill then intervened to note that he had just heard from General Wilson (Chief of the Imperial General Staff) of the conversations he [Wilson] had had in Paris with Lloyd George and Foch. 'Foch was opposed to encouraging the [White] Russians to go in at this point … Wilson went on to suggest that before sending a mission to the Baltic it was necessary to wait for a decision on Russian policy from the Supreme War Council; but when that would be obtained he had no idea.'[10]

First Lord Walter Long now commented that the Admiralty had 'suggested the formation of a committee … which should advise upon the policy for the Baltic Provinces and should review this policy from time to time. Such a committee could at least formulate questions for the Supreme War Council to which the Cabinet could request an answer.' Possibly in this way definite pressure could be put on President Wilson. He agreed with the Secretary of State for War (Churchill) that 'we were running the risk of grave disaster and we should be confronted with questions in Parliament to which it would not be easy to reply'.[11]

The oft-times frustrated Rear Admiral Fremantle, in one of his last appearances as an *ex-officio* member of the committee before moving on to a new posting, and no doubt pleased to shed this particular albatross, noted that there was an urgent need 'for some co-ordinating policy. We were at present rendering naval and military assistance in a thoroughly unsatisfactory fashion [and] we had lost a valuable light cruiser, with eleven lives.'[12]

But it was Lord Privy Seal Andrew Bonar Law who got to the nub of the issue. Britain could not afford to protect the Baltic States on its own; unless America came in the costs of the actions in Russia were unsupportable. And the USA was adamantly staying out. And Chancellor of the Exchequer Austen Chamberlain agreed with Bonar Law. He was convinced that 'the United States would do nothing to help such a policy. The French borrowed what they [the

USA] were lending for spending, and the burden in effect fell on us. He had just returned from Paris, where the French had asked him to assist them at a rate equal to our total pre-war expenditure. The Americans expressed their disinclination to do more for France or for us, other than to assist with purchases made in the United States.' Chamberlain then flatly stated that 'there was no way out for a ruined Europe unless the United States would untie her purse-strings. It was impossible for Europe to shoulder these ever-accumulating burdens without the assistance of the United States'.[13] And America, with an isolationist Congress, was unlikely to do that.[*]

Chamberlain would have felt vindicated had he read the contents of a telegram sent by US Acting Secretary of State Frank L Polk. On 8 March, and referring to the White Russians, he stated to his Vice Consul at Viborg (then in Finland), who was the US contact with the Whites, that 'this Government [is] not in a position to offer any support or assistance but wishes to be kept advised of developments. You are to exercise extreme caution not to encourage false hope.'[14]

Bringing the meeting to a close, Bonar Law made the point that 'we had undertaken to support the Baltic States against the menace of Bolshevism'.[15] But no-one seemed able to square the circle as to how best to provide that assistance. Eventually, the meeting agreed that

> (a) The War Office, the Admiralty, and, if they wished to do so, the Treasury, should send Memoranda to the Foreign Office, dealing with the assistance required to protect the Baltic States from Bolshevism, and the probable cost of such assistance; (b) On the basis of these Memoranda, the Acting Secretary of State for Foreign Affairs should prepare a despatch to the Prime Minister, asking for the direction of the Supreme War Council as to the policy to be pursued in regard to the Baltic Provinces: (c) In the meantime, no Naval or Military Mission should be sent to this area.[16]

The can rattled further down the road. As First Sea Lord Rosslyn Wemyss wrote despairingly to Rear Admiral John Green at Archangel on 24 March:

---

[*] Although an American Expeditionary Force under General William S Graves had been sent to Siberia in September 1918, largely to keep an eye on a similar Japanese force in the same region.

Alas, what you say about the lack of instructions is absolutely true. You are not the only person who feels it. Every department that has to deal with Russia is complaining and we find ourselves in some difficulty in contending with the situation in the Baltic for that very reason. The fact of the matter is that the government do not know what policy to put forward.[17]

Walter Long was prescient regarding questions in Parliament. Lloyd George was forced to make a statement to the House on 16 April. He explained that:

We are supplying all these countries with the necessary equipment to set up a real barrier against an invasion by force of arms. The Bolshevists may menace or they may not. Whether they do so or not, we should be ready for any attempt to overrun Europe by force. That is our policy. But we want peace in Russia. The world will not be pacified so long as Russia is torn and rent by civil war. We made one effort [Prinkipo]. I make no apology for that. That was an effort to make peace among the warring sections, not by recognising any government, but by inducing them to come to together, with a view to setting up some authority in Russia which would be acceptable to the whole of the Russian people, and which the Allies could recognise as the Government of that great people. We insisted that it was necessary they should cease fighting before they started to negotiate. With one accord, I regret to say, they refused to assent to this essential condition, and, therefore, the effort was not crowned with success.[18]

The first question (of what would be many inquisitions on the subject from this particular MP) came from Lieutenant Commander the Honourable Joseph Montague Kenworthy, MP for Kingston upon Hull Central and an Asquithean Liberal*. He asked if the Soviet Republic had acceded to this proposal.

'No' replied the Prime Minister; 'they would not accede to the request that they should cease fighting. On the contrary, they

---

* He later joined the Labour Party in 1926 and became the 10th Baron Strabolgi in 1934.

suggested that we were doing it purely because our friends were getting the worst of it ... But there are unmistakable signs that Russia is emerging from the trouble. When that time comes, when she is once more sane, calm, and normal, we shall make peace.'[19]

So Britain was keen to make peace; but its sailors were still fighting a war.

The Return

Cowan was granted his wish; early in March he was ordered to return to the Baltic. His despatch was in part due to the government's desire not to increase the resources committed to the Baltic; Fremantle and the Admiralty had argued for a deployment in force, including the 1st Battle Squadron (five battleships armed with 15in guns). Lloyd George, whilst accepting that the Supreme War Council must be convinced to supply arms, food, money and equipment, refused to countenance the deployment of such a force. So, on 25 March, back went Cowan, now with Geoffrey Mackworth, recently advanced in rank, as his flag captain.

With his flag again in the 'C'-class light cruiser *Caledon* and accompanied by ten destroyers he sailed first for Kristiania (Oslo) to deliver a consignment of 12 tons (222 boxes) of gold bullion (and be received by Queen Maud of Norway, youngest daughter of King Edward VII) and then on to Copenhagen, where he tarried for a week. At the beginning of April, with reports from Cameron that the situation in Latvia was rapidly deteriorating ringing in his ears, Cowan took *Caledon*, together with the destroyers *Seafire* and *Scotsman* to Libau; these were 'S'-class vessels, launched in 1918 and armed with three 4in guns, a 2pdr and two twin 21in torpedo mounts. *Seafire* was captained by Commander Andrew Browne Cunningham, a future First Sea Lord and much decorated Admiral of the Fleet.* It is interesting to note that *Seafire* sailed with only around 60 per cent of her normal complement such was now the difficulty of finding crews for foreign service.

They sailed through thick fog, minefields and navigational hazards at a steady 22 knots, ignoring the dangers as was Cowan's wont, and arrived 3 April. Cunningham was soon ordered to Windau 'a small port with two long breakwaters and ample quay space';[20] the Bolshevik front line was not very far away.

---

* Cowan's destroyers also included HMS *Wolfhound*, commanded by another future Admiral of the Fleet, John Cronyn Tovey.

Here Cunningham found the population starving; although possessed of British sovereigns and other coinage, there was no food to be purchased with them. Starving, skeletal children, wailing piteously, crowded round the ship on the quayside crying 'Mister, Mister, please bread'.[21] The Royal Navy sailor is notoriously soft-hearted. As one historian noted, 'enduring months at sea, often in bad weather and continual danger, closed men in on themselves. Things that needed to be said in the navy were said briefly and bluntly. In confined space emotions had to be supressed.'[22] But when this carapace was cracked open by some perceived injustice or appeal from an underdog, repressed emotion could pour out. In no time *Seafire*'s crew had set up a soup kitchen on the shore and 'we had the satisfaction of knowing that for the three or four days we were there the small people were tolerably well fed'.[23] On one occasion, a small child paddled an ice floe up to the side of the ship and begged for food. It was more than Gunner (T) Michael O'Leary could bear. He ran down to the mess, seized a large quantity of rice pudding and a spoon and passed them over; they were wolfed down in seconds. The crew also dispensed considerable quantities of 'The King's Yellow'* to the women on shore. On the fourth day, *Seafire* departed for Libau.

At Libau

The food situation in Libau was no better than at Windau. On 4 April Cowan was moved to write to the Admiralty that 'unless food is sent very shortly, Libau will be the scene of serious disturbances and probably bloodshed'.[24] First-hand evidence of the deprivation was seen from the decks of HMS *Cleopatra* when she arrived there.

Stoker Richard Frank Rose, born on the leap day of 1896 in Bognor, had added two years to his age to join the Royal Navy in 1910. When war came he served on HMS *Birmingham* when she sank the first U-boat of the war and then was in the stokehold of a series of destroyers. Just before the cessation of hostilities he was at Haslar Camp in Portsmouth when he was assigned to HMS *Cleopatra*. In April 1919, *Cleopatra* sailed from Rosyth for service in the Baltic as part of the 2nd Light Cruiser Squadron. Before Rose left on this duty, he took the precaution of getting engaged to be married.

* Soap.

When his ship arrived at Libau, Rose was part of the motor boat crew who landed their captain, Charles Little, ashore. Whilst waiting for his return, the sailors 'at once became the centre of curiosity of the natives and soon discovered that they needed one thing to barter for foodstuffs etc – "tabac" as they called it'.[25] Incautiously, Rose gave one supplicant a cigarette. Immediately 'they invaded the boat and nearly caused it to sink'.[26] Disaster was averted when the bowman produced a revolver which caused all to scatter. Nevertheless, the sailors soon established a good trade in which cigarettes were exchanged for 'doubtlessly looted' jewellery.[27] But the dreadful and hungry plight of the locals impressed itself on the battle-hardened stoker and his mates. In no time a receptacle for spare bread and another for clothing was placed on the mess deck and each day the donations amassed were collected up and given to the poor of Libau.

Meanwhile, on 15 April Cunningham was ordered to go to the assistance of SS *Saratov* which had suffered engine failure whilst in the naval harbour (Libau had three harbours, two inner, one of which was the 'naval' and one commercial, and one outer). Cowan wanted the merchant ship, with its load of arms and ammunition, moved to the outer harbour where it was safer from a repetition of the seizure attempt made in March. *Seafire*'s engineer officer went aboard and reported that it would take until the next afternoon before she was capable of movement. Cunningham settled down to wait. There were many German sailors on the quayside and they crowded round his ship; he posted armed sentries at the bottom of the gangways and they had from time to time push the soldiery away.

Coup d'État

In the light of the deteriorating relationship between Ulmanis's government and Goltz, it is perhaps unsurprising that, on Wednesday 16 April, the Baltic Germans staged a coup d'état. Together with *Freikorps* solders they eventually replaced the government with a puppet regime headed by Pastor Andreas Needra, who Goltz believed was more open to German interests, especially the granting of citizenship to the *Freikorps* veterans who wanted to stay and farm the proffered lands. This would, of course, further the Germanisation of the area.

Cunningham discovered this disconcerting news as he was

enjoying a morning cup of tea and a chinwag with a fellow officer from another destroyer, whilst he waited for *Saratov* to be repaired. Suddenly he was presented with a large and dishevelled soldier who had demanded an audience with him.

In a mixture of German, Latvian and sign language, Cunningham came to understand that the HQ of the nascent Latvian army had been attacked and taken by the Germans. Cunningham immediately went to see for himself, discovering the building looted, in flames, and a brass band triumphantly playing as the perpetrators marched away. It was, he thought, 'no time for a ship full of arms to be lying alongside the jetty'[28] and hurried back to his destroyer.

There he found the *Saratov* repaired and ready to sail, so he ordered her to follow and set off for the outer harbour, gun crews closed up and everyone at action stations. There was a swing bridge at the exit to the harbour and Cunningham ordered storming parties to be readied in case it wouldn't open for him, but in the end he gained free passage into the outer basin.

The Germans were busy rounding up the ministers of the deposed government. Cowan, having been informed of what was happening by Cunningham's erstwhile tea-drinking partner, now signalled Cunningham to take the destroyer *Scotsman* under his orders and sail to the commercial harbour to embark any members of the now defunct legislature who wished it. They entered harbour stern-first, in case of the need for a quick exit, and moored near the customs house. Two German machine-gun teams were positioned on the wharf, threatening the harbour. Cunningham sent them a polite message that they would be blown to pieces if they did not move away immediately; it had the desired effect.

Next a German officer was admitted with a head wound. It transpired that he had been ordered to seize the customs house, failed and had attempted to kill himself – and missed; he was treated and sent on his way. Two ministers from Ulmanis's government were embarked, one of whom, the Minister of Commerce, was ensconced in the charthouse where he comman-deered the only typewriter on the ship and began churning out propaganda. Ulmanis himself had taken refuge with the British Mission, under Major Keenan.

Another German officer appeared saying that he wanted to search the customs house; having no orders to participate in any action on land, Cunningham assented and sent Lieutenant

Commander Delorest John Dumergue Noble, captain of *Scotsman*, to accompany him. When Noble had failed to return after two hours, Cunningham himself landed; the German sentries attempted to block his entry to the customs house but, in the best tradition of naval presumption, he 'told them to go somewhere else in the best German at my command'[29] and pushed past them. The Germans were interrogating some 'suspects' but in actual fact they found no-one of importance.

Cowan, meanwhile, had taken control of the situation; All his messages to Goltz were transmitted through *Seafire* and Cunningham thought them 'frigidly polite, always firm and sometimes acrimonious'.[30] Cowan's later report details the political activities that he was forced to involve himself in. On the night of the coup,

> two young Baltic-German Officers came off to my ship (their leader in crimson plush breeches) and announced that they were the Heads of the Committee of Safety until the formation of a new Government and asked me if I could guarantee them the support of His Majesty's Government in this movement.
>
> I pointed out to them that until I had some satisfactory explanation for the events of the day, I could listen to and recognise no such proposals. I then sent them on shore again and heard nothing more of them.
>
> On my requiring an explanation from von der Goltz for these happenings, he denied all responsibility or knowledge for them, saying that his troops were out of hand, and that the Baltic-Germans were not under his orders. In consequence of this I called a meeting of the Allied representatives, and with them demanded the following from von der Goltz: first – that the unit which raided the Lettish Headquarters should be at once removed from the Libau district: and second – that the commanding officer of the offending Baltic – German unit be relieved of his command.
>
> We also gave him the time and date by which we required the fulfilment of these demands. Both were complied with within the time.[31]

Cowan also demanded that Goltz release the members of the legislature he had imprisoned in the coup and restore the legitimate government to power. Goltz cavilled at the first part of this request, claiming that they were all Bolsheviks, and ignored the second. He knew that Cowan had no way on land of enforcing his demands.

The admiral transferred Ulmanis and his colleagues to the *Saratov* and for the next ten weeks the legitimate government of Latvia was housed in a freighter, under the protecting guns of Royal Navy warships.[*] Unsurprisingly, the presence of the British warships at the inner harbour quay piqued popular interest and crowds gathered to see the spectacle daily. Adventurous children would run past the line of German sentries, who were stationed to prevent people getting too near the destroyers, and would almost always be rewarded by a thick slice of bread and jam or other titbit from the RN sailors. On one occasion, as a small girl was rushing back to the crowd proudly bearing her 'prize', she was clattered to the ground by a sentry. As one man, the sailors on *Seafire*'s and *Scotsman*'s decks roared for revenge and swarmed over the rails seeking physical retribution. World War might have reignited had their officers not managed to restore order.

The following morning, Cunningham awoke to discover a party of carpenters building a high wooden barricade on the quay, abreast of the destroyers. On enquiring why, he was told it was to keep the crowds away and ensure that they would not be further disturbed. Cunningham waited until it was finished, with a German sentry posted at its only door, before moving both his ships along the jetty until they were no longer covered by the newly-erected barrier; the people and the children came as before. This produced an explosion of anger from von der Goltz, but there was no further effort to quarantine the ships.

Shortly after this contretemps, the Germans attempted to put to sea in two armed trawlers, loaded with two platoons of soldiers; after they had gone about 600ft from the jetty, the 'instant readiness' destroyer steamed up with guns manned and aimed. The trawlers went back to their mooring. Cowan might not rule ashore; but he did at sea.

The coup prompted the Allies to demand the immediate recall of the *Freikorps* to Germany. Ebert responded by saying that a German withdrawal would inevitably lead to a Bolshevik victory in the Baltic, unless the governments in London and Paris were prepared

---

[*] Ulmanis was restored to power on 3 July, *vide infra* chapter 11.

to send troops in to replace them. Nonetheless, on 9 May Ebert signalled his government's willingness to order a withdrawal, as he was anxious to maintain good relations during the Paris talks. But Allies were resolutely unwilling to send their own troops; and they recognised the truth of Ebert's assertion. Now they changed tack and again insisted on Article XII being adhered to and the Germans staying and fighting, as instructed.

Meanwhile, on 24 April, Pitka had arrived at Libua in *Lennuk*. He brought with him a Russian naval captain, Knupffer, who represented the White Russian Northern Army. They were eager that Cowan should co-operate with them in an advance on Kronstadt. Such an offensive required the support of coastal bombardments and they wanted monitors and aircraft; Cowan had, of course, neither of these.* Knupffer also suggested an initial operation where leaflets were dropped promising food in return for surrender. Pitka stayed until the morning of 26 April when he informed Cowan that he had received a radio telegram that informed him Kronstadt was ice-free and the Red Fleet was at sea. Pitka immediately set sail, helped by the donation of fuel for his ship.

For Cowan, the news that the Reds were out was all the motivation that he needed to leave the political minefield of Latvia and within the hour *Caledon*, *Seafire* and *Scotsman* were headed north; at the same time Cowan ordered *Cleopatra* and destroyers to depart Copenhagen and join him in Reval. Might he finally get into a fight?

---

* Apart from a scout aircraft, carried by *Caledon* on a raised platform above the forecastle.

Top: A painting by Charles
Dixon of HMS *Cardiff*
leading the German High
Seas Fleet into internment.
(© NATIONAL MARITIME
MUSEUM BHC0670)

Above: HMS *Cardiff*, flagship
of Rear Admiral Alexander-
Sinclair, at Reval.
(© IMPERIAL WAR MUSEUM
Q19366)

Right: HMS *Curacoa*,
flagship of Rear Admiral
Cowan in May 1919, until
mined.
(© IMPERIAL WAR MUSEUM
FL5370)

H.M.S. CURACOA.

Above: The forward 6in gun of the light cruiser/flotilla leader *Royalist*.
(AUTHOR'S COLLECTION)

Below: Divers going down to examine the propellers of the light cruiser
HMS *Calypso* which were damaged when she ran aground entering Libau.
(© IMPERIAL WAR MUSEUM Q19338)

Above: The light cruiser HMS *Caradoc* bombarding Bolshevik positions from off the Estonian coast, December 1918. The clock-like instruments are range dials, which visually indicate the gun range the ship is using. This was so consorts could concentrate their fire, using a simple calculator to derive their corresponding range, given their offset and relative bearing to target.
(© IMPERIAL WAR MUSEUM Q19345)

Below: HMS *Princess Margaret* loading mines at Grangemouth. (PHOTO: ALAMY)

Above: 'L'-class submarines similar to *L-55*, which was sunk with all hands in June 1919. (AUTHOR'S COLLECTION)

Below: Aerial view of Kronstadt harbour, 26 July 1919, showing the positions of Bolshevik warships before the attack by British CMBs in August 1919. (© IMPERIAL WAR MUSEUM Q107944)

Left: Agar's boat *CMB-4* at the Imperial War Museum, Duxford. (AUTHOR'S COLLECTION)

Right: *ML-22*, a typical example of a Motor Launch, a type which was used in the Baltic for mine clearance. (AUTHOR'S COLLECTION)

Below: The Russian pre-dreadnought battleship *Andrei Pervozvanni*, seriously damaged in Commander Dobson's August attack. (AUTHOR'S COLLECTION)

Above: The Russian battleship *Petropavlosk*, sunk by CMBs in the August attack. (AUTHOR'S COLLECTION)

Right: The Russian cruiser *Pamiat Azova*, sunk by Dobson and Steele, August 1919. (AUTHOR'S COLLECTION)

The Russian cruiser *Gromoboi* pictured here in 1901. She was laid up at Kronstadt. (AUTHOR'S COLLECTION)

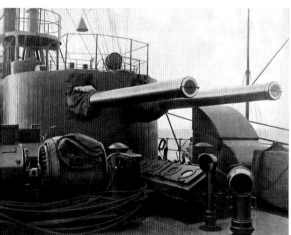

Above: The Russian protected cruiser *Oleg*, sunk by Augustus Agar, June 1919. (AUTHOR'S COLLECTION)

Left: Aft turret on the *Oleg*, 1905. (AUTHOR'S COLLECTION)

Below: A Russian *Orfei*-class destroyer, similar to *Azard* which sank HMS *L-55*. (AUTHOR'S COLLECTION)

Above: British squadron in Kaporia Bay in October 1919. The destroyer in the foreground is HMS *Winchelsea*. (AUTHOR'S COLLECTION)

Below: A copy of a painting by Cecil King (1881–1942) of Libau Harbour in February 1919 depicting HMS *Caledon* with the destroyers *Wrestler* and *Valhalla*. (AUTHOR'S COLLECTION)

Above: A restored CMB on the River Thames. (PHOTO: DR V A MICHELL)

Right: A close-up view of the torpedo launching trough aboard the CMB. (PHOTO: DR V A MICHELL)

Below: The French armoured cruiser *Montcalm* pictured in 1902. She was sister-ship to *Gueydon* which was sent to Riga, but never got there. (AUTHOR'S COLLECTION)

The crew of *CMB-4* that sank the *Oleg*: Midshipman Hampsheir (left), Lieutenant Agar (centre) and Petty Officer Beeley (right). Hampsheir looks somewhat dazed as shock takes hold. (AUTHOR'S COLLECTION)

Admiral Rosslyn Wemyss.
(LIBRARY OF CONGRESS)

Admiral Walter Cowan.
(© NATIONAL PORTRAIT GALLERY)

Johan Pikta, Estonian naval chief.
(AUTHOR'S COLLECTION)

Johan Laidoner, commander of the
Estonian Army.
(AUTHOR'S COLLECTION)

Konstantin Päts, Estonian political
leader. (AUTHOR'S COLLECTION)

Kārlis Ulmanis, first Prime Minister
of independent Latvia, pictured in
1919. (LIBRARY OF CONGRESS)

Left: David Lloyd George, British Prime Minister during the Baltic campaign.
(AUTHOR'S COLLECTION)

Below: The Estonian Army High Command in 1920. From upper left: General Major Ernst Põdder, Dr Arthur Lossmann, General Major Aleksander Tõnisson, Colonel Karl Parts, Colonel Viktor Puskar, Colonel Jaan Rink. From bottom left: General Major Andres Larka, General Major Jaan Soots, Commander-in-Chief General Lieutenant Johan Laidoner, Admiral Johan Pitka and Colonel Rudolf Reiman.
(AUTHOR'S COLLECTION)

General Gustav Adolf Joachim Rüdiger Graf von der Goltz. (AUTHOR'S COLLECTION)

Baron Mannerheim, Regent of Finland (seated) with his aides. (AUTHOR'S COLLECTION)

An old postcard of Dunbeath Castle, home to Rear Admiral Alexander-Sinclair. (AUTHOR'S COLLECTION)

An old postcard of Wemyss Castle, ancestral home of Admiral Rosslyn Wemyss. (Author's collection)

Memorial to four RN admirals, Alexander-Sinclair, Cowan, Fremantle and Thesiger, erected in Tallinn by a grateful Estonian nation and sited in the Old Town outside the Maritime Museum.
(Photo: Ernest Bondarenko)

The exterior of the Church of the Holy Spirit, Tallinn.
(Photo: Ernest Bondarenko)

Memorial plaque to the Royal Navy sailors who died in the Baltic Campaign, Church of the Holy Spirit, Tallinn. (PHOTO: ERNEST BONDARENKO)

Inside of the Church of the Holy Spirit, Tallinn, showing the memorial plaque to the Royal Navy. (PHOTO: ERNEST BONDARENKO)

Cowan's rear admiral's flag, now rather worn with age, hanging in St Peter's Church, Kineton. (AUTHOR'S COLLECTION)

Admiral Sir Walter Cowan's tombstone at the New Cemetery, Kineton. (AUTHOR'S COLLECTION)

A Sopwith Camel 2F.1 such as was flown from HMS *Vindictive*. (AUTHOR'S COLLECTION)

CHAPTER 9

On the Offensive, Gulf of Finland, May 1919

After the initial success of General Laidoner in driving the Russians out of Estonia, things went less well. In the second half of February 1919, the Red armies started a new offensive to recapture the country. To this end the communists established what was referred to as the new 'Estonian' Red Army. It comprised more than 80,000 conscripts, but it was not so much an army as a *levée en masse*.

Once again Narva came under attack from the east and was heavily bombarded, leaving 2,000 people homeless. But it was not taken; the Estonian 1st Division and their allied White Russian Northern Corps repelled the Seventh Red Army's attacks and the bulk of the Bolshevik gains were around the southern border where they made significant progress during early March. A reinforced Estonian 2nd Division counter-attacked and by the end of the month the 'Estonian' Red Army was pushed behind the Optjok River.

Thus Cowan arrived in Reval to find the Estonians pressed not just militarily but also politically, the latter because of a Hungarian* offer to mediate between them and the Bolsheviks. The American diplomats observing the situation certainly thought so. On 4 May the US *Chargé d'Affaires* in Copenhagen, Ulysses S Grant-Smith, wrote to Assistant Secretary of State Polk that 'Esthonian [*sic*] situation requires immediate affirmative action by Allies [and] America. Unless Government receives prompt help peace with Bolshevists likely. Esthonia will then gradually or quickly but inevitably succumb completely to Bolshevism.'[1]

He further pressed on the American Relief Administration (ARA)

---

* Not a disinterested party, for the Hungarian Soviet Republic had been formed under Bela Kun on 21 March. Kun's rule would last until 1 August.

and its head, Herbert Hoover, that starvation was a very real threat in both Latvia and Estonia and could be a cause of Bolshevik victory. Hoover did not let his diplomat down. From America's vast riches, food could be spared. On 11 May Hoover telegraphed:

> Your recommendations adopted and steamer *Dancey* loaded with 2,000 tons foodstuffs, which we advanced on credit as substantial evidence our great sympathy Esthonian [*sic*] people, will arrive Reval Monday 12th. Please see that this information properly disseminated. Colonel John Groome leaving Rotterdam Tuesday via boat for Libau with a relief mission and will have charge our work in Esthonia, Lettland [Latvia] and Lithuania, reporting direct to me. He will be followed by two relief ships.[2]

The Americans would not fight but they were prepared to provide humanitarian assistance.

Meanwhile, on Cowan's arrival, Knupffer and the local commander urged him to support the transfer of General Yudenitch and his White Russian forces from Finland to Estonia to lead an offensive towards Petrograd. However, Cowan may have been aware that the Estonians would not welcome Yudenitch, as they realised his overall objective was to recreate Great Russia with Estonia as a subservient part of it. The majority of the newly-elected Finnish parliament was also against any participation in an offensive against Petrograd.

But Cowan's first instinct was always to attack. Consequently, on 1 May he attempted to start operations against the Bolshevik navy, taking two cruisers with four destroyers to counter a rumoured landing operation east of Reval. Finding no Russian force there he continued to Hogland Island, halfway to Kronstadt. But no enemy did he find here either. In his report to the Admiralty, however, he underlined his position that the situation in both Libau and the Gulf of Finland forced him to remain in the Baltic for the foreseeable future.[3]

On 7 May, Cowan transferred his flag to HMS *Curacoa*, a half-sister to *Caledon*, now due for relief and return to Britain. *Curacoa* was a veteran of the Harwich Force and had been Commodore Reginald 'Black Jack' Tyrwhitt's flagship in that body; she now came under the command of Captain Geoffrey Mackworth who had become Cowan's flag captain in *Caledon* in March; he followed his admiral to *Curacoa* as flag captain.

Two days later, Cowan sailed *Curacoa* to Helsingfors to visit the British Minister, Sir Coleridge Arthur Fitzroy Kennard, Bt,* and to pay his respects to the Regent of Finland, Baron Carl Gustaf Emil Mannerheim. A remarkable character, Mannerheim, an ex-general in the Tsarist army, had led the White Finnish forces against the Bolshevik Red Finns in the Finnish Civil War. In this endeavour he had received much support from von der Goltz and his Germans. Mannerheim had then led the Finnish forces in Estonia assisting Laidoner to drive out the Red Army in January and February. Cowan was much impressed by the Regent noting that he was 'the handsomest foreigner I have ever met'.[4]

On 13 May, *Curacoa* had returned to Reval and was on passage for Libau when at 0830 she struck a mine with her stern, 70 miles east of her intended destination. Captain Mackworth mustered all hands by ledger and found one crewman, Ordinary Seaman George Plunkett, was missing and three others were seriously injured. Plunkett had in fact been reading the patent log-line and was thrown up into the air by the explosion and drowned. Cowan had been enjoying a bath in his admiral's quarters when the detonation occurred; it threw him and his bathwater out onto the deck. Naked, he grabbed a fur coat and raced for the bridge to be followed by his coxswain bearing a pair of trousers. He later recalled that prior to the arrival of said apparel he 'was in great discomfort'.[5] Despite this sartorial disaster on the part of his admiral, Mackworth still berated a sub lieutenant 'for presuming to approach the bridge of one of His Majesty's ships wearing flannel trousers'.[6]

Surgeon Lieutenant William Oliver Lodge had only joined the ship via a 'pier head jump' in place of a Welsh colleague who had refused to sail on the grounds that he had not volunteered for war service. He now found himself treating twelve men for 'mushroom' fractures to their ankles, caused by the ship jumping upwards with the impact. It was, he later wrote, 'as though a lift in a skyscraper had dropped to the basement'.[7] He set and splinted the fractures but 'doubted if the patients would ever walk [properly] again'.[8]

---

* An exotic character, he wrote a number of privately-printed books, some of them obscene, very much in the style of the *Yellow Book*, which was perhaps unsurprising as his mother had been an admirer of Oscar Wilde and had paid for the famous Epstein tomb of Wilde in the Père Lachaise cemetery, Paris.

The stricken vessel, which had taken on a 30° list and had the wardroom full of 'salt water and oil fuel',[9] was navigated into Reval with great difficulty, her stern shattered and steering gear out of action and Pitka brought his two destroyers out to cover her retreat to safety. Cowan transferred his flag and his staff to *Cleopatra*. With some help from the local dockyard, *Curacoa* was patched up sufficiently to attempt the voyage back to Britain, in which she was accompanied by Commander Cunningham and *Seafire*. Even so, her return was fraught, for her rudder fell off while passing The Skaw (Skagen Odde) and the ship could only be steered with her engines for the last 500 miles to Sheerness dockyard; she eventually paid off at Chatham on 11 June. Another man dead, another ship crippled.

At a court of inquiry, held on 18 August, Mackworth was found to have been at fault for failing to heed a report that a mine had been sighted. He nonetheless continued to be trusted by Cowan, for his services as flag captain were retained.[10] In mitigation, it was noted that the mine was a Russian hornless type which was supposed to have a cutter attached to its moorings similar to the T-cutter for the *Actaeon* sweep used by the Royal Navy. The anonymous author of this note added dryly 'but up to the present no known instance of it having worked has occurred'.[11]

The Reds Come Out

The capture of the Russian destroyers in 1918 had made an impact on Trotsky; he realised that the Baltic Fleet was not fit for purpose, ruled as it was by sailors' soviets and with its officers, generally described as 'counter-revolutionary swine',[12] reviled, executed or ignored.

But Trotsky needed a fighting fleet if he was to contest the Gulf of Finland and the Baltic Sea generally. On 17 January 1919, the remaining officers at Kronstadt were stunned to be summoned to meet the navy's titular leader. He told them that 'it was fully understood that, belonging to the old school, they could not readily acquiesce in all the innovations of the proletarian regime; that it was hoped that in time they would come to adapt themselves to it; and that if in the meantime they could "give their knowledge to the revolution" their services would be duly recognised'.[13]

Furthermore, their authority was restored; a ship's commissar's overall control of the warship was abolished and the post now had responsibility only for political matters and none in purely naval affairs. Clearly in matters of revolutions pragmatism also had a part to play. The Baltic Fleet was soon to be back in business and ships began to be restored to working order.

By the end of April, Cowan had resolved that he needed to keep a close watch on Kronstadt to be in a position to intercept the Russian fleet if it came out to interfere with the ongoing operations of both the Estonian and White Russian forces, as they pushed along the coast in an attempt to take Petrograd.

Consequently, Cowan moved out from Reval on 14 May and lay firstly in Narva Bay and then reconnoitred eastwards as far as Kaporia Bay. Here the Estonians were landing troops covered only by the old, slow gunboat *Lembit* and a destroyer, both of which were in any case short of fuel and dependent on Cowan for resupply. So short of resources were the Estonians that their landing vessels included unarmed merchant ships and even the Nekmangrund Light Vessel.

British forces were only *Cleopatra* plus four destroyers but Cowan maintained a watch in the Bay and supported the Estonian troops with bombardment when they came into contact with the Bolsheviks. However, he still felt that he was too far away from the Bolshevik naval base to be able to react quickly enough to any excursion by Soviet forces.

Accordingly, Cowan moved further east and took position at Seskar (Seiskari) Island, in the Gulf of Finland, due north of Narva. From here he was able to keep Kronstadt under surveillance through lookouts posted at the mast head of his cruiser. This proved to be an irritation beyond bearing for the Baltic Fleet and on 17 May, Cowan observed that they were preparing to come out. At this time the admiral's forces were a light cruiser and a destroyer leader, *Cleopatra* and *Shakespeare*, the latter a Thorneycroft-designed vessel sporting five 4.7in guns and a 12pdr, together with the destroyers *Scout* and *Walker*.

Flying an enormous red flag, a destroyer of the *Avtroil* class led four other similar vessels to the edge of the protective minefields and then opened fire on the British ships. To the east the cruiser *Oleg* could be seen to have steam up and it was reported that a battleship, *Petropavlovsk,* was also out. Cowan's forces would be severely overmatched by such ships but without hesitation they left their anchorage and at full speed closed the range to 16,000 yards before returning fire.

A hit was spotted on one Russian destroyer, which seemed to reduce its speed to 10 knots, but Cowan's ships then came under 12in gunfire from the 'Grey Horse' shore battery and he decided to haul off. The Russians themselves ventured no further, which was a pity as British forces had recently been reinforced by the 7th Submarine Flotilla under the command of the legendary submariner, Captain Martin Eric Nasmith VC.[*] They might have found some sport if the Soviets had pressed on.

Such brief sallies became the norm through the spring and summer and a steady trickle of reinforcements, especially destroyers, found their way to the Baltic to counter them. These additions to the forces in the Baltic seemed at variance with the politicians' desire to reduce both the cost and the level of involvement in Russian issues. But as no-one really knew what they should do, the navy kept trying to support their squadrons as best they could.

Prisoners

On 22 May, HMS *Wallace* of the 1st Destroyer Flotilla, a newly-commissioned Thornycroft destroyer leader armed with five 4.7in guns, arrived at Copenhagen from Rosyth. There, in conditions of great secrecy, she took on board two Bolshevik prisoners for transit to Helsingfors. One of them was Fyodor Fyodorovich Raskolnikov, the quondam Commissar of the Baltic Fleet captured on the *Spartak* the previous December. The Soviets rated him so highly that they seemed prepared to exchange him for eighteen British prisoners of war. *Wallace* was to take him to Finland.

Neither captain nor navigator had been to the port before and 'the route looked very complicated due to the numerous minefields, German and Russian'[14] which she had to pass through. In company with the destroyer *Versatile*, *Wallace* left Copenhagen on the 23rd. They soon encountered drifting mines, and *Versatile* sank one, but both passed though the German minefield off Riga without incident. Navigational difficulties continued to worry them. *Wallace*'s torpedo officer, Lieutenant Commander Algernon Usborne Willis, noted that this was due to 'light vessels etc not being in their right positions or removed altogether'.[15] On arrival in the waters off

---

[*] Who from 1923 adopted the surname Dunbar-Nasmith, following his marriage in 1920 to Beatrix Justina Dunbar-Dunbar Rivers.

Helsingfors they found that 'the outer light vessel had been moved about eight miles further in and was useless. [The] place is stuffed with submerged rocks one to three fathoms deep.' Further complications were caused because they 'picked up the wrong markers on the way in but fortunately found out and stopped before we had gone too far'.[16] Captain, navigator and Willis held a conference on the bridge and then located the leading marks and got in safely just as the sun was setting. It was a close call and demonstrated the difficulties inherent in operations in the Baltic.

They were met by representatives of the Danish Red Cross who were to be the liaison for the prisoner exchange. But there now followed two days of rather annoying inactivity before on the 27th Raskolnikov* and his companion were sent up to the Finnish/Russian border with a Danish Red Cross representative in charge. 'We were very glad to get rid of them' noted Willis.[17]

Biorko

By 31 May, Cowan's forces at Seskar comprised the light cruisers *Cleopatra*, *Dragon* and the flotilla leader *Galatea*, together with seven destroyers including *Walker* and two submarines out on patrol. That same day a Bolshevik destroyer was sighted coming west, accompanied by a dreadnought battleship with other small craft waiting immediately behind the minefields. Stoker Rose thought that these were troop carrying vessels under escort.

Lieutenant Commander Ambrose Thomas Norman Abbay in *Walker* unhesitatingly advanced to confront the Russian ships and was attacked by an aeroplane which dropped two bombs within 30 yards of her starboard beam. On being fired at the intruder flew off. Abbay pushed on to the east and engaged the Bolshevik destroyer but the battleship opened a heavy and well-controlled fire at the same time.

Cowan immediately took his ships out and *Dragon* fired four salvoes at the larger Russian vessel. The Soviet destroyer fell back on its heavier consort, and both manoeuvred behind the minefields while keeping up a heavy fire on *Walker* as she retreated to meet her own ships; to add to Cowan's problems the Russian fort at Krasnaya Gorka ('Red Hill') opened fire, aided by having a kite-balloon up for

---

* He went on to be a diplomat, writer and censor before being branded an 'outlaw' by Stalin. Raskolnikov published a critical 'Open Letter to Stalin' from Sofia in 1939, whereupon he promptly died by falling from a window. Assassination was the most likely cause.

observation. The submarines HMS *L-15* and *E-27* fired torpedoes at the retreating Soviet ships, without effect.

Always eager for a scrap, Cowan trailed his coat for half an hour at the edge of the defensive minefields between Diamond Bank and Kaporia (Kaporje, Koporye) Bay but the Soviets ventured no more than they had done and he was disappointed. *Walker* had discharged 156 rounds of 4in and claimed a hit on one of the smaller vessels. She had been straddled four times and had come under 12in shellfire from the fort as well as the battleship. The Russians obtained two hits on the destroyer without significant damage being caused, bar a splinter puncturing a torpedo warhead, and *Walker* suffered only one casualty, Able Seaman Edward Ignatius Quinn,* who was wounded during the action.

After the action, Cowan called all the commanding officers and Captain 'D' together and 'strafed them for not obeying signals quickly enough'. But he gave *Walker* 'a pat on the back for his effort which was really very good'.[18] To the sailors, the encounter became known, perhaps ironically, as 'The Battle of Diamond Bank'.[19]

These two incidents of 17 and 31 May, in which he was unable to arrive at the minefields quickly enough to engage the enemy to advantage, convinced Cowan that he needed a base even closer to Kronstadt; and maybe an air arm too. Additionally, he was very concerned to ensure that the Soviets were denied the opportunity to lay further mines west of the existing defensive minefields, which would make it even more difficult for any aggressor to safely approach the Red Fleet's harbour.

Cowan now called for help to his new friend and Regent of Finland, Count Mannerheim. The Finns, as worried about the Bolsheviks as the Estonians were, granted Cowan a base at Biorko Sound (Björkö Sound, Korsholm) – an island in the outer archipelago of Korpo on the Finnish coast. Not only did they offer the mooring but also accommodation ashore and harbour services. Cowan moved his forces there on 4 June. Now the admiral was significantly nearer to Kronstadt and through the establishment of a look-out in a Finnish lighthouse at Stirs Point, he had eyes nearer still. Two sub lieutenants, three able seamen and some signalmen were permanently stationed there, with a communications link to the Biorko base.

---

* Quinn had joined the navy as 'hostilities only' in March 1916. He would not escape its clutches until 29 February 1920.

Biorko was not, however, a prepossessing place in the opinion of most of the sailors who saw it. 'It consisted of a small, roughly constructed jetty made from trunks of pine or fir trees. On landing, the shore ran back for a couple of hundred yards then rose steeply and was covered with a snow capped forest of pines and firs for as far as the eye could see ... a most desolate place.'[20] As for the inhabitants, 'the people are a bit down in the mouth as about a year ago the Bolsheviks were in occupation and, before they left, killed or commandeered everyone between the age of sixteen and thirty-five ... [but] they are a most exceptionally good natured and kind people'.[21] Cowan delighted in his new base however, and not just because of its location. Each evening, his burly Irish coxswain would take him ashore where the admiral, carrying his favourite walking stick, would set off at a brisk pace and walk for three or four miles through the forest. On returning to his ship he would inform the crew that such exercise would also do them a great deal of good; 'his advice not being well received' according to Richard Rose.[22]

Riga

Von der Goltz's army reached and 'liberated' Riga on 22 May, only to replace a Bolshevik reign of terror with one of its own. Grant-Smith, the US *Chargé d'Affaires* in Copenhagen, sailed to Latvia to witness the situation first hand. He telegraphed to the Peace Conference in Paris that

the Red Terror is worse than the White but the latter sufficiently shocking. Soldiers of the attacking forces who took the city, only to find mothers, sisters and pastors murdered in cold blood by the Bolsheviks and wives forced to work in public baths where they had been raped by Bolshevist soldiers, can be expected to show little mercy. In this war power swings alternatively to the extremists of either side and justice is administered by those whose passions are hottest. Consequently, what is called justice is largely reprisals and vengeance. Losses in field actions comparatively light but slaughter by shooting squads is appalling. Bolshevists shoot prisoners and civilians indiscriminately often in the legs and then club out their brains with rifle butts. Whites are generally less barbarous but carry out wholesale executions.[23]

Three thousand inhabitants of the city were killed by the combined German/*Landeswehr* forces in the short period of occupation. Needra's puppet regime was installed and Goltz began to look north towards Estonia, his German Baltic dream seemingly that little bit nearer fulfilment.

Cowan had already decided that he must focus on the eastern Gulf and so the Admiralty sent him a second in command. Forty-five-year-old Commodore (Second Class) Arthur Allan Morison Duff CB arrived in the Baltic on 29 May, having been appointed to command *Caledon* and the newly-reconstituted 2nd Light Cruiser Squadron on the 14th of the month.

He had entered *Britannia* in 1887 and, after taking first-class certificates in seamanship, pilotage, gunnery, and torpedo, was made lieutenant in 1894. Duff had the distinction of serving under some of the biggest 'names' in the pre-war navy. Flag Lieutenant to Admiral Sir Cyprian Bridge on the Australia Station; Gunnery Lieutenant of the *Majestic*, flagship of Sir Arthur Knyvet Wilson VC in 1901; and then in the same ship he served under Admiral Lord Charles Beresford. At the end of 1903 Duff was made commander at the early age of twenty-nine. He became executive officer in the *Exmouth*, once more serving on Wilson's flagship. In 1909, Duff was advanced to captain and in 1911 he became Flag Captain to that hard taskmaster and disciplinarian Rear Admiral Lewis Bayly in the 1st Battlecruiser Squadron. He had attended the Royal Naval War College in 1910 and was rated 'first class', being placed 'first out of seven captains in order of merit'.[24] In 1914, Duff had the distinction of sinking the first U-boat of the war when his light cruiser HMS *Birmingham* rammed and sank *U-15* on 9 August. He commanded *Birmingham* at the Battle of Jutland and then went on to captain the battlecruisers *Inflexible* and *Tiger*. He now joined Cowan at a crucial point in the campaign; perhaps to add brain to Cowan's more aggressive approach. The admiral immediately deployed Duff to the Western Baltic and Latvia, where he 'by his quick and accurate grasp of the whole German situation there, freed me from a very considerable portion of my preoccupations'.[25]

Additionally, Latvian waters now entertained a French destroyer flotilla, belatedly despatched in April to bolster the Allied naval presence and, not coincidentally, to ensure that French interests were represented and pursued there. Commodore Jean-Joseph Brisson in *Mécanicien Principal Lestin* – armed with two 100mm

(3.9in), four 65mm (2.6in) guns and two twin 450mm (18in) torpedo tubes – brought with him another eleven destroyers, although they were reduced in number through progressive withdrawal. For Cowan this was not an unalloyed blessing. The French navy had already suffered a mutiny in their Black Sea flotilla during April, with matelots refusing to work their ships in any way which would be detrimental to their Red 'comrades' ashore. Reporting to Cowan in May, Brisson was obliged to state 'Admiral, I will do anything for you, but you must not ask me to fight the Russians'.[26] He was concerned that his sailors would not obey his commands.*

New Resources

Apart from the addition of the French ships, during the late spring and early summer vessels continued to arrive to swell Cowan's command. In response to his earnest request for shallow-draft vessels to operate both as minesweepers and minelayers, the Admiralty sent him a type of boat developed during the late war.

These were the Motor Launches or MLs, the brainchild of the American Elco Company of Bayonne New Jersey, whose General Manager Henry Sutphen and Chief Naval Architect Irwin Chase conceived and designed the launches in conjunction with representatives of the Royal Navy. The first fifty were built in the USA, and then Canadian Vickers became the prime contractor to get around American neutrality issues. Once built they were sent by train to Halifax, Nova Scotia, and then deck loaded onto British freighters to cross the Atlantic.

They were twin engined, much faster than a trawler (c.19 knots), just about seaworthy (they were wet ships and rolled a lot), armed with one 3pdr gun (and Type D depth charges when available) plus machine guns and carrying a crew of nine, two officers, two engineers and five deckhands. They had been developed as anti-submarine vessels, the precursors of the American 'sub-chaser' classes, but during the war found themselves undertaking escort duty, boarding merchant ships and detonating mines, amongst many other tasks, especially the Coast of Ireland Command and the Dover Patrol. Command of them had been almost entirely the preserve of RNVR officers. Cowan put them to work in the heavily

---

* Brisson later resolved this problem by insisting that although the Red Army forces wore Russian uniforms, they were in reality German.

shoaled and littoral areas of the Gulf of Finland sweeping, and occasionally laying, mines.

They were not, however, entirely without defects, the most dangerous of which were the Hall-Scott engines. These originally used petrol, a significant fire hazard, and problems with the engines overheating resulted in a decision in mid-1916 to use a mixture of one part petrol to two parts kerosene. Another quirk of the engines was that they had to be stopped and restarted when going from ahead to astern or vice versa. Starting was achieved with a burst of compressed air from cylinders carried aboard and was not always reliable. Manoeuvring could thus be tricky on occasion.

Another new class brought forth by the Great War which now joined Cowan's forces were the P-boats or coastal sloops. They had originally been designed to replace destroyers in coastal operations. Twin screws, a large rudder area and a very low freeboard gave then a small and fast turning circle and with ram bows of hardened steel they had been intended primarily to attack submarines. Indeed, a resemblance to large submarines had been deliberately designed in to give the boats a chance to close the range and sink a German U-boat by ramming or gunfire. A low, sharply cut-away funnel added to that impression.

They carried a crew of fifty, could exceed 21 knots and were armed with one 4in gun, one 40mm anti-aircraft weapon and two 14in torpedo tubes, taken from older torpedo boats. Twenty-four ships of this design had been ordered in May 1915 and another thirty between February and June 1916, although ten of this latter batch were altered in December before launch for use as Q-ships (ships which look like an unarmed merchantman to lure U-boats to the surface but which carry concealed weapons) and were renumbered as PC-class sloops. Eighteen shipyards were involved in building them and they supplemented the navy's larger *Flower* class sloops.

These vessels were now intended for use in the Baltic in an anti-submarine capacity and had been fitted with some, rather primitive, underwater detection equipment. HMS *P-31*, for example, under her captain Lieutenant Commander Thomas Gilbert Carter OBE, carried both a K-tube device and a Portable General Service Hydroplane (PGS) The K-tube was a triangular metal frame with listening devices fitted at each of its three angles. Because of the noise of the P-boat itself, the ship had to stop to deploy the K-tube, making it an easy target if a submarine was in the vicinity! The tactical doctrine was to cruise for ten minutes and then stop and listen for ninety seconds while the multi-point detectors allowed for an estimate of position and course of the enemy to be made. The PGS, first deployed in 1915, was a disc, lowered into the water to pick up vibrations. It was non-directional – the operator could know that there was a submarine somewhere, but not where it was.

A Military Mission

Cowan had long argued that a military presence was necessary; or failing that at least some sort of military mission to advise and liaise with the Baltic States' land armies.

At Churchill's urging the role was finally given to General Sir Hubert Gough, unfairly or otherwise sacked from the command of the British Fifth Army in 1918. His role was to assess the situation on the ground and to liaise with the various local commanders to ensure that they received appropriate supplies and tactical advice. Lord Curzon privately briefed him to avoid being pushed by Churchill into formal military intervention.

On 24 May Cowan met Gough at Reval on board HMS *Galatea*, in which the general had taken passage, and accompanied him over to Helsingfors 'to assist at his ceremonial landing, and to salute him there';[27] to that end *Galatea* fired a fifteen-gun salutation as Gough disembarked. Cowan then went with the general to meet with the Finnish authorities. When the admiral departed with *Cleopatra* on the 28th, he left *Galatea* as Gough's personal transport.

The admiral held generals, British or White Russian, in slight regard, however, remarking that 'they always want to move from one port to another, preferably in a British cruiser'.[28] But Gough's presence would remove from Cowan the necessity to involve himself in endless diplomatic discussions; and thus get on with the fighting, as he preferred.

CHAPTER 10:

Single Combat, May – June 1919

L-55

June 1919 did not start well for the Royal Navy in the Baltic. His Majesty's Submarine *L-55* was a modern 'L'-class boat, armed with six torpedo tubes and two 4in guns and capable of 14 knots on the surface and 10.5 knots underwater. Built in 1918 at Govan, she was commanded by an experienced submariner, thirty-year-old Lieutenant Commander Charles Manners Sutton Chapman, DSC and Bar. He had won his first medal at the battle of Heligoland Bight in 1914 and a second was awarded in 1917 for 'services in submarines in enemy waters'. Chapman was used to the solitary duels of the underwater war and had previously fought in submarines in the Baltic during the recent conflict as second-in-command to the legendary submarine 'ace' Commander Max Horton.

L-55 had deployed to the Gulf of Finland as part of the reinforcements for Cowan's burgeoning fleet, as had *L-12*, which was commanded by Chapman's friend and fellow Baltic war veteran, Lieutenant Ronald William Blacklock. On 4 June, both submarines were on patrol in Kaporia Bay, off the Estonian coast, operating as a pair. In the late afternoon, Blacklock and Chapman saw two Red destroyers, *Gavriil* and *Azard*, entering their patrol area. These vessels were equipped to lay mines and were tasked with reinforcing the protective minefields in front of Kronstadt whilst also conducting general scouting activities.

Both destroyers were engaged at long range by British forces and withdrew, their track taking them nearer to *L-55*. Seizing the opportunity for an attack, Chapman trimmed down and at 1737 fired two torpedoes, both of which missed their targets.

Unfortunately, the discharge of the weapons affected the buoyancy of the submarine and she porpoised to the surface, coincident with the destroyers observing the torpedo tracks and turning to engage.[*]

Azard's gunfire immediately hit the conning tower and the submarine crash-dived to avoid further attack. But shortly afterwards there was a massive explosion and a roil of the sea caused by escaping air; *L-55* had blown up and sunk with all hands. In the mosaic of minefields in the area her forward hydroplane had caught a mine cable and pulled it against the hull near the control room. Blacklock was in the act of turning his boat to gain a firing position when he heard the noise of the blast and both destroyers then turned and ran for home. When the destroyers had withdrawn, *L-12* surfaced and Blacklock searched for her companion as far as the minefield but found no trace excepting the odd patches of oil on the surface of the sea. The following day Captain Nasmith flew out in a seaplane to meet *L-12*'s commander; they agreed that *L-55* had sunk well inside the minefield and that nothing more could be done.

Forty-two sailors were killed. They included 24-year-old Lieutenant Henry Kenneth Martin Southwell, son of The Right Reverend and Venerable Henry Southwell, Bishop of Lewes; and Henry George Hazelden French, a boy telegraphist from Hastings, aged just seventeen. Blacklock 'had lost an old and valued friend in Chapman; we had been through so much together in the past that it was doubly hard to see him killed like this'.[1] Lieutenant Commander Willis thought the sinking was 'a blow and cast gloom on the proceedings'.[2] It was the biggest British loss of the campaign so far.

The same day that *L-55* was sunk, the Russians also sortied to attack two Estonian vessels operating in Kaporia Bay. *Versatile* and *Vivacious* were called upon to chase them off and got within 8,400 yards range. However, 'they don't seem to have got anything in spite of a large expenditure of ammunition'.[3] Once the Russian gained their protective minefields, the British ships had to give up the chase.

---

[*] One of the issues for both submarines and surface ships was that torpedoes didn't run as predicted in the Baltic. Lieutenant Commander Willis believed that it was because the water was fresher than the open sea; 'consequently' he wrote 'there is a loss of about fifty pounds of buoyancy'. For *Wallace* and the 1st Flotilla he decided 'to lighten the heads by putting in wood or cork to displace about thirty pounds of water' (Diary 29 May, WLLS 3/1, CAC).

The Knight Errant

In February 1919, a slim, pale naval officer was escorted into a building in Horse Guards. When he came out again, he had joined the intelligence service.

Twenty-nine-year-old Lieutenant Augustus Willington Shelton Agar RN was descended from a long line of Kerrymen. Born in Kandy, Ceylon (Sri Lanka), the thirteenth child[*] of a planter from County Kerry, John Shelton Agar, he was an orphan by the age of twelve, losing his mother one year after his birth and his father in 1902, killed in a cholera epidemic in China.

Educated at Eastman's Naval Academy and HMS *Britannia*, he passed out as a midshipman in 1905. Agar gained a pilot's certificate in 1913, unusual for a naval officer in those times, and served with the Grand Fleet in the North Sea during 1914–15, before taking part in the evacuation of Gallipoli. Further service in the White Sea followed from whence he was transferred, initially as a torpedo and mining officer, to a top secret Coastal Motor Boat (CMB) base on Osea Island, in the estuary of the River Blackwater in Essex. Here he saw action with the Harwich Force and in Operation 'ZO', the attack on Zeebrugge and Ostend (an action which was entirely 'volunteers only'), where Agar commanded a smoke-laying CMB.

Agar had not been considered by his previous commanders as a particularly competent officer. In mid-1913, his captain evaluated him as being 'capable when he tries but at times shows lack of interest'. By mid-1916, he was thought to be 'clever but unreliable; apt to do foolish things; deaf one ear'. Six months later the same commander again noted that Agar was 'clever but unreliable'. And in early 1918, a Lieutenant Commander Parker wrote that he was 'hard-working, at times spasmodic, not tactful, violent temper, conceited but good knowledge at bottom'.[4] Hardly 'officer-like qualities'; but in the freewheeling world of CMBs, Agar had at last found his metier.

CMBs, popularly known as 'Skimmers', were first developed by the Thornycroft company in the summer of 1915. Shortly afterwards, three lieutenants[§] of the Harwich Force approached the

---

[*] He regarded thirteen as his lucky number all his life.
[§] They were later named by Air Commodore Francis Banks as Lieutenants Geoffrey Hampden, William Bremner and John Anson (FROB2/1, CAC). Hampden, who had been wounded in both legs during the pursuit of the SMS *Emden*, and had only a quarter vision in his right eye, was probably the leader of the trio. In 1918, his commanding officer stated that 'the development of the CMBs in His Majesty's service was largely due to him' (ADM 196/152/4, NA).

company and stated that their commodore (Reginald 'Black Jack' Tyrwhitt) had given them permission to speak to the management and ascertain if the boats had a role in warfare. The idea developed by these officers was that a very fast, shallow-draught vessel would be ideal for attacking German ships in their harbours. It would be able to pass over the defensive minefields without triggering one and its high speed would allow rapid strike and escape.

Introduced in 1917, the boats made use of the lightweight and powerful petrol engines becoming available and a variety of armament was carried, including torpedoes, depth charges or mines, together with light machine guns, such as the Lewis gun. They were of monocoque construction with a 'skin' of Honduran mahogany backed by oil-soaked calico which 'fed' oil to the wood over time to prevent it drying out.

They were initially propelled by 250 brake horsepower V-12 aircraft engines made by Sunbeam and Napier and later used engines of Green's and Thorneycroft's own manufacture. This made them very fast (they could hit 40 knots and average 35) and able to skim over the top of minefields by aquaplaning. CMBs were the navy's equivalent of fighter aircraft and were manned by young and adventurous men (usually a crew of three or four), as were their aerial equivalents. They were dangerous and difficult to handle; but they were also beautiful to look at. One naval officer wrote 'I do not know who invented the CMB but this little vessel was a masterpiece of ingenuity, so much so that I wept with envy when I saw the first one go over from Dover to Dunkirk'.[5]

CMB commanders, like their alter egos in the air, were seen (and often saw themselves) in Arthurian terms. The dominant moral codes of the late Victorians and Edwardians were derived from their reverence for the chivalric, the lost Eden of Arthurian legend, Camelot, the Round Table and from their obsession with England as a new Rome. The educational system was founded on the classics for that very reason. Thus public schools and colleges produced a breed of men who were devoid of guile and conditioned to believe in romantic notions of honour, glory and sacrifice. These educational establishments raised boys to believe in chivalric values that were all the more potent because they had not been tested in the real world. And as one historian has written, 'every public schoolboy was familiar with the *Iliad* and the *Odyssey* and the poetry – with its emphasis on honour, discipline, athleticism and courage in the face of death – spoke across the ages about what it meant to be a gentleman and a scholar at the height of empire'.[6] They were the modern-day knights errant and CMBs were their chargers.

Nonetheless, service in CMBs was not without its problems. For example, their petrol-powered engines were prone to catching fire (during the year 1917–18, five CMBs were lost through fire, three of them whilst still in harbour); and the restriction on weight necessary to obtain the high speed and low draught, meant the torpedo could not be fired from a normal torpedo tube but was instead carried in a rear-facing trough. On launching, it was pushed backwards by a cordite firing pistol and a steel ram and entered the water tail-first. A tripwire between the torpedo and the ram head would start the torpedo motors once pulled tight after release. The CMB would then turn hard over and get out of the way. Clearly this was an operation fraught with danger – but there is no record of a CMB ever torpedoing itself.

Nor were they comfortable. They carried a commanding officer, a second-in-command, who also functioned as observer, and one or two engineers who sat crouched under the deck in front of the two officers. This position was particularly exposed and uncomfortable, perched beside their machinery whilst all the water breaking over the bows fell on them; they had to sit chin on knees, doubled up, managing the temperamental petrol engines.

With the war over, Agar had resigned himself to a long and boring period of relative inactivity; at the armistice 'all thoughts of the Big Attack had of course to be abandoned', he fretted.[7] He and the other officers continued to work on Osea Island, 'keeping our boats and base up to concert pitch'.[8] They found it difficult work as 'many of the Hostilities Only young seamen and mechanics were longing to be demobilised and sent back to their homes'.[9]

But then, whilst on leave in London, he was contacted by his commander at Osea, Captain Wilfred Frankland 'Froggie' French, and told to report to the Admiralty for an important meeting. From there he was conducted to Horse Guards; and inside he met 'C', the legendary Mansfield George Smith Cumming,* head of Britain's Secret Intelligence Service. Cumming was running agents in Russia; but the flow of information had ceased and his normal couriers had

---

* The man on whom Ian Fleming allegedly based 'M' in the James Bond novels.

been either killed or imprisoned. He needed to be able to get agents and messages in and out of Russia, especially Petrograd, and a CMB, able to pass over the defensive minefields and travel quickly and stealthily, seemed the ideal vehicle.

Agar was given £1,000, told to pick his own crews and furnished with two CMBs. His orders instructed him to make his own way to Finland in secret and set up base there. Once there and united with his boats and their crews, Agar planned to establish his operations at a derelict yacht club at Terrioki, 30 miles north of Biorko and just three miles from the Finnish/Russian border. He had selected five men he knew from Osea Island; two sub lieutenants, Edgar Robert 'Sinbad' Sindall and John White Hampsheir together with Midshipman Richard Nigel Onslow Marshall, all reservists RNR, and two Chief Motor Mechanics, Hugh Beeley (an RNVR member, Rolls-Royce trained and known as 'Faithful Beeley') and Albert Victor Piper. All the men had volunteered for this special service

Agar had been instructed to contact Cowan for assistance and did so, requesting a destroyer to tow his little vessels to his new base and the admiral so ordered *Voyager* on 4 June, telling Captain 'D' that it was for 'running our spies to a place well up the coast'.[10] Agar also asked Cowan for two torpedoes; as Agar himself put it, 'I had been told to avoid all operations which could involve us in a hostile act, as our boats were supposed to be civilian in character, yet these torpedoes might come in very useful in self-defence if we found ourselves up against Russian ships'.[11] Cowan firstly ordered Lieutenant Commander Willis to see Captain 'S' about putting 'four [18in] Mark VIII torpedoes for the CMBs on board *Voyager*'.[12] But at some point he must have had cold feet for Agar found him unwilling; 'the thought of men in civilian clothes using weapons … did not appeal to him'.[13] But Agar pointed out that 'C' had given them permission to take one set of naval uniforms with them and promised that, if he did have to engage an enemy, he would ensure they wore their uniforms and flew the White Ensign.

It suited Cowan's warlike nature to allow Agar his torpedoes; but he wanted no responsibility for the act. Instead he said that he would order a small oiler to be available with petrol and oil for the CMBs, adding that 'it might be carrying on its deck two torpedoes for our submarines'.[14] Later, when they were alongside the oiler, Agar discovered that there were two long objects under canvas on its decks. He recalled afterwards that 'the master of the oiler told me that he had picked them up floating at sea and I could have them as they were not on his charge'.[15] Agar had got his torpedoes.

However, the first problem to overcome was an engine failure in one of the boats. Agar and his team had to rig sheer legs to hoist the engine out and repair it. But by 10 June, both vessels had been tested and were ready for work. The destroyer HMS *Voyager* towed them out of harbour and they set course for their new base.

Agar's assigned task was to deliver into Russia a courier, code-named 'Peter', who would make contact with one of Cumming's key operatives inside the country, designated only as 'ST 25' but in reality the accomplished espionage agent Paul Dukes. Agar was then to bring either both agent and courier, or 'Peter' only, out again.

While Agar was preparing to depart his new home with 'Peter', he gained information which would have a key part to play in the events of the coming few days. The small Royal Navy team shared their yacht club with a detachment of Finnish border guards whose commandant had been encouraged to accept them and 'look the other way'. He now told Agar that on 10 June the garrison at the fortress of Krasnaya Gorka, which guarded the southern entrance to Kronstadt, had revolted, arrested their commissars and hoisted a white flag as a signal to White Russian and Allied forces to come and rescue them. The commandant was sure that the Bolsheviks would send a force to recapture the strongpoint and use warships to bombard it from the rear.

But Agar's first priority was to deliver 'Peter'. A local smuggler had been hired to act as a pilot and, taking Beeley with him, they departed Terrioki after dusk on 13 June in *CMB-7* and headed for Russian soil. On the open sea they increased speed to 20 knots until the fortress of Kronstadt came into sight and then throttled back. At 8 knots the boat was practically silent and Agar aimed for a gap between the sixth and seventh forts in the line of defences, expecting at any moment to be illuminated in a searchlight beam and fired upon. The minefields were laid at a depth of 6ft so were harmless to a CMB but the breakwaters were believed to be only three feet below the surface, giving his boats a mere 3in clearance. It would be a risky endeavour to cross between the forts and over these hazards.

Miraculously they made it through to the other side of the line. The sunken breakwaters proved no hazard and, free of the defensive line, Agar called for top speed; at 36 knots they sped towards land.

'Peter' was successfully landed in Russia, within walking distance of Petrograd.

Now Agar headed towards the Tolbuhin Lighthouse so that he could observe any vessels drawn up to bombard the rear of Krasnaya Gorka. Sure enough, he could distinguish two heavy ships, which he identified as *Petropavlosk* and *Andrei Pervozvanni*, and a number of shielding destroyers. They had left the sanctuary of their harbour and were standing out in the roads, admittedly covered by the protective minefields and the guns on Kronstadt itself, but still out in the open – but these defences rendered Cowan impotent to intervene with his warships. In his subsequent report, Agar stated that he thought of attacking the Red ships there and then, but his engine malfunctioned, rendering him unable to attain sufficient speed for a torpedo launch. Instead *CMB-7* returned to base.[*]

Agar had agreed to return to the drop-off point in forty-eight hours' time to effect a pick-up rendezvous. While he waited, he was able to see the Red ships bombard the unfortunate fort at regular intervals. The would-be warrior was disturbed; 'I was tempted at first … to attack those battleships with the torpedoes we carried in our boats. But I soon gave this up, as our duty to ST 25 must come first', he wrote.[16] A knight has a responsibility to help those weaker than himself; but Agar had conflicting priorities.

Then, on the 14th, Agar observed a strange little vignette which also saw the Estonian navy gain another vessel. During the gunfire from the fort, he spotted a small Russian gunboat, the *Kitoboi*, emerge from the environs of Krasnaya Gorka flying a large white flag. She approached HMS *L-12*, which was on patrol in the area, and Lieutenant Blacklock, exercising considerable caution, launched a boat and sent an officer across to ascertain what the Russian wanted. It transpired that the crew, unimpressed by the Bolshevik regime, had mutinied and forced their captain at gunpoint to sail out and surrender to the Royal Navy. Seeing no alternative, the Russian had complied but told *L-12*'s officer, with tears rolling down his cheeks, that the result would be that the Bolsheviks would slaughter his wife and family. Nonetheless,

---

[*] Agar wrote about his actions in the Baltic in two books and they are in conflict. In the book written first but published last, *Baltic Episode*, and in his official report, his story is as above. But in the book penned later, *Footprints in the Sea,* his autobiography, Agar claims that he was in *CMB-4* and passed between forts number 3 and 4. This author has chosen to follow his earlier account, which was written in 1935, rather than the later 1959 version.

Blacklock escorted the gunboat out of the area and then turned her over to a destroyer. Cowan presented her to Pitka. The Russian captain immediately joined the White army but, Lieutenant Blacklock was later informed, was captured and crucified by the Reds.

The gunboat crewmen were perhaps encouraged in their actions by a radio broadcast made by Cowan on 6 June, in which he had invited the ships in Kronstadt to leave their base, raise a white flag and surrender. Perhaps unsurprisingly, they declined, with the single exception of the *Kitoboi*. The Bolshevik command replied 'asking if we were not tired of war after five years of it and why we "could not mind out own business"'.[17] Nonetheless, Kronstadt was allocated a call sign and told to use the 800-metre band if they changed their mind.

*　　*　　*

'Peter' was duly collected, without Dukes who had decided to stay on and collect more intelligence, and thus Agar's immediate mission was completed. He was now without tasking, until further instructions arrived from Cumming in London.

A lack of orders did not deter Agar; he knew that he was both in a position to take some offensive action and equipped to do so. He also surmised that the Krasnaya Gorka garrison could not hold out for much longer in the face of continued bombardment. Agar resolved that he would act. But first he would seek authority to do so. Via an agent of SIS based locally, Agar sent a coded message to Cumming asking for permission to attack. The reply came back 'Boats to be used for intelligence purposes only, take no action unless specifically directed by SNO Baltic'.[18] This response did give some 'wriggle room' in its second phrase. There was, in any case, no time to seek Cowan's endorsement if he was to seize the moment; but Agar felt confident, given the Admiral's reputation, that Cowan would support him. 'I was quite certain in my mind,' he wrote, 'what his [Cowan's] wishes would be and decided to attack the Red ships that very night.'[19]

On Monday 16 June, Lieutenant Agar left his base at 2215 hours (Finnish time) and set course for Kronstadt with both CMBs; *CMB-7*, now commanded by Sindall and Agar himself in *CMB-4*. From courtesy, Agar had sent a message to Cowan giving his intentions. He and his men had their naval uniforms with them and both boats were flying small White Ensigns.

The plan was to again pass through the Russian defences and attack the ships now in the roads with torpedoes, at around midnight. But disaster struck. While rounding Tolbuhin Light, *CMB-7* struck a submerged obstacle, probably a 'dud' mine, which broke her propeller shaft. Marshall, although a non-swimmer, went over the side to see if he could fix the problem, to no avail. Agar took her in tow and they returned to Terrioki. Sindall's mechanic, Piper, immediately dived overboard to examine the shaft, but surfaced with a look on his face which required no further explanation. The shaft was beyond repair; and they had no spares.

From a lookout point in a nearby church steeple, Agar was able to observe that the two battleships seen earlier now had steam up and were under way, back to harbour. In their place had arrived a large cruiser, the *Oleg*; the destroyers were still in position. That afternoon, the cruiser restarted the bombardment of the fortress. It was now or never. The fortress needed help; there was a target of opportunity in the roads; and he still had one CMB. Lieutenant Agar determined to attack that night, the 17th.

Hampsheir, Beeley and Agar once more put on their uniforms and mounted their charger. At 2230 local time, *CMB-4* slipped out of harbour. They were off to challenge the Russians to single combat. The weather was worsening with a heavy swell, not ideal conditions for a small 40ft-long motor boat, but they reached the position of the cruiser around midnight. She was protected by a destroyer screen and the first task was to slip through it unobserved.

To ready the torpedo for launch, Agar ordered Hampsheir to remove the safety pin from the cartridge in the firing chamber. There was a sudden noise, the boat shook and Hampsheir reappeared with an agonised look. While trying to remove the safety pin from the firing pistol lanyard, it broke, leaving the pin still in. As Hampsheir fought with the device, the pin suddenly came out and the pistol fired. Fortunately, the linkage to the explosive firing charge was also faulty and the torpedo launching mechanism itself did not fire.

They now had to stop the boat and reload the cartridge, difficult on land, even more so when the vessel was rolling in a sea. Beeley took over and removed the starting pistol and replaced the cartridge. At 2350 it was ready to use. The whole process had taken fifteen minutes, all the while with Russian destroyers 200–300 yards to either side of them and the big cruiser in silhouette ahead. As Agar wrote later 'I, of course, dared not leave the wheel and controls. I could see the black hulls of the destroyers and waited for gun flashes. We were a "dead sitter" but, luckily for us, remained unseen.'[20]

When Hampsheir finally popped up the hatch to say all was well, Agar slipped the clutch and went to full speed. The little craft tore down on the cruiser. Holding on until the range was 500 yards, he fired the torpedo and turned almost a complete circle, now heading back the way they had come, followed by the wind and, more worryingly, the first gunfire.

The torpedo hit abreast the foremost funnel and a huge column of black smoke rose up from the stricken ship. Both forts and destroyers opened fire on them, fortunately going high, and they gave three cheers for themselves, unheard above the engine's roar, as they fled away. Shells exploded in the sea around them, soaking the men and their craft but none stuck home. At 0300 they re-entered Terrioki; Agar and his crew had just sunk a large Russian armoured cruiser of twelve 6in guns, 576 men and 6,975 tons.

The wait to reload the torpedo cartridge had been nerve-wracking and only Beeley's steadiness had got the job done; as Agar said, 'no fuss, no worry, Faithful Beeley indeed'.[21] But reality had intruded into the Arthurian world. Hampsheir's nerves had not been up to it. 'He was in a poor way, principally from shock'[22] and would not, in fact, recover; Agar had to send him to a sanatorium in Helsingfors, where a nervous breakdown was diagnosed and he was cared for by an English matron.

By borrowed car, and then on horseback, Agar set off to find Cowan, locating a boat from HMS *Dragon* instead and, after a problem convincing them who he was, he gained permission to await Cowan's arrival with her. At midnight, the flagship arrived and Agar rowed himself across. Cowan received him, despite the hour, and sat up in bed in his sleeping cabin while Agar told his tale. Cowan was pleased. 'This allows me to show them that I have a sting which I can always use if they show their noses out of Kronstadt,' he declared[23] and the admiral told Agar that he approved of his action and would defend him if the Foreign Office played rough. Sinking *Oleg* was not enough to save the Krasnaya Gorka fortress, however. The next day, red flags were once more flying over it.

Anxious to hide the exact nature of the secret weapon that he possessed, Cowan wrote to all his commanders that the Bolshevik cruiser *Oleg* had been sunk at Kronstadt on the night of 17 June by Lieutenant Agar in a CMB but that he was anxious that the methods of sinking should not become known on the shores of the Baltic. But when Agar brought his CMBs back to Biorko for repairs, one towing the other, Cowan formed up his fleet in two lines; as the little boats passed through them, each and every warship 'manned ship' and cheered them through.

There was even a little rejoicing in Parliament. On 13 August, in what was obviously a 'planted' question given both were members of the government, Lord Curzon asked Walter Long 'if he is in a position to give any particulars as to the sinking of the Bolshevist's [*sic*] cruiser?' Long replied that 'the Bolshevist cruiser *Oleg* was sunk by British naval forces which encountered her when patrolling. It is obviously undesirable to give the exact means by which this was accomplished.' Cowan's wish for anonymity of method was respected. And the ever-persistent Lieutenant Commander Kenworthy chipped in with a follow-up question. 'When will dispatches be published showing the excellent work of the Royal Navy in the Baltic since the Armistice?' Financial Secretary to the Navy, Dr Thomas James Macnamara swatted that one away. 'I do not think I can answer that. There are a great many difficulties which I cannot at present measure. I quite agree it is desirable that the splendid work done should be known.'[24]

For his bravery in action, and on Cowan's recommendation, dated 26 August, Lieutenant Augustus Agar was awarded the Victoria Cross. Because of the secret role he had been engaged on, and his 'unofficial' presence in the Baltic, the citation for the award merely stated that it was 'in recognition of his conspicuous gallantry, coolness and skill under extremely difficult conditions in action',* for which reason it became known as 'the mystery VC'.[25] Chief Motor Mechanic Hugh Beeley RNVR, twenty-four years old, was also recognised with the bestowal of the Conspicuous Gallantry Medal, with the same citation given as for his commander. He also received a £10 per annum gratuity in recognition of 'his management of the engine of an obsolete type of motor boat which failed during a previous attempt'.[26] And 21-year-old Sub Lieutenant John White Hampsheir RNR gained the DSC.§

* *London Gazette* 31516, 19 August 1919.
§ Possibly, the experience did little to prolong Hampsheir's life. He was demobilised in January 1920 but died on 11 December 1936 aged only thirty-eight.

CHAPTER 11

Dangerous Shores, Latvia and Estonia, June – July 1919

The frustration of the forces deployed in the Baltic at what they perceived as the British government's inaction continued to grow. Lieutenant Commander Algernon Willis, newly arrived in the battle zone, thought that 'von der Goltz's idea is obviously to overrun the whole place, take Petrograd, all probably under the plea that he is fighting the Bolsheviks ... in reality he is working hand in glove with them'.[1] The lack of perception, as he saw it, of the politicians irked him; 'the government and Paris conference don't seem to be able to see this although they have been told often enough by Cowan,' he confided to his diary, 'and possibly it's too late – the Hun has been organising for the last six months and we have done nothing to stop him'.[2]

But the military activity in and against Russia was becoming progressively less acceptable to the British public and support for it was leeching away. In all classes of people, not just those of a left wing mind-set, opinion was moving against the intervention. In June, Sir David Shackleton, a senior civil servant at the Ministry of Labour, offered a warning to the Cabinet. A man of humble origins, he had started work aged nine at a cotton mill in Rawtenstall, Lancashire. By dint of sheer hard work and self-education he became an MP in 1902 and chairman of the Trades Union Congress in 1906. Four years later, Winston Churchill asked him to join the Civil Service and he swiftly rose to the position of permanent secretary at the new Ministry of Labour. He was thus well equipped to understand the beliefs of many different sorts of people. He told his lords and masters of the growing 'extent to which men of all classes are now coming round to supporting the Labour [Party] view that the Soviet government ought to be given a fair chance'.[3] In other words it was not just the political left which was supporting the Bolsheviks, but increasingly other shades of political thought as well. This seemed to fulfil Lloyd George's admonition that conducting a war against the Bolsheviks, as Churchill wished to do, would cause a revolution. As the Prime Minister had stated, 'Our people would never permit it' (*vide supra*, Chapter 6). But the fact was, there were men fighting in Russia, at sea and on the ground, and they wanted to know what the Cabinet wished of them.

At the Admiralty, First Sea Lord Admiral Rosslyn Wemyss was becoming considerably frustrated by what he perceived as a lack of direction and purpose from his political masters, the 'frocks' as they were known to the army and navy. With the negotiations in Paris finally coming to a head, and a peace treaty apparently imminent, Wemyss and his First Lord, Walter Long, presented a paper to the War Cabinet on 18 June. In it they expressed the view that the situation in the Baltic needed re-consideration in the light of the forthcoming agreement. 'The Terms of Armistice', Wemyss stated, 'which provided for the German forces evacuating the Baltic provinces, have not yet been carried out, and it is not unlikely that the enemy will attempt to evade these particular terms after the peace has been signed in the same manner as he has so far succeeded in doing during the seven months of Armistice.'[4]

Furthermore, Wemyss considered that 'it is evidently the German policy to over-run and occupy the Baltic provinces if he can, and the question therefore arises whether the blockade should be instituted and maintained, even after peace has been signed, until the Germans have withdrawn their forces from these provinces'.[5] He then questioned the role the politicians expected from his forces; 'the reason for the presence of British naval forces in the Baltic is to safeguard the flanks of our friends, but if the Germans succeed in occupying these provinces, the flanks will not be existent and there will be nothing for our naval forces to do in this direction'.[6]

So, in these circumstances, should the Royal Navy be withdrawn from the Baltic or should it remain? If the RN left, Britain would potentially suffer a loss of prestige; and if the White Ensign stayed, the navy and the government would have to beg support from the Danes, Swedes or Finns, which he thought 'a most undesirable state of affairs'.[7]

But answer came there none; the policy muddle continued.

Latvia

In Latvia, Commodore Duff was finding things difficult. German provocation, and unwillingness to cooperate as they had been enjoined, was a continuing problem.

As an example, on 10 June the destroyer HMS *Waterhen*, under the fourth son of the Rector of Loughkeen and Ballingarry Parishes in County Tipperary, Commander Edwin Anderson Homan, was moored alongside the harbour wall at Libau. At 1430 a considerable number of armed German troops gathered around the ship and started to behave in a threatening manner; by 2100 they had taken to marching up and down beside the vessel singing the *Deutschlandlied*, 'Deutschland, Deutschland über alles', and formed up by the port quarter of the warship. Homan took no chances; he went to action stations and trained weapons towards the crowd, which eventually dispersed. However, the following day it was the German womenfolk who took the lead, catcalling and pointing to the ship while drawing their fingers across their throats.

Not everyone took such provocation lying down. The German cavalry had the habit of coming down to the quay near to where the French ships were moored and conducting their drill. One morning when they arrived, the French sounded their siren and the noise 'rather upset the Hun horses which started dancing about and unseating their riders'.[8] Von der Goltz sent a letter to Brisson demanding enormous damages but the French commodore ignored it.

As well as provocations, there were also constant attempts to break the British blockade and bring arms or other supplies in by ship. On 3 July, the SS *Hannover*, escorted by two German torpedo boats, attempted to get to Riga. Passing Libau at dusk to avoid observation, she was nonetheless spotted by the destroyer *Vancouver* at Windau and Duff despatched the light cruiser *Danae* to intercept the German force. Armed German naval vessels were explicitly banned from the Baltic and the torpedo boats were turned back whilst *Hannover* was escorted to port for inspection.

By early July, Duff was moved to write to the Admiralty from his flagship, *Caledon*, in harbour at Libau:

> The Allies out here may make arrangements which appear to them necessary but which they have no power to enforce; and if met, as has generally been the case, by a flat refusal to carry out these arrangements, they can only refer the matter to Paris.

By the time it has been possible to obtain any decision, the German has already done what he intended – thanks to having the force to do it; and by the time a decision has been taken in Paris, it has been too late.[9]

And it was proving remarkably difficult to get von der Goltz to leave the Baltic. On 18 June the Allies had 'invited' Germany to recall him and his government ordered him to leave Riga, an order he cunningly evaded by putting his Iron Division under the control of the Latvian Provisional Government of Pastor Andreas Needra on that same day. As he explained the rationale to his men 'The entrance of the Division into Lettish services was due to the fact of the German Government, for political reasons, being bound by obligations to the Allies not to employ German troops on the north side of the Dwina [Dvina].'[10] If he had departed Riga as ordered, he explained, then it would have left only the *Landeswehr* in the city and that would have meant their defeat and the fall of Riga to the Bolsheviks, 'thus the crushing of all prospects of colonisation, a new Bolshevist invasion of the country, and the Germans and German-Balts being compelled to leave the country. The German Government is endeavouring to prevent, with all means at its disposal, such a flight *en masse* of the German-Balts. Therefore, it has left to the Head Command to take appropriate steps.'[11] Thus his government could say with a straight face that there were no German troops on the northern side of the Dvina and 'no member of the Iron Division will lose his German citizenship by entering the service of the Lettish Government. All claims for provision remain as before. The remuneration of troops will undergo no change. The treaty concluded with the Lettish Government is valid up to the 1st of July and must then be renewed.'[12] It was a neat trick but, nonetheless, the German forces were about to be evicted.

For, whilst the Royal Navy and Cabinet considered their positions, the land war continued to grind on. Having taken Riga and imposed German control and savagery, von der Goltz now turned his attention to Estonia and the chance to extend his domains northwards. In June, the Iron Division struck towards the Estonian border; but German ambitions met with a setback in northern Latvia when his force was decisively beaten by a joint army of Estonian and Latvian troops (the Estonian 3rd Division which included the 2nd Regiment of the North Latvian Brigade) at the Battle of Wenden (Cēsis) on 23 June. Within four days Goltz's troops had been pushed back 40 miles and the Estonian forces were advancing into the outskirts of Riga.

To add to his misfortunes, the Treaty of Versailles was signed on 28 June and the peace finally settled.* And another locally-negotiated treaty, brokered by Lieutenant Colonel Stephen George Tallents, who had been appointed British Commissioner for the Baltic Provinces the preceding February, ended the fighting in Latvia. Tallents arranged an armistice (the 'Ceasefire of Strassenhof or Strazdumuiža', 3 July) which required all *Landeswehr* and other German troops to evacuate Riga within forty-eight hours of signature and all German troops to be out of Latvia as soon as possible. It also gave General Gough the right to appoint a new commander for the *Landeswehr*, a command which went to Lieutenant Colonel Harold Alexander[§] of the Irish Guards, a member of Gough's mission. He led them out of Riga to the Bolshevik front and succeeded in keeping the formation focused on fighting the Reds and away from Goltz's influence. It was a relief for the citizens of Riga, albeit one which would turn out to be temporary.

Gough issued a notice to the people of Riga. 'An Armistice has been concluded. The Ulmanis government has resigned with a view to forming a new representative government. The first duty of the new government will be the re-establishment of normal life in Latvia. Pending the establishment of a new government, Colonel Tallents, the British Commissioner for the Baltic Provinces has been appointed Acting Governor ... '[13] Ulmanis was finally going to be able to exercise some degree of executive control; he sailed from Libau to Riga in SS *Saratov* on 7 July.

Not that the War Office staff in London found the situation completely to their liking; 'as regards the Landwehr, which is now under the command of a British officer', they reported to the War Cabinet,

the Germans in it have been returned to Germany, while the Balts are being formed into a unit of the Latvian Army. There

---

* Although there was some alarm that Germany might later reject the punitive terms involved. The final signing of the Treaty of Versailles did not take place until 28 June 1919, the fifth anniversary of the assassination of Archduke Franz Ferdinand.
§ Who was to serve with distinction in the Second World War, becoming Field Marshal Harold Rupert Leofric George Alexander, 1st Earl Alexander of Tunis, and a Governor General of Canada.

is evidence to show, however, that unofficially considerable numbers of German troops are being equipped and transported from Germany for service in the Baltic States. In addition the German authorities are recruiting and equipping Russian ex-prisoners of war in Germany for despatch to a pro-German Russian force under a certain Colonel Bermondt at Mitau.[14]

Estonia

The Red Baltic Fleet made several sorties in June; on the 21st and 22nd six destroyers and minesweepers came west to within gun range of Biorko and the British ships exchanged shots with them, across the minefields. On both nights Cowan moved out with two cruisers and his destroyers to try to engage the Soviets, but on the second venture two of his destroyers, *Vivacious* and *Whirlwind*, damaged their propellers in the shallow waters and had to return to Copenhagen.

Meanwhile, during May and June, the White Russian North Western Army, commanded by General Alexander Rodzyanko but under the ultimate control of General Yudenitch (in Helsingfors), and with Laidoner and the Estonians to their rear, was pushing east along the Estonian coast in an attempt to take Petrograd. This force placed frequent demands on Cowan for artillery support. For example, at the request of the White Russians he shelled and set on fire Bolshevik positions at Kernova and Dolgaya, in Kaporia Bay, and the Rekopesh Glassworks between 23 and 26 June. But he was becoming disenchanted with these demands for gunnery support. 'I do not propose doing any more of this,' he wrote to the Admiralty on 1 July, 'there is not enough definiteness [*sic*] in the plans and actions of the Russian command to justify the expenditure of ammunition or the entry into shallow waters … also I think it probable that innocent people suffer more than the Bolsheviks.'[15]

He was also deeply suspicious of the Russians' motives, accusing both navy and army commands of 'plotting and intrigue', chiefly against the Estonians, Finns and Latvians 'whose independence they are all against', adding 'I feel that they [the White Russians] are far from worthy of support' and believed that if they did take Petrograd it and they would soon fall under German influence.[16]

Nonetheless, British opinion was at this time sanguine about Yudenitch's chances of success. The *Spectator* magazine reported in June that the Russian and Esthonian [sic] forces under General Yudenitch made a further advance last week towards Gatchina, twenty-five miles south of Petrograd. Some of the Bolshevik troops mutinied and many were captured... . The island fortress of Kronstadt, covering the minefields, alone prevents our ships from reaching Petrograd forthwith. It will doubtless surrender when General Yudenitch reaches the capital, and the food transports which starving Petrograd awaits with impatience can then ascend the Neva. Bolshevism stands for hunger and rapine, but the Allies can offer Russia food.[17]

But in fact, by the end of June, Yudenitch's march on Petrograd ran out of steam. He gave up the attempt and moved his army to occupy a strip of land east of the River Narva and beyond the Estonian border, which was chiefly Russian in population. At Yudenitch's back, Laidoner and his army remained generally inactive; they were simply pleased to have seen the White Russian forces, whose antipathy to Estonian independence was well known, off their territory.

The ending of activity on this front also allowed some Latvian volunteers serving with the Estonians to return home. On 30 June, *Dragon*, *Velox* and *Viscount* took 1,600 Latvian troops to Libau from Reval where they were to displace the White Russian troops under the German Balt Prince Lieven, who had garrisoned the town when the Germans left it.

And the British had something to celebrate too. Late on 24 June, an Admiralty telegram had informed Cowan that Germany would sign the Paris peace treaty. Late that night all the RN ships on the harbour turned on their searchlights and sounded their sirens in relief. The population of Reval took the celebrations to mark Midsummer's Eve, especially since the following day was the Feast of St John, a public holiday in the city. They therefore joined in with gusto, firing cannons and discharging rifles into the air.

Mines

As part of the general rotation of ships, on 25 June Cowan transferred his flag to the brand new *Danae*-class light cruiser HMS *Delhi*, commissioned only that month. Home to over 450 men, she carried six 6in, two 3in and two 2pdr guns at a maximum speed of

29 knots. Captain Mackworth again transferred with Cowan to take command. Forty-year-old Captain Geoffrey Mackworth DSO was the ninth child and fifth son of Sir Arthur William Mackworth, 6th Baronet Mackworth of the Gnoll, Glamorgan. The reason for the predilection by Cowan for Mackworth's services is now difficult to discover. Both men were considered 'strict, often uneven and excessive, disciplinarians'[18] and it was a combination which would eventually bring its own problems to the Baltic. *Inconstant*, *Phaeton* and *Royalist* also went home and were replaced by *Danae*, *Dauntless* and *Dragon* (all *Danae*-class cruisers) and *Princess Margaret* returned with a fresh load of mines and small-arms ammunition for the Latvians.

Cowan felt oppressed by the need to keep the Baltic Fleet's larger ships from breaking out. If the battleships got into open water they could destroy his own much smaller ships and cause havoc along the Estonian and Latvian littoral. He also had to ensure that he had sufficient freedom of the seas to operate anywhere at any time and this meant keeping the seaways free from obstructions, mainly mines. And the admiral was concerned that the Reds could deploy aircraft against him and wanted planes of his own, both to prevent this and to carry reconnaissance and bombing missions into enemy territory.

The 20th Destroyer Flotilla under Captain Berwick 'Budge' Curtis CB, DSO* had joined the Baltic Squadron in June. The flotilla had been formed in February 1918 as a highly trained and high-speed force of destroyer-minelayers, tasked with filling the holes created by German minesweepers in the Heligoland Bight area. From its inception, the formation had been led by Curtis in the flotilla leader HMS *Abdiel*.

Their work, although dangerous, created few 'headlines' until on 28 March they had, almost literally, run into three German armed trawlers. Sighting them at daybreak, Curtis detailed two destroyers to tackle each trawler. Commander Taprell Dorling in *Telemachus* was ordered to take the centre enemy vessel, but as he closed the German rolled a depth charge into the water between them. Dorling promptly went full speed astern. It was fortunate that he did. 'The depth charge blew the stern off the enemy vessel. Another few seconds it would have pulverised our bows as well. We rescued the

---

* Described by Admiral Fremantle as 'that most competent and enterprising officer' (Fremantle, *My Naval Career*, p 237).

crew from the boat and made them prisoners.'[19] Curtis had hoped to capture the trawlers and take them into harbour but his wireless picked up signals indicating that enemy light cruisers were closing on his position and he decided instead to blow up both the remaining German ships. They took off the crews and sank them with gunfire and explosives. This little escapade brought Curtis and his men £360 in prize money, £5 per head for each man captured, a welcome supplement to a sailor's pay.

Now they were in the Baltic, their speed and minelaying capability were a splendid addition to Cowan's forces and he was not long in getting them into action. On 25 June Their Lordships gave permission for the mining of Petrograd Bay, in an attempt to block the Soviet ships' egress. *Princess Margaret* and the 20th Destroyer Flotilla, undertook the mission on 12 July and laid mines to the north and west of the Russian's own fields. As Cowan later put it, he 'kept pecking at them in this way and that so as to prevent them breaking out and roaming at large all over the Baltic'.[20]

But just as important as laying mines was sweeping them. On 26 June the 1st Fleet Sweeping Flotilla arrived at Biorko, under the 'eccentric and unstable'[21] Lieutenant Commander Barry Victor Sturdee as SNO. This comprised 'Flower'-class fleet sweeping vessels, although throughout the war they had been used in many other roles as well, including submarine hunting, convoy escort and as Q-ships. They were simply constructed, based on merchant ship plans and built in ordinary commercial yards which were accustomed to such designs. The vessels had been built in double quick time (the first batch ordered in December 1914 and commissioned in May 1915 for service with the Grand Fleet) and lacked either comfort or subtlety. Initially armed with two 12pdr guns (later classes had 4in), very economical on coal and capable of 16 knots, they were lively in a seaway with a tendency to pitch; but they proved to be durable and capable.

However, whilst fine for sweeping in sea channels, their draught meant that they were unsuitable for clearing mines in shallow waters and harbours, both of which abounded in Cowan's territory. This was a particular problem in Riga where the retreating Germans had mined the harbour after their collision with, and defeat by, Estonian forces in June. As another expert noted, 'the lack of tidal rise and the shallow laying of mines in these waters ... means that most of the clearances are only practicable with the lightest draught vessels'.[22] Underwater wrecks and other obstacles made the situation worse. Previously, Cowan had urgently requested shallow-draught paddle steamers to join his command (and later received some, *vide infra*) and meanwhile 'asked the Estonians to clear the entrance with their shallow draught minesweepers (in reality fishing vessels) and promised to pay them on the same scale as RN for all mines destroyed'.[23] Although arduous, minesweeping could produce the occasional moment of entertaining distraction. On one occasion a light cruiser signalled to HMS *Godetia*, Sturdee's ship, 'there is a mine astern of me; please get rid of it'. However, a racing boat crew in the harbour saw an excited crowd of watchers on the cruiser's quarterdeck all staring intently and pointing astern at a bobbing object and reached the conclusion that it had been accidentally dropped overboard. With the 'proverbial courtesy of the sea they secured it and towed it alongside the cruiser and it was not until they observed a tendency on the part of the onlookers to disperse rapidly and unobtrusively that they realised the situation'.[24]

But generally, sailors hated mines. They were so random and untargeted in their destruction. Lieutenant Roger Selby thought that 'there's no doubt about it, mines are the hell of naval warfare; it's the only thing which isn't human directed so you have no-one to hit back at … and you can never be absolutely certain that you are clear of them'.[25]

HMS *Banbury*

On 23 May, the Improved 'Racecourse'-class paddle minesweeper HMS *Banbury* had arrived at Reval, together with her sisters *Lanark* and *Hexham* in response to Cowan's urgent plea for shallow-draught minesweepers. Powered by coal and driven by two side-mounted paddle wheels, she was armed with one 12pdr and one 3in high angle anti-aircraft weapon. Their beam was 58ft[*] at the paddles so manoeuvre was more than a little complicated in tight spaces. All three ships had been put to work clearing mines from the so-called 'Red Route', the supposedly mine-free channel linking Reval, Libau and Copenhagen, the necessity for which had been re-iterated by the mining on 28 May of the fleet tanker *War Expert* in the same field as had accounted for *Cassandra*.

[*] Her beam can be compared to 33ft for a 'Flower'-class sloop. *Banbury*'s draught was around 7ft compared to circa 12ft for a 'Flower'-class sloop.

Banbury soon ran into problems. On 7 July she went aground whilst casting off her moorings. She had been moored up very close to a shoal and had failed to clear it in trying to get under way, damaging her bottom and holing the reserve feed tank. The reason that *Banbury*'s captain gave for mooring in such an unpropitious position shines a light on the general lack of preparedness that had seen her sudden rush to answer Cowan's call.

Lieutenant Commander John Wales RNR told the court of enquiry into her accident that

> my reason for mooring where I did – with such a small scale chart – was that the means of landing liberty men are very poor, we only having small lifeboats. Also a considerable number of the men have never been properly kitted up and have had no opportunity of obtaining their uniform. Therefore, it is only when I anchor at small uninhabited places that I am able to land them for exercise.[26]

No chart and no uniforms; a sad state of affairs.

The Loss of *Myrtle* and *Gentian*

Minesweeping was self-evidently a dangerous occupation. First World War mines were unpredictable, unreliable and prone to misbehave. During the conflict the Royal Navy's minesweeper force comprised primarily trawlers, generally taken up from fishing ports.

By the end of the war these auxiliary minesweeping forces comprised 412 trawlers, 142 drifters and 52 paddle steamers out of a total of 726 designated minesweeping vessels. Most of the trawlers were hired by the navy but some simply commandeered and purchased off their builder's slips. Ships and crews came wholesale and, with the addition of a small signalling staff, the trawlers largely remained under their own skippers – who became warrant-ranked Skippers RNR. In all 214 British minesweepers of all types, including small patrol craft, were lost to mines (all but nine of them in Home Waters) during the war while sweeping over 30,000 mines.

Early British minesweeping was limited to the towing of a ground chain from two spars set across the stern of a vessel. Clearly this resulted in an extremely narrow swept path and the chain was easily snagged by seabed obstructions. The next development was a serrated wire sweep towed between two ships. Otter boards, used by fishermen to keep open the mouths of their nets, were employed to increase the width of wire in contact with the seabed. But again, this design frequently became snagged on rocks and wrecks. Finally, HMS *Vernon*'s technical experts got around this problem through the introduction of redesigned otter boards known as 'kite otters'. These were also able to maintain a specified depth. This development was the basis for the British Type *Actaeon* sweep used for most Royal Navy minesweeping operations during the war. It was effective for depths down to 50 fathoms. Minesweeping was usually carried out in pairs towing the sweep between them. A single 2½in wire was towed between two ships steaming 500 yards apart, with its depth regulated by a water-kite 12ft long and weighing a ton. The kite was lowered from the sweeper by means of the pulley on the gallows at the stern. In 1916 serrated wire was introduced, rendering the cutting of the mooring cable more certain. The wire cut the mine mooring rope and the weapon floated to the surface where it was destroyed. On occasion the serrated sweep wire would fail to do its job and the mine, mooring rope and sinker would become entangled in the sweep. To cope with this crisis there were three potential methods used. Firstly, the sweep wire could be slipped immediately – both ends of the sweep were cast off from the sweepers so that the mine would sink and the position was marked by laying buoys. Secondly, the mine might be towed into shallow water away from the shipping lanes before slipping took place. And thirdly the mine could be towed to a designated dumping ground before being slipped.

Cowan was constantly ill at ease regarding the minefields around his bases. 'The repeated appearance of mines in the swept channel between Reval and Libau are a great anxiety to me,' he noted in a report to the Admiralty.[27] Hence he had pressed the minesweeping sloops into action as soon as they arrived, despite the disadvantages of their relatively deep draught.

On 15 July, four 'Flower'-class sloops of the 1st Fleet Minesweeping Flotilla were out in the Gulf of Finland, sweeping mines to the east of Ösel Island. They were using the *Actaeon* method, operating in two pairs, *Lupin* and *Lilac* and *Myrtle* and *Gentian*. During the afternoon, the latter pair was ordered to slip their sweeps and sink four mines which had been swept up to the surface by the former duo. As they closed these 'floaters', *Gentian* hit and detonated an unseen mine. *Myrtle* closed to render assistance but she too set off a mine; the explosion killed some of the hands in the engine room and after boiler room of the ship, and many others of the crew were wounded. There were now two wrecked Royal Navy ships in the middle of an uncharted minefield. *Lupin* and *Lilac* steamed towards them but anchored up because they could not be sure which area had been swept. They called to shore for help, specifically a shallow-draught tug to try to pull the sloops to safety. But *Myrtle* was badly damaged: her forepart had broken away and she was sinking. Her captain, Lieutenant Commander Richard James Rodney Scott RN, had left his ship with her crew but hearing that the fate of one of his men had not been definitely ascertained, returned alone to what was left of the ship. *Myrtle* was drifting through the minefield, rolling heavily and burning fiercely; but regardless of the risk, Scott made a thorough search for the missing man, although without success.

Shortly after Scott left the ship for a second time, she sank, ninety minutes after hitting the mine; her survivors had used the small boats of both vessels to transfer to *Gentian*. From here they were transhipped to safety by the boats of a passing American Food Relief vessel, the liner *Lake St Clair*, which was on passage home but stopped and 'rendered every assistance with her boats'.[28]

The only available tug was Estonian and her owner was reluctant to sail because of the difficulty in getting insurance. Eventually the problem was resolved and the destroyer *Wrestler* towed her out to the remaining stricken ship. But the weather was worsening and towing proved impossible; indeed, it took *Wrestler* three days to get the tug back home. At 1500 on the 17th, almost forty-eight hours to the minute after she had been mined and in strong winds, *Gentian* turned over to port and sank. Twelve crewmen, six from each ship, had lost their lives, all but one of them in the engine rooms when the ships were struck. Lieutenant Commander Scott was awarded the Albert Medal in Bronze for Gallantry in Saving Life at Sea for his actions and 22-year-old Lieutenant Henry Crawford Macdonald RN, also of *Myrtle*, received the DSC for displaying 'seamanship of a high order'.[29] Cowan would take no more risks in shallow water; the sloops were not fit for purpose there. The 1st Fleet Sweeping Flotilla was ordered home.[*]

All was not complete doom and gloom, however; on 19 July the

---

[*] The 'Red Route', a swept channel from Copenhagen to Reval, had finally been completed by mid-summer.

Official Celebrations for the signing of the Peace Treaty at Versailles were held. The so-called 'Peace Day' was celebrated all over Britain and the Empire and the new Cenotaph, initially built of plaster and wood to a design of Edward Lutyens, was unveiled and dedicated in London. In newly-liberated Libau and Riga 'ships were dressed overall and, in the afternoon, a very successful sports meeting was held on shore [comprising] of land and aquatic sports'[30] reported Duff. There was a band and local officials and their families, together with French and American officers and men, were invited along. Tea was provided for some 600 souls and in the evening there was a short firework display. It was almost like civilisation again. And at Reval, all ships contributed foodstuffs for a party for the town's children, held in a local park. According to Stoker Richard Rose, 'they enjoyed every minute of it'.[31] Then, as darkness fell, all ships fired off fireworks and very lights in celebration.

HMS *Vindictive*

Cowan's desire for some form of air power led to the despatch of HMS *Vindictive* to join his forces. She had started life as a *Hawkins*-class heavy cruiser and was laid down under the name *Cavendish* but was converted to an aircraft carrier while still being built. Renamed in June 1918, *Vindictive* was completed a few weeks before the end of the war and saw no active service with the Grand Fleet. She had eight oil-fired and four coal-fired boilers in an attempt to provide her with motive power whatever the fuel supply situation.

The conversion from cruiser to aircraft carrier involved removing some guns and the conning tower, thus allowing the forward super-structure to be remodelled into a hangar housing six aircraft. The hangar roof, with a small extension, formed the 106ft long flying-off deck. Aircraft were hoisted up through a hatch at the aft end of the flying-off deck by two derricks. The 193ft landing deck required the removal of more guns and a port side gangway connected the landing and flying-off decks to allow aircraft with their wings folded to be wheeled from one to the other. Despite these modifica-tions she still managed 29 knots on her trials.

Commanded by Captain Henry Edgar 'Dasher' Grace, the tennis playing second son of the famous cricketer, Doctor W G Grace,* she

---

* Another Grace child, William Gilbert Jnr, had naval connections, being a master at the Royal Naval College, Osborne, at the time of his premature death from appendicitis, aged thirty.

set sail from Rosyth for Reval on 2 July, arriving at Copenhagen the next day (and where she fired a 21-gun salute), and departing for Estonia twenty-four hours later. Her journey from Denmark to Estonia was enlivened by encountering two floating mines. One she sank with a 2in gun, the other passed within 6ft of her hull.

Vindictive carried a mixed bag of seventeen aeroplanes (ten land and seven floatplanes). There were Grain Griffin reconnaissance aircraft, Sopwith 2F-1 Camel fighters, Sopwith 1½ Strutters and Short Type 184 seaplanes, all 'somewhat long in the tooth but better than nothing at all'.[32] They were under the command of Squadron Leader David Grahame Donald RAF.

The land planes carried by *Vindictive*, the Camels and 1½ Strutters, were stored in a hanger in two hinged sections. When required the plane was hoisted up onto the flying-off platform and the fuselage and tail section was joined to the rest of the aircraft by means of longerons. The rudder and elevator controls were then connected. Take-off from the platform was always perilous and it was usual for Camels operating with the fleet to be fitted with flotation bags which were designed to keep the tail above water after an emergency ditching in the sea. Although thankful for the thought, pilots were less than enamoured with the reality. At higher altitudes, the air in the floatation bags expanded, causing them to press against the control cables; pilots then had to fly whilst trying to deflate them by hand. The planes themselves were of variable quality. Camels had given sterling service on the Western Front, having entered service in June 1917. They quickly achieved a reputation for being difficult to fly although an excellent fighter plane in experienced hands. But towards the end of the war, and after only a year of service, the type was mainly being used as a ground attack aircraft, having become obsolescent as a day fighter as its climb rate, level speed and performance at altitudes over 12,000ft were outclassed by the latest German fighters and aircraft on both sides had made rapid and significant progress.

The 1½ Strutter was an older type, first introduced in December 1915 as a two-seater reconnaissance fighter. It was a very lightly-built aircraft and its structure did not stand up particularly well to arduous war service. It was also far too stable to make a good dogfighter and the distance between the pilot and the observer's cockpits hampered communication between them. The last operational 1½ Strutters in the Royal Flying Corps were replaced by

Camels by late October 1917, but the navy persisted with the type.

Vindictive also carried two types of seaplanes. The Grain Griffin was a carrier-based reconnaissance aircraft developed and built by the RNAS Marine Experimental Depot at Port Victoria during the First World War. A development of the unsuccessful Sopwith B1 bomber, it was a two-seat single-engined biplane. Only eight were ever built and they did not see action during the war; three of them were now with *Vindictive*. Finally, the Short 184 was a two-seat reconnaissance, bombing and torpedo-carrying, folding-wing seaplane first flown in early 1915. They served with the navy throughout the Great War but were distinctly obsolescent by 1919.

However, the deployment of all these aircraft was to be unfortunately delayed. On 6 July, while making for Reval at 15 knots in moderate visibility, *Vindictive* struck hard on the Middel Grund Shoal at the harbour entrance and became firmly stuck. Taking *Cleopatra* and *Delhi*, Cowan rushed to the scene, to find his new carrier in water that was 3ft less than her draught and in a tideless area. There now followed an eight-day struggle to re-float the stricken ship. First, they tried to lighten ship, discharging oil and ammunition. The following day they offloaded the seaplanes; Cowan himself came aboard to assess the situation and at 2330 *Cleopatra* and two tugs tried to pull her off, but to no avail – the tow parted. On the 8th they unloaded more planes and most of the provisions. A floating crane came alongside to assist the offloading. On the 9th, divers examined the ship's bottom and the following day all hands unloaded *Vindictive*'s coal, a messy job under any conditions. *Cleopatra* and *Delhi* attempted a joint tow; again the cables parted. On the 11th *Vindictive* was still de-coaling, lighters were taking off stores and the floating crane returned. The 12th saw the tugs *Assistans* and *Karin* bring out airbags which were deployed during the day. Grace tried to pull her off with her own engines but failed. The next day they prepared airbags and 'camels',* Then, on the 14th, with *Cleopatra* and a tug pulling and a strong wind which caused an unusual rise of water by 8in, off the shoal she came. Only then did they realise that the area all around was actually mined. If it had not for the wind-backed tide she might well be there still.

There was a fair amount of damage. She was badly strained and went straight into Reval harbour to refit. It was not until the 20th, at

---

* 'An apparatus for raising a sunken ship, consisting of one or more watertight chests to provide buoyancy' (*Oxford English Dictionary*).

0630, that she was able to depart for Biorko with her maximum speed reduced due to damage to the hull. She sailed with a Camel on the flying-off platform at two minutes notice, with the flyers keeping four-hour watches. Pilots were given £10 in gold, a revolver and a 'meat bribe ticket'[33] in case of forced landing.

When *Vindictive* arrived at Biorko the weather was glorious. Many sailors went swimming; one didn't come back. Thirty-nine-year-old Chief Petty Officer Frederick Rampton of *Princess Margaret* drowned; what a pointless way to lose a life, in the middle of a war zone. That same day, the Reds sent two aircraft over to bomb in the vicinity. Captain Williams RAF in a shore-launched Strutter and Captain Randall RAF in a Camel, launched from *Vindictive*'s flying-off platform, chased them away but failed to catch them. The two Soviet planes henceforth became regular visitors to Biorko from this point. The sailors named them 'Ivan the Terrible' and 'Alexander the Awful'.[34]

At Biorko Cowan's miniature air force now had to make an aerodrome to fly from. A thin strip of land on the mainland at Koivisto was chosen, just across the narrow channel from the island base. The land was cleared, using much of the loose explosives that the squadron possessed and an airstrip 300 yards long and 100 yards wide, barely an adequate size for air operations, began to take shape.

30 July; Operation 'DB'

Now he had an air arm, Cowan was determined to mount raids on Kronstadt as often as possible. On 26 July, Donald was finally able to fly a reconnaissance mission over the fortress. Then, at 0200 on 30 July, Squadron Leader Donald carried out the first bombing raid on the Red base with a strike force comprising three Short seaplanes, two Sopwith 1½ Strutters, one Griffin and three Camels. Lieutenant Eric Bremerton RAF flew one of the 1½ Strutters. He took off from the carrier on the dark and nearly hit the water. Remarkably, it was the first time he had flown that aircraft type.[35]

Cowan christened this Operation 'DB' after his hero, Admiral David Beatty. The planes were met with anti-aircraft fire but dropped sixteen bombs between them. The Grain Griffin was hit and was observed to be in distress and heading back to the carrier, so Captain Grace increased to 20 knots and proceeded towards the shore to give what succour to the pilot he could.

The main objective of the attack had been a destroyer depot ship with five destroyers alongside, which had been identified from Donald's photo reconnaissance of four days earlier, and Cowan claimed at least one hit on the vessel. And while the aircraft had bombed the harbour, Agar led two CMBs out from Terrioki and attacked a Red patrol craft with a torpedo (which missed) and machine-gun fire; the Russian turned around and fled for its base.

But the raid did not take the Bolsheviks by surprise, for there were clearly eyes and ears sympathetic to the Soviet cause lurking on or around Biorko Island. Cowan reported that 'an unknown individual twice called up on the telephone one of our shore stations asking when the raid was to begin'.[36] And when the planes took off again at dawn, rockets were observed to be sent up from the southern end of the island.

The foray had coincided with a meeting of the revolutionary sailors in the Alexandrovsky Garden. Two 112lb bombs landed amongst the crowd and an agent in place reported that 100 people were killed or wounded, although the Soviet press stated only two dead at first and then twelve. The agent overheard some sailors say that if the bombing continued 'they shall hoist up over Kronstadt a white flag'.[37] The dead, or at least some of them, were buried with great pomp in Marsovoe Pole – the Field of Mars.[*] Perhaps in retaliation for the attack, a Soviet plane came to visit Biorko the following day, causing Captain Grace to delay a regatta 'pulling contest' in order to close up his anti-aircraft weapons. Nonetheless, the regatta was a 'great success'.[38]

Now Cowan had an air force in the game, and he kept them hard at work. All through August there were daily missions over Kronstadt as Cowan tried to use his new resources to cause maximum inconvenience to the Bolshevik fleet. On 5 August, Lieutenant Bremerton took up a Griffin, the third aircraft type he had flown since arriving in the Baltic, and bombed a factory in the port area, starting a fire. To achieve tactical surprise, he had glided in from 8,000ft to 1,500ft with the engine off. Nonetheless, there was 'anti-aircraft [fire] all around us but we got away with it'.[39] Then on the 8th he took out a 1½ Strutter loaded with two 100lb bombs.

---

[*] The Champ de Mars had become the main public space of commemoration, the altar of the cult of the revolution, during and after 1917. The choice of name was deliberate, referencing the French Revolution of 1789.

On the 13th, Bremerton again went up in a Griffin, for a further reconnaissance flight. He had only been in the air for ten minutes when the oil pressure gauge suddenly plunged to zero. He turned back for home but the engine seized up and instead they came down in the water, five miles from the shore and close to one of the Kronstadt outer forts. The plane sank with only the tail staying above water. Fortunately, a Finnish motor boat had observed the crash and rescued both crew members. The machine was salvaged but was proved to be beyond repair. There was now only one serviceable Griffin left.

All this activity was noticeable to the sailors. Stoker Rose recorded that 'the next few weeks became quite hectic, the planes flying at regular intervals during the daylight hours, bombing shipping lying in Kronstadt harbour. The sound of gunfire and exploding bombs was quite audible on the prevailing wind.'[40] And the raids had more than just irritation value. Two bombs also struck the tanker *Tatiana,* killing one seaman. Severe damage was caused to the harbour facilities. Intelligence on the ground suggested that fires were started in the wood store, oil depots and coal and food supply warehouses, an assertion which seemed to be confirmed by the Bolsheviks themselves.[41] Another agent reported that 'all the steam launches on the jetty near the cruiser *Gromoboi* were destroyed. Stern of an oil transport was damaged. Eight men were killed while attending a meeting. In the sailors' engineering school one officer was killed and nine men wounded. Small damage was done to destroyer *Azard*.'[42]

Despite these successes, in reality the hitting power of Cowan's air force was limited. The bombs were too small to cause damage to armoured ships and anti-aircraft fire further reduced the accuracy and efficiency of the bombers by keeping them at high altitude. But their nuisance value was high. 'Altogether, the air raids keep the sailors and garrison of Kronstadt in a state of apprehension', reported an unknown source.[43]

But the continuous operations – photo reconnaissance twice daily, bombing attacks every two to three days – took its toll on the machines themselves. In early August Cowan was already asking for six more Camels to be sent out, 'bifurcated in *Princess Margaret'*.[44]

Red Threat
If the Russians were reluctant to venture out with their capital units,

that was not the case with the submarines. On the night of 23/24 July, the *Vepr* was despatched to attack British ships in Kaporia Bay but suffered engine trouble and had to return. The *Pantera* had been sent out at the same time and on the 26th she spotted two British submarines, *L-12* and *E-40*, travelling on the surface. Keeping the sun at his back to conceal his position, her commander, Alexander Bakhtin, launched an attack with a single torpedo fired at the furthest British submarine, *L-12*, which saw it early enough to evade.

Pantera now focused on the nearer vessel, HMS *E-40*, and fired two torpedoes at her, before turning away and diving deep to avoid retaliation. The British submarine evaded the torpedoes and as her bows came round on the diving Russian, fired off one of her own, which passed alongside the Red vessel. A nearby destroyer, HMS *Watchman*, conducted a depth-charge attack as well but *Pantera* eluded her and retuned to Kronstadt. The destroyer later found two Russian torpedoes floating and picked them up.

Now repaired, *Vepr* made a second sally on the 27th. Early the following day, she detected two British vessels and fired a brace of torpedoes towards them, again without success. In return, the destroyers *Valorous* and *Vancouver* attacked with depth charges and the Red submarine was badly damaged, losing her electrics. She was, however, able to limp home, despite the subsequent attentions of HMS *L-15*. Commander Robert Gerald Hamond of *Valorous* was subsequently commended by Cowan for this attack and for his 'prompt and correct action'.[45]

Although no ship had yet been lost to a Soviet submarine, the threat they posed worried Admiral Cowan. He increased his mining activities around the exits from Kronstadt and deployed submarine nets to protect his own harbours. Cowan also requested of the Admiralty that they send him more vessels equipped with hydrophones.

At Home
Back in London, as the month of July drew to an end, the questions in Parliament that Walter Long had feared would come began now in earnest. The self-appointed scourge of the Admiralty, Lieutenant Commander Kenworthy MP, rose to ask Long a question on 23 July. Was the First Lord of the Admiralty

aware of the increase in efficiency of the Russian Soviet warships in the Eastern Baltic during the last few months; if he is aware that, among other modern vessels, these include two ships of the line and several modern destroyers; that the shooting of these ships is as accurate as was the shooting of the German men-of-war; whether he will state the object of keeping British ships of war in these waters; and will he state whether he is satisfied that our forces there are sufficient and in no danger of being overwhelmed by a sudden attack?

Long gave what he hoped was a suitably anodyne yet sarcastic reply;

The answer to the first and second parts of the question is in the affirmative, and to the third part in the negative. The object of keeping British ships in the Baltic is to prevent unprovoked raids on the coastal towns of the Baltic States and Finland, to prevent interference with the arrangements to feed the needy populations of these Border States, and to prevent the spreading of Bolshevik militarism. The answer to the last portion of the question is in the affirmative.[46]

It was interesting that this was the first time any politician had mentioned Finland; an attempt at securing a wider justification perhaps?

CHAPTER 12

Operation 'RK', Kronstadt, August 1919

Cowan had been impressed by the success of Agar's single-handed CMB raid and the destruction of the *Oleg*. His constant nagging fear was that his forces were insufficient to deal with the Russian heavy ships, should they break out. It now seemed to him that with an air force and these small strike craft he might be able to even up the odds. His mind moved ineluctably towards the use of his forces in an attacking manner.

The admiral sent for Agar and questioned him closely on what might be needed and how he might use the CMBs to attack the Bolshevik ships in the very heart of their harbour and base. His thinking was modelled on Operation 'ZO', the raids on Zeebrugge and Ostend in April and May 1918, which had made his mentor Roger Keyes into a national hero. The fact that the raids were a failure and that many brave men had lost their lives in vain[*] did not register with Cowan. 'You see Agar,' he told the lieutenant, 'I want this to be a blow, the same as Roger did in Zeebrugge but without landing troops and demolition parties, who only clutter up the main striking force with paraphernalia.'[1] It was with his hero Keyes in mind that he designated the nascent plan Operation 'RK'.

In Cowan's eyes, secrecy was essential; 'I don't mind the Russians knowing about our aircraft as we can't hide them in the sky, but they must not know about the CMB flotilla as that is to be our striking force,'[2] he told Agar. Agar suggested towing the CMBs out from the UK, two at a time behind a destroyer, as opposed to freighting them out, as he had done for his spy mission. It would be

---

[*] For details of Operation 'ZO' see S R Dunn, *Securing the Narrow Sea* (Barnsley: Seaforth Publishing, 2017).

143

much quicker and would be under Royal Navy control at all times.

A planning committee of Agar, Flag Commander Chichester-Clark and the *Delhi*'s navigator, Lieutenant Charles Morgan, was quickly constituted and developed a five-point plan for the attack. They recommended that such a raid should be carried out when least expected, made by CMBs approaching by the same route as Agar had used, be preceded and accompanied by air bombardment on the garrison town as a distraction, focus on attacking the ships in harbour during the air diversion and, if unsuccessful, use the CMBs to lay mines across the harbour entrance. Speed, they noted, was essential.

But speed would have to wait for Cabinet approval; this was not a mission that could be undertaken without Admiralty and political agreement. And Cowan needed more CMBs to be sent to him. He forwarded the plan to Wemyss and asked for resources and permission. The operation was now in the First Sea Lord's hands.

Wemyss

First Sea Lord Admiral Sir Rosslyn Erskine Wemyss had taken office on 27 December 1917 after his predecessor, Admiral John Jellicoe, had been defenestrated by First Lord Eric Geddes on Christmas Eve, by letter. He was a monocle-wearing throwback, from an aristocratic family (a cadet branch of the Earls of Wemyss and March which had inherited Wemyss Castle and 7,000 acres of land in Fife in the eighteenth century), and on good terms with royalty having George V as a long-standing friend. Wemyss was a 'battleship navy' man, socially adept but no thinker. He was self-important, patrician, aloof and possessed a low opinion of democracy and politicians, once exclaiming 'when every crossing sweeper has a voice in matters it is quite impossible for any government to rule'.[3] The economist John Maynard Keynes knew Wemyss and thought he was a 'lightweight ... with a comical quizzical face and a single eyeglass'.[4] His appointment caused much resentment, for Jellicoe was both loved and respected by many in the navy.

However, he had his supporters. Deputy Chief of the Naval Staff Sidney Freemantle thought him 'a man of optimistic and sanguine temperament'[5] and his avuncular 'hail-fellow-well-met' personality had helped the cause of teamwork and efficiency at the Admiralty. On Wemyss becoming First Sea Lord, 'Jacky' Fisher gave to George E Buckle of *The Times*, in response to the question 'but has he brains?', the evasive answer 'he has tact'.[6] Certainly, Wemyss had handled a difficult situation well as the British representative at the Armistice negotiations.

Wemyss had found his job increasingly trying during 1919. Firstly, the lack of any coherent political direction was both frustrating and time-consuming; secondly, he was presiding over a considerable cut-back of naval budgets and resources; and thirdly, he was the target of a vituperative campaign in the Northcliffe press to have him replaced by Admiral Beatty, soon to be Earl Beatty. This was a campaign with which Beatty was in complete agreement, if not its instigator; he desperately wanted Wemyss's job and felt he deserved it. As early as January 1919 *The Times* had written that 'it is understood that Sir David Beatty will almost immediately come to the Admiralty, an appointment which will help remove a very widespread anxiety about the navy during a difficult period of transition',[7] which understandably made Wemyss furious. His anger was stoked by the lack of any supportive response from the government 'which undoubtedly wrecked my position in the eyes of the public'.[8]

By August Wemyss had determined to resign and, indeed, would send his first resignation letter (which was seemingly ignored) on 20 August, having trailed it in a note dated the 6th. It was in that frame of mind, therefore, that he had obtained for Cowan permission to go ahead with Operation 'RK'. He ambushed the Cabinet by stating that 'in view of the impending danger and actual losses' he had to place before the Cabinet the options of withdrawing completely or sanctioning the attack and succeeded in gaining their 'grudging consent' to the latter.[9] As Wemyss wrote to Cowan 'the permission for you to attack was obtained, so to speak, on a snap vote, and I took the opportunity. But they don't, won't or can't understand the situation.'[10]

Resources

Despite the desire for a speedy execution of the plans for 'RK', owing to a shortage of skilled motor mechanics the CMBs could not be sent until the end of July. Part of the 20th Destroyer Flotilla was ordered to return to Britain to collect the motor boats. They were a larger version of Agar's vessels, 55ft long instead of 40ft, carrying two torpedoes rather than one and up to four Lewis guns.

The towing destroyers were to transport the motor boat spares, engines, torpedoes and the like, and one officer and one rating was to be on board the little craft while they were being towed. This latter instruction seemed to offer an uncomfortable passage to the unfortunates chosen. Eight CMBs were to be brought out to Biorko.

Such an exercise wasn't as easy as the orders made out, as demonstrated by the travails of HMS *Venturous*. She was a 'V'-class destroyer, launched in 1917 and under the command of Lieutenant Commander Guy Percival Bowles. On 25 July *Venturous* was ordered to sail with *CMB 67A* in tow; firstly from Harwich to Immingham to collect some mines and then on to Copenhagen. However, it wasn't until four days later that she finally left the Humber in company with *Abdiel*, *Gabriel* and *Vanquisher*. In line ahead they proceeded towards Denmark at 16 knots, each towing a CMB. On passage, in the early hours of the 30th, the weather deteriorated markedly and the sea became very rough. A signal lantern was washed overboard and speed was reduced to 6 knots. Then at 0615 the tow parted. Bowles stopped his ship and just under an hour later managed to get underway, with the line reattached. This lasted until 1855 when the bull-ring of the CMB was torn out and the tow lost again. Once more *Venturous* halted; the two men in the CMB were now taken on board the destroyer for safety and after another hour's delay the destroyer proceeded once more, now at 8 knots.

At noon the following day, the tow parted and took forty-five minutes to repair, only for it to part again at 1940. Now the CMB was also full of water, so Bowles ordered her to be made fast alongside and pumped out, before reattaching the tow and setting off again, at low speed. Everyone on board the destroyer might now be justified in feeling thoroughly sick of acting as a tug boat.

But worse was to come; with the wind now force five, at 2230 the tow parted for the final time; water logged and windswept, the CMB sank, taking with her an electric torch, ropes and harness, pillows, a lantern, a hatchet, two number eleven buoys and other salvage paraphernalia that *Venturous* had expended in trying to rescue her charge. She eventually arrived in Copenhagen just after midnight; and no doubt received little sympathy.

All in all, the 20th Flotilla suffered a total of sixteen breaks of tow on the voyage 'so they had a pretty rotten time'.[11] But Cowan's strike force eventually made in to Biorko on 8 August; and so did the man detailed to lead them, 34-year-old Commander Claude Congreve

Dobson DSO. Dobson was a submarine specialist and had won his decoration in a 'tethered goat' action in the North Sea; in HMS *C-27* he had sunk the U-boat *U-23* on 20 July 1915.[*] He was clearly a brave officer but he was also an only recently recovered one, having been unfit for sea duty since 15 August 1918 due to neurasthenia.[§] He had been passed fit again as late as 24 April 1919;[12] this assignment was his first opportunity to exercise command once more.

The Plan

The plan for the raid was comprised of three elements. Firstly, the striking force of CMBs; six were to be deployed in an attack on the ships in the harbour whilst two guarded the entrance and, if necessary, neutralised the harbour barrier (see Appendix 4 for details of the CMBs involved). These vessels would have to pass through the forts and the harbour mouth, which was only 50 yards wide, without being detected. Secondly, a supporting group, consisting of the light cruisers *Delhi*, *Danae* and *Cleopatra* together with HMS *Spenser* and a flotilla of destroyers would be stationed outside the minefield to act as rearguard should a Soviet vessel slip out or gunnery intervention against heavy ships be necessary. And finally, air support would bomb the garrison, diverting attention to the sky.

In was decided that 18 August would be the attack date, and the leading CMB was to enter the harbour at exactly 0130, whist the aircraft dropped their bombs. Four targets had been designated by Cowan. The two battleships, *Petropavlovsk* and *Andrei Pervozvanni*, were obvious candidates; the submarine depot ship *Pamiat Azova* was chosen as putting her out of action would severely inconvenience Red submarine operations; and the heavy cruiser *Rurik* was selected as she was reported to have on board some 300 mines which would go up like a Brock's Benefit if she were to be hit.

On the 12th, Lieutenant Bremerton took Dobson on a reconnaissance mission over Kronstadt; whilst they were away, a Red plane dropped propaganda leaflets over the Biorko base. And then the day

---

[*] For the details see S R Dunn, *Southern Thunder* (Barnsley: Seaforth Publishing, 2019).
[§] An ill-defined medical condition characterised by lassitude, fatigue, headache, and irritability, associated chiefly with emotional disturbance. He had been treated for syphilis in 1909, a disease which might have been a contributing cause to his health troubles.

before the operation Dobson and Lieutenant Bremner flew over the harbour to mark down the ships' positions. They also noted that *Gavriil* was at anchor outside the dockyard basin as guardship, and she was now added to the target list.

The boats would have to travel at speed, both for surprise and because otherwise the torpedoes would not function, and manoeuvre in a confined and crowded space. And inevitably all this would have to be done in the face of searchlights and enemy gunfire; the risks to life and success were great.

The fact that the operation was to take place at all was something of a miracle of planning and opportunity; the CMBs had been towed 2,000 miles to be there. The aircraft were old and obsolete, operating from a makeshift airfield and a primitive aircraft carrier. And the crews of the CMBs were young and all volunteers, at a time when many in Britain simply wanted peace and demobilisation (four of the boat skippers were RNR). And, of course, the raid had only been sanctioned at all as a result of Wemyss's cunning.

But now it was a fact. The die was cast and the men prepared. At 2130 on the 17th the flotilla started their engines and shoved off from HMS *Vindictive* where they had berthed during the day. Leaving Biorko at 2200 they proceeded in two groups, one led by Agar, one by Dobson, to the rendezvous at Inonemi Point. Dobson took a Finish smuggler with him to act as pilot. The game was afoot.

Attack

No plan survives contact with the enemy; and so it proved. Things went awry from the very start. Ten aircraft had been detailed to take part, a Camel, three 1½ Strutters, two Griffins and four Short 184 seaplanes. Two of the seaplanes, carrying two 112lb bombs each, could not take off from the water owing to the load. A 1½ Strutter crashed on take-off and another had serious engine problems mid-flight. Six made it to the target. They included Eric Bremerton, who had slept from 1900 to 2230; now he was aloft in a 1½ Strutter as part of the air attack.

Dobson arrived at the meeting point and his flotilla joined him at midnight, while Agar, having piloted two other boats to the rendezvous, proceeded independently to patrol the harbour mouth. The flotilla then set out at 19 knots towards the North Channel. Dobson passed south of fort No 4. He was now slightly behind time and the air attack had started but difficulties in navigation made him chary of increasing speed. He could also see just two boats, *79* and *88* (Lieutenants William Hamilton Bremner and Archibald Dayrell-Reed respectively), following him but decided that he should capitalise on the air diversion and attack immediately.

With Bremner, whose boat was full of cable-cutting equipment in case of a harbour barrier, in the van, they proceeded up the Petrograd canal and found *Gavriil* still on guard duty but with no one on deck. Bremner, finding no barrier at the entrance, roared into the basin and launched his torpedoes at the depot ship *Pamiat Azova*. Dobson, in *CMB-31BD*, followed him in and his number two, Lieutenant Russell MacBean fired two torpedoes into *Andrei Pervozvanni*. Behind him, Dobson saw *CMB-88* running in and thought she put one torpedo into *Andrei Pervozvanni* and another into *Petropavlovsk*.

In fact, all was not well in *88*. Dayrell-Reed and his number two, Lieutenant Gordon Steele,[*] heard the explosion as the depot ship was torpedoed and suddenly came under fire from both sides of the boat. Steele ducked down involuntarily and when he looked up again the whole surface of the water was pockmarked with shell splashes. The motor boat was headed straight towards a hospital ship and Steele had just remarked 'where are you heading' to his skipper when he realised the 'although still standing up and holding the wheel, his head was resting on the wooden conning tower top in front of him'.[13] He had been shot through the head. 'Mossy' Dayrell-Reed was a big man and it was with some difficulty that Steele lowered him to the cockpit floor so that he could take command. He was right on top of the *Andrei Pervozvanni* and must fire now or never. He fired and then stopped one engine to make an emergency turn away, firing at *Petropavlovsk* as he did so. As the boat turned, Steele saw and heard Dobson's torpedoes hit *Andrei Pervozvanni*, an explosion which drenched *88*'s crew with water and yellow picric acid powder before seconds later he observed his own weapons make their mark. The Soviets were now fully alert and there was a considerable volume of rifle and machine gun fire being directed at the motor boats as all three CMBs began to retire.

Meanwhile, *CMB-72A*, under Lieutenant Edward Bodley, assigned to attack *Rurik*, finally arrived on station having had

---

[*] Steele was an experienced 'special ops' officer having served in the Q-ships *Vienna* and *Baralong*, the latter at the time when she sank *U-27*, which was attacking the American cargo ship *Nicosian*.

trouble with her steering gear. The problem had not been rectified which made it impossible for Bodley to manoeuvre into the basin but he tried to launch his weapons anyway at a destroyer (presumably *Gavriil*) he saw as he approached the harbour entrance, only for the mechanism to misfire (it had in fact been shot away).

Now Lieutenant Lawrence Napier and Sub Lieutenant Osman Cyril Horton Giddy in *24A* entered the fray. Napier thought he had succeeded in torpedoing *Gavriil*,* but in trying to make good his escape his boat was disabled by nets or the breakwaters and sunk by gunfire. Behind them came Acting Lieutenant Commander Frank Brade in *62*. As Bremner was racing out, both boats collided and *79* was almost cut in half. The two boats were locked together, obstructing the entrance to the basin. Brade went to full speed, dragging both boats clear and then took *79*'s crew into his own vessel, while Bremner blew up his craft with guncotton. Brade then attacked *Gavriil* with his torpedoes but missed. *CMB-62* was now under fire from the destroyer's aft gun and a machine gun. The first shell fired hit the rear part of the cockpit and wounded all on board, Brade himself fatally. Bremner took command and ordered the firing of green Very lights, the signal for a disabled ship. Their Lewis guns had jammed and would not clear and the Russians therefore had uninterrupted target practice; their second shell hit the boat amidships and passed clear through whilst a third exploded on the cockpit, as did a fourth. Bremner, who had been wounded in three places whilst on his own boat, was now suffering from no less than eleven wounds. At this point a fifth shell hit forward and all the crew were blown into the water as the motor boat blew up.

Agar, with Marshall and Sindall alongside him in the repaired *CMB-7*, had remained outside the harbour intending to attack any shipping that came out. At about 0200 he retired to Petrograd Bay and waited to assist any boats in trouble. When he decided that no more CMBs were likely to emerge, he went back in himself and fired his single torpedo into the military harbour; it exploded but Agar could not distinguish what he had hit.

Dobson withdrew through the North Channel forts in company with *88* but then waited to see if any stragglers emerged. Coming under fire at first light he again moved away and proceeded back to the flagship.

---

* In fact his torpedo had hit the harbour wall behind the Soviet destroyer.

Sub Lieutenant Francis Howard in *86BD*, who had been intended to attack the *Rurik*, had overwhelming problems with his steering and engine and had been left behind, unable to manage more than 7 knots. Nonetheless, although clearly not in a fighting condition, he proceeded through the forts under heavy fire and patrolled Petrograd Bay, ready to attack any hostile craft and cover the retirement. But with his engines failing due to a seized big end, and hardly able to move at all, the guns zeroed in on his vessel. Fortunately, Sub Lieutenant Roland Hunter-Blair arrived in *72A*, and in the nick of time. On *86BD* Howard's number two, Sub Lieutenant Robert Leslie Wight, hastily prepared the crippled vessel for towing and *CMB-72A* took her under tow.

Their passage back to safety was fortuitously aided by an airman, Captain A K Randall in a Sopwith Camel. He had suffered engine failure half-way to Kronstadt but his machine restarted just as he was about to attempt a landing and, despite the risk involved, he once more set course for the harbour. Although late to the party, he chanced upon *72* and *86* in trouble. Randall dived down and machine-gunned a searchlight, which had caught the vessels in its beam, saving the CMBs from certain destruction. The rest of the aviators had made it home. Lieutenant Bremerton landed at 0145 having spent three hours and fifteen minutes in the air. He was 'dead tired when I landed and fell asleep on the aerodrome in a drizzle of rain after reporting'.[14]

On board *88*, they administered morphine to Dayrell-Reed who recovered consciousness once and tried to speak. Near Biorko they saw a destroyer and asked for a doctor. As they passed *Delhi*, Cowan left the bridge to speak to them and when they reached their berth alongside *Vindictive* the aircraft carrier's crew gave them a cheer. Dayrell-Reed died shortly afterwards.

Three Russian ships had been sunk, *Petropavlovsk*, *Andrei Pervozvanni* and *Pamiat Azova.* But there had been a cost. Three CMBs had been lost and two damaged. More importantly, brave men had died. Four ratings, Sidney Holmes, a leading seaman, William G Smith, able seaman, and two Chief Motor Mechanics Francis Stephens and Francis Thatcher, and four officers, Sub Lieutenant Hector Forbes MacLean, Acting Lieutenant Commander Frank Tomkinson Brade, Sub Lieutenant Thomas R G Usborne and Lieutenant Archibald Dayrell-Reed, were killed in the attack. Thirty-one-year-old Dayrell-Reed was a reservist, a mariner who had served his apprenticeship in sailing ships, as his piratical beard suggested. He had taken part in Operation 'ZO' in 1918; now he was laid to rest in the small Koivisto General Cemetery with full naval honours. As the service concluded, two small Finnish girls ran out from the crowd of onlookers with bunches of wild flowers for 'Mossy's' grave. Apart from Dayrell-Reed, none of the dead have a grave. Napier, Bremner,* Giddy, two chief motor mechanics and an able seaman were taken from the water by the Bolsheviks and made prisoners of war, where they endured harsh conditions which nearly killed them too. The morning following the raid, the Soviets bombed Terrioki, but caused no damage to the CMBs. Nonetheless, Marshall asked for permission to set up the two Lewis guns from the much-damaged *CMB-4* on the roof of the Terrioki Yacht Club.

The Red fleet had been disabled; never would the big ships again threaten the Baltic littoral and Cowan had achieved command of the sea; but at a cost.

Success

Congratulations for the success of Operation 'RK' poured in from all over the Baltic. Major General Laidoner in Estonia was first off the mark. On the 19th he wrote:

> In name of Estonian Army and Navy I have the honour to congratulate the Royal British Navy on the event of its admirably heroic deed by Cronstadt [*sic*], simultaneously the Estonian Army and Navy wish to express their highest gratitude to the British Navy and to you, sir, for the great service rendered to the young Estonian Republic by the power of the British Navy and sacrifice of hands.

Cowan replied that it was 'our pride and pleasure to do everything in support of your country'.[15]

Next came greetings from the German Balts, perhaps a less-expected quarter. The *Hauptmann* of the *Ritterschaft* of Estonia (the president of the local Baltic Barons) sent his congratulations via Colonel Pirie-Gordon of the military mission.

---

* In 1918, Bremner's commanding officer had written of him that he was 'a very great gentleman' who was 'physically and morally most courageous' (ADM 196/145/642, NA). He would need all of those qualities to survive his period as a prisoner of the Soviets.

The Estonian Foreign Minister, Poska, then wrote on the 23rd to express his own congratulations and to aver that 'Estonia is especially jubilant over this success, as it removes the danger, which threatened her from this quarter'. Cowan replied that 'Any help or service we have been able to render to Estonia has been given very gladly, as our admiration for the dauntless and untiring resistance your forces have maintained against all aggression is very great, and our wishes for the realisation of all your hopes are warm and sincere.'[16]

Three days later, Pitka, now styled an admiral, wrote 'I congratulate you, British heroes, on your late feat of unparalleled courage, through which the enemy's navy is ultimately defeated. You will remain eternally in the minds of the Estonian nation and Estonian Navy as example of courage and bravery.'[17]

And from Helsingfors, on the 26th, Mannerheim fulsomely expressed his admiration for the action.

> I cannot refrain from writing once more to you, to express my deep admiration for the splendid way in which small craft from the naval forces under your command entering the harbour of Kronstadt delivered the Baltic from some of the most dangerous units of Bolshevik sea-power.
>
> Deeds of that kind have in times past built up the fame of the English Navy and this feat has once more shown to the world, that when England strikes, it strikes hard.
>
> I know that my feelings of admiration and respect for the men participating in the plucky raid are shared by every true soldier in this country and that we all deplore the loss of some of the gallant officers and men, who had their share in this splendid achievement.[18]

Even the Danes joined the chorus; Commodore Bornsdorff at Copenhagen simply telegraphed 'cheers for British Gallantry'.[19]

Cowan himself wrote personally to each individual who had participated in Operation 'RK' on 20 August. 'I venture to think that the end of those three boats [*sic*] will have as great an effect in keeping the remainder of the Bolshevik navy quiet as will the devastation you have wrought in their harbour – the strongest naval fortress in the world – ravished and blasted by under fifty disciplined, dauntless Britons.' Warming to his theme, Cowan perhaps let hyperbole take control of his pen, continuing 'those who are dead we can only envy', possibly not the foremost emotion of the survivors. Nonetheless, his closing paragraph was no doubt heartfelt. 'Between you, you have written another brilliant chapter in our navy's history and its faultless execution is due to your splendid discipline and also to what is our service's strongest and fairest characteristic, namely the sympathy, trust and understanding between all ranks.'[20] As later events would show, this latter point was perhaps a slight exaggeration.

Admiral Charles Madden, CinC of the Atlantic Fleet, echoed Cowan's thoughts when he wrote from his flagship, HMS *Queen Elizabeth*, that 'this successful enterprise will rank among the most daring and skilfully executed of naval operations of the war. On no other occasion during hostilities has so small a force inflicted so much damage on the enemy. Rear Admiral Sir Walter Cowan deserves generous recognition for the able foresight, planning and preparation, which led to such a great naval success.'[21]

Cowan could have been excused for feeling a little swollen-headed by now. From Britain, Wemyss wrote to Cowan on 26 August.

> I have been waiting for further news of your brilliant action before writing to you but can no longer wait to congratulate you and all concerned. It appears to have been an extraordinarily gallant and successful attack and I am in hopes that as a result we may get some permanent relief from the strain of the Baltic ... you probably realise how almost impossible it is to get real help or guidance from our so-called Cabinet with their slipshod methods and want of a definite policy.[22]

But, as it transpired, the 'so-called Cabinet' was less than happy with the action. As the First Sea Lord's biographer noted 'Wemyss's satisfaction at so gallant an action was far from shared by the Cabinet. The admiral sent over to announce it met, greatly to his surprise, with an anything but cordial reception ... for ... while openly disavowing the Bolsheviks, they had been secretly negotiating with them and the sinking of their fleet was the last thing they desired.'[23] In fact, a negotiated withdrawal of British forces from Archangel had been under discussion.

Belatedly, in October the Admiralty put out a press statement regarding Operation 'RK'; it was at best dissembling, at worst mendacious, and no doubt couched in terms dictated by the politicians. 'The Bolshevik warships in Kronstadt harbour constituted a formidable threat to our minesweeping operations,' Their Lordships wrote, 'which were being undertaken with the ultimate object of sending food ships to Kronstadt and Petrograd. It was necessary in order to safeguard our position that this menace be destroyed as soon as possible.'[24] No mention of supporting the White Russians, Estonians or Latvians; and no mention of the ongoing fight against the Bolsheviks. Apparently, it was all purely humanitarian.

Reward

A considerable number of medals were awarded for Operation RK, despite the Cabinet's lack of enthusiasm. Dobson and Steele were both awarded the Victoria Cross. Dobson's citation noted that

On 18 August 1919 at Kronstadt, Russia, Commander Dobson was in command of the Coastal Motor Boat Flotilla which he led through the chain of forts to the entrance to Kronstadt harbour. *CMB-31BD*, a 55ft boat, from which he directed the general operations then passed in under heavy machine gun fire and hit the battleship *Andrei Pervozvanny* [*sic*] with both torpedoes, subsequently returning through heavy fire to the open sea.

That of Steele noted:

Lieutenant Steele was second-in-command of Coastal Motor Boat *88*. Steele's boat became illuminated by an enemy searchlight. Very heavy machine gun fire followed immediately, the captain being killed and the boat thrown off course … Lieutenant Steele took the wheel and steadied the boat, lifting the dead officer away from the steering and firing position, and torpedoed the battleship *Andrei Pervozvanni* at 100 yards range. He then manoeuvred the CMB in a very confined space to get a clear shot at the other battleship *Petropavlosk* before making for the safety of the bay.

Agar received a DSO to go with his shortly-to-be-gazetted VC and there was a liberal distribution of the DSO, DSC and CGM.* The navy was proud. But what exactly was it meant to do next?

Spy Mission

What to do next was at least clear to Agar. Despite his participation in the Kronstadt raid and his sinking of the *Oleg*, Agar's real task was still to extract and deliver the couriers for Paul Dukes, alias 'ST 25'. The team at Terrioki had already made twelve trips across the water to Petrograd. Now they received pressing instructions that they must make a thirteenth and take out Dukes who was urgently required back in London, not least to provide information for the politicians to help deflect the constant attacks of the Labour party and its left-wing supporters on the policy of intervention in Russia.

On 23 August, Agar set out in his 40ft CMB; it was his thirteenth trip, his lucky number. He took a courier, Gefter, Chief Motor Mechanic Beeley and Midshipman Marshall, together with a smuggler as a guide, departing the yacht club at 2200 as usual. The weather was calm, with some cloud. Several searchlights were sweeping the sky and a powerful one from the large fort on the northern end of Kronstadt was trained so as to sweep at sea level, along the line of the chain of forts, looking for an intruder such as a CMB.

Soon a nasty swell from the south-west got up and made the boat bump unpleasantly as it skimmed the water. Then two more lights were trained on the little craft from dead ahead. By now the boat was going very fast indeed as Agar used his top speed to dodge the first beam and steered by compass for what he thought to be the line of forts (but transpired to be the Island of Kronstadt).

Gunfire opened up on them and things soon became a little too hot to handle. Agar had also become disoriented by the glare and the twisting and turning as they tried to evade the probing beams. He determined to head back to Terrioki as he could not shake off the searchlights but he didn't really know which way to go.

It was a predicament. To reduce speed would be to ensure being

---

* There was a generous allocation of DSCs to the junior officers who took part in the raid. Amongst those who received the medal was twenty-year-old Acting Sub Lieutenant Norman Eyre Morley RNR, who had been on *CMB-88*. He would go on to be the only naval officer to win the DSC and three bars – i.e. awarded the medal four times – in the history of the Royal Navy. Another was Sub Lieutenant John Christian Boldero who won a bar to his DSC in the Second World War, when in command of the gunboat HMS *Cicada* and despite having lost an arm in 1941.

hit by shells from one of the forts, so whatever he did he had to keep at full throttle. This gave no time for reflective thought and re-orientation. Moreover, the boat was now not really answering to the wheel and seemed to be travelling in circles.

In fact the boat had described, firstly, a complete circle and then a large semi-circular arc of three miles towards the northern end of Kronstadt Island. But suddenly there was a terrific bump followed by a bang, and everyone on board was precipitated into the bottom of the boat. It was as if they had run into a brick wall, from 40 knots to zero in an instant. They had hit a rock or a breakwater and all of the crew were momentarily stunned and in shock. The motors had stopped at the impact and as Agar picked himself up he saw Beeley sprawled over the engines. For a moment Agar feared his mechanic was dead, but then 'Faithful' Beeley pulled himself upright and muttered 'I'll get her going again, sir'.[25] Fortunately, the searchlights for some reason or other abruptly switched off, bar one which was mounted too high and so swept over their heads.

In typical navy fashion, rum was deemed to be necessary and Marshall handed round a tot to everyone. Agar could now discern that they had run onto a rock breakwater near the northern end of Kronstadt Island. The boat was filling with water and badly holed. Fifteen miles of water separated them from the Finnish shore and there were two forts between them and the shore.

Marshall plugged the large hole in the side of the boat with leather clothing. Using boathooks, they pushed the CMB off the obstruction and began to bale for their lives, using empty petrol cans; Marshall used his sea boots. Utilising what canvas they could strip off their vessel, and a couple of boathooks for masts, the crew fashioned a makeshift sail. For a rudder they tied two or three empty petrol tins together at the end of a rope, control of which was given to the courier, Gefter, to use as a sea anchor. Slowly they were able to move across the walls of the fort and towards the Finnish coast.

Steadily the broken vessel drifted and sailed to the north, aided by a current which pushed them towards Terrioki at no more than two knots. By dawn, they had managed to travel six miles but we were still only half way to the Finnish coast and by now exhausted. But providence was about to intervene. Two small fishing boats appeared. Agar ordered his Lewis guns trained on them and under such persuasion the fishermen parted with their masts and sails, which were mounted in the cockpit of the CMB.

Now Agar could make better progress and by noon the craft had reached the entrance to the Terrioki base. A badly-damaged motor boat, with two holes in its bottom, together with five worried men, had somehow escaped from the very face of the Kronstadt forts and travelled 16 miles across the Gulf of Finland in just under twelve hours. It was some sort of miracle.

As for Dukes, he made his escape overland.

CHAPTER 13

Attrition, August – October 1919

As spring turned into summer, Cowan had established three standing patrols in the Gulf of Finland. That at Stirs Point, on the northern shore near the lighthouse, went as far as the start of the Soviet minefields and was also hemmed in by British-laid mines protecting the northern shore and the approaches to Biorko. Ships often moored to the lighthouse in order to give them protection from Bolshevik attack. Another was in and around Kaporia Bay on the southern shore, the last coastal inlet before the southerly edge of the Bolshevik mined area was reached. And a third was maintained at Biorko, protecting the coastal channel and the southern side of the island itself. All of these patrol areas offered dangers in the form of mines (which might be British, Tsarist Russian, Red Russian or German), shoals and submerged wrecks. Additionally, Royal Navy submarines were deployed across the face of the Soviet minefield, in order to attempt an interception of any Red vessel which used the swept channel to exit into the open sea.

Acting Sub Lieutenant Edward Reignier Conder sailed for the Baltic with the destroyer HMS *Vectis* on 7 August. He was the son of Edward Baines Conder, a former opera singer turned clergyman and now a canon of Coventry Cathedral, and his artist wife Eleanor Charlotte Henrietta Eames. Conder had just returned from leave (at the Abbey Hotel, Kenilworth) and was raring for action. Arriving at Biorko on 15 August, he found the small harbour and approaches to be occupied by *Delhi*, *Danae*, *Cleopatra*, *Vindictive*, the 20th Destroyer Flotilla, two submarines, ten CMBs and a frozen meat ship. Additionally, there were two Finnish torpedo boats, two Finnish seaplanes and a collection of MLs armed with depth charges. At night the numbers were swelled by two paddle minesweepers from the 11th Fleet Sweeping Flotilla, which were based at Helsingfors but would come into Biorko for shelter. High-angle anti-aircraft guns on the destroyers were kept closed up during darkness in the event of air raids and there was always a destroyer maintained at one hour's readiness in 'X-berth', at the end of Biorko Island, in case of a submarine sighting. 'It is difficult to see what she could do unless at ten minutes notice,' thought Conder.[1] It was a very busy little port.

Vectis was soon into the dreary but dangerous routine of sentry-go. Two days after her arrival she was patrolling in Kaporia Bay; then she manned the Biorko patrol which consisted, according to Conder, of 'steaming slowly up and down from about one mile south of Verita port to beyond the end of Biorko Island'[2] while the fortress at nearby Kronstadt shone a searchlight towards them and occasion-ally sent up an observation kite balloon.

By 27 August, *Vectis* was back in Kaporia Bay where she met an Estonian destroyer which requested that she bombard some Bolshevik positions as 'they were rather short of ammunition'.[3] The Estonians sent an officer over to point out the targets and at 1008, *Vectis* opened fire from Nos 3 and 4 guns at a range of 7,000 yards. Their target was a small wood where the Red soldiers were said to be sheltering and, after plastering it with both common shell and Lyddite, they shifted focus to the alleged location of the Bolshevik HQ. After firing thirty-eight shells, *Vectis* ceased firing at 1140 and resumed patrol. At 1630 hours, the captain, Commander Raymond Jocelyn Harris-St John, decided to have another shot at the enemy; but such usage was already beginning to tell. The director circuits failed and only one gun could fire, and that only one round.

Early the following morning, *Vectis* spotted a floating mine, which was destroyed by rifle fire, and then supported *Abdiel* and minelayers as they laid a field to the north-east part of the bay, with *Delhi* and *Danae* in attendance. Then on the 29th, gunnery problems repaired, *Vectis* was back on bombardment duty, this time opening up at 0645 on the smoke of the Bolshevik cooking fires. 'If they were eating their breakfast at the time, they probably suffered from indigestion,' thought Edward Conder, 'as our shooting appeared to be pretty good.'[4]

Such bombardment operations, planned or opportunistic, had been conducted throughout August. As Cowan reported to the Admiralty on 8 September; 'I have carried out constant bombardments in Kaporia Bay, to ease and maintain the left flank, which is now held by the Estonians.'[5]

The Loss of HMS *Vittoria*

On Sunday 31 August, the destroyer-minelayers HMS *Abdiel* and *Vittoria* of the 20th Destroyer Flotilla had been on patrol off Seskar Island, directly in front of the Kronstadt minefield. It was 1900 and not yet dark, but Captain (D), Berwick Curtis, had given permission for them to anchor up.

On board *Vittoria*, the Officer of the Watch, Gunner (T) Charles A Bacon, was taking a last navigational bearing before dusk, when he found himself staring straight at a periscope, 400 yards on the starboard bow. To his horror he also spotted two torpedo tracks. 'Green forty-five load' he screamed at the only gun crew closed up, the fore superimposed position. But it was already too late. One torpedo missed 30 yards ahead; the other struck the starboard side at the aft engine room bulkhead. Gunner's Mate Albert Webb Clarey and Gunlayer Second Class Ernest Arthur Miles continued to try to fight their gun as ordered, but the ship was already listing badly and they could not get sufficient depression to fire at the submarine's last noted position.

Bacon ordered 'out boats' as the captain, Commander Vernon Hammersley-Heenen, reached the bridge. The destroyer's back had broken and there was no choice but to abandon ship; the boats were loaded and lowered in an orderly manner. Men who jumped into the sea were rescued by the ship's motor boat and *Abdiel* was quickly amongst them lowering her whalers and boats too.

On board *Vectis*, in harbour at Biorko, the quartermaster reported observing a 'big flash at sea ... but we ignored him' wrote Conder, 'as he is a little deficient mentally'.[6] But at 1907, HMS *Spenser* started to raise steam and *Vectis* was ordered to 'raise steam for full speed with upmost urgency'.[7] As they prepared to sail, the destroyers picked up *Vittoria*'s dying signal; 'Cannot last much longer now, fast going'.[8]

Clarey and Miles were amongst the last to leave the ship, as they had been hoping to get a shot off at the enemy somehow. Their dedication to duty killed them, for as they went over the side they were both struck by one of the ship's funnels which collapsed as she heeled to port and sank. By the time *Vectis* arrived at the scene, many of the survivors had been rescued. *Abdiel* asked *Vectis* to cruise around to keep the submarine down while she completed her search for men in the water. A few survivors had landed on Seskar Island itself. Here they discovered that 'the inhabitants of the Island are very Red and they inform the Bolsheviks of the usual anchoring points of our destroyers'.[9] The stranded sailors were taken off by an ML the following morning. Eight men died that day. Miles's wife, awaiting him in Davies Street, Hertford, would never see him again, and nineteen-year-old seamen Ernest Hutchings from Chiswick and John Edward Pettitt of Sudbury would never reach manhood at home. Their parents might have felt justified in asking 'Why?'

Vittoria's nemesis had been the *Bars*-class submarine *Pantera* ('Panther'), which had first deployed against British warships in July (*vide supra* Chapter 11). Armed with four torpedo tubes but possessed of numerous shortcomings, including a lack of internal bulkheads and a slow diving time, she was commanded by Alexander Bakhtin. Despite these disadvantages, Bakhtin had just scored the Soviet navy's first submarine success against the British forces. In 1923, Bakhtin's achievement was recognised by the award of the Order of the Red Banner.[*]

The court of inquiry into the loss, under the chairmanship of Captain Grace, found that 'Captain Curtis had committed an error of judgement in allowing his ships to anchor before nightfall'.[10] In mitigation it was noted that no submarine activity had been observed in the area for six weeks. But Cowan did not propose taking any further action against Curtis formally 'especially in view of his exceptional record during the war and out here'.[11]

To the Admiralty, Cowan wrote 'the loss of *Vittoria* through a Bolshevik submarine, I very much regret'.[12] But, demonstrating that lack of empathy for which he was unfortunately well known, he sent a message to all the ships in his command 'cutting up her skipper and abusing her generally and charging the survivors with a lack of destroyer spirit'.[13]

HMS *Verulam*

HMS *Verulam* was a 'V'-class destroyer launched in 1917 and

---

[*] His fame would be short lived. A year later, after Stalin's rise to power, his noble heritage was discovered and he was stripped of all his revolutionary accolades and sent to the Solovki gulag in the Solovetsky Islands. There he suffered five years of hard labour until he was released in 1929. Two years later he contracted tuberculosis and died, unnoticed by the communist dictators he had fought and killed for.

which had only recently joined Cowan's forces. At 0045 (local time) on 4 September* she was undertaking the Stirs Point patrol, heading south. This was a much unloved duty generally as the patrol area started and finished with minefields and was in a tightly confined area.

The Stirs Point light had been extinguished and the land was difficult to make out in the darkness; thus the only way that her captain, Lieutenant Commander Guy Langton Warren, had of ascertaining her true position and the point at which he should turn again to the north was by measuring the course and distance run from his last known position at the Serkolada Beacon.

Unfortunately, Warren stood on just a little too far. As he made a sixteen-point turn to starboard, the ship struck a moored mine on her starboard side, abreast the mainmast. A British mine in a British-laid minefield. The detonation also set off the ship's depth charges and wrecked her motor boat. The 'whole of the ship from the after tubes to the stern was on fire,'[14] noted an eyewitness. Boats were quickly swung out and loaded. But just as the ship's whaler and dinghy were making away from the destroyer, the flames touched off the warheads of *Verulam*'s torpedoes, capsizing both boats and tipping the men in them into the water.

Vectis saw a flash from the direction of Stirs Point but HMS *Vidette* was the first to respond, going to 25 knots and quickly reaching the sinking ship. She launched her own boats and Carley floats and used her searchlights to hunt for survivors in the water. Twenty of the men were not found until the morning, brought off from Stirs Point by a Finnish vessel and 'stark naked'.[15]

This time sixteen men lost their lives, including six officers; the dead men had been mostly stationed aft, officers in their cabins, the after lookout and the pantry staff. Sub Lieutenant Conder knew two of the dead officers, Midshipmen Alexis William Ashley from Teddington and Arthur Wilfred Edgecombe of Harrogate, both of whom were eighteen years old and had been in his term at Britannia. In his diary he simply noted that they 'went'.[16] Another officer who died, Lieutenant Charles Cunningham Dumville Lees, aged twenty-five, had obtained five first-class certificates in passing out of Greenwich and Whale Island and was clearly marked for future command. Only three of the dead were ever recovered; the

---

* 3 September GMT.

bodies of Engineer Lieutenant Joseph House DSC and Stoker First Class John Elliott were found immediately. Sub Lieutenant Owen Philip Powell's corpse did not wash ashore until ten days after the event. All three were buried at Stirs Point Cemetery.[*]

Verulam had a mascot, a bulldog bitch named Lummy, who had 'a regrettable taste for beer and football'.[17] The night before the ship's sinking, the wardroom of HMS *Westcott* had entertained their friends on *Verulam* to dinner. Lummy came too. At the end of the evening, Lummy point-blank refused to go back home and stayed aboard *Westcott*. The following day she 'was all morose'.[18] At the sound of the explosion which killed her ship, she raised her head and howled. The dog knew.

The court of enquiry found that Warren was to blame. As Admiral Sir Charles Madden, CinC Atlantic Fleet, noted on the findings; 'no useful purpose was served by standing on to the southern safe limit of the patrol as the minefield protected that area. By doing so without a proper fix, Lieutenant Commander Warren ran an unjustified risk.'[19] On 8 November, Warren received an 'Expression of Their Lordships' Displeasure'.

Cowan told his masters that '*Verulam* was also lost, through striking one of our own mines off Stirs Point ... This is a new flotilla which has scarcely yet become accustomed to the difficulty of conditions or maintaining the patrols under the cramped condition of manoeuvring space which must obtain whilst we remain here.'[20] But to his commanders he sent another snotty note. The captain of *Vectis*, Commander Harris-St John, was so disgusted to receive it that he refused to pass the contents on to his officers. 'Our admiral is not very popular now,'[21] remarked Conder.

There was a strange predella to the sinking. On 16 November Captain Colin Kenneth Maclean, Captain (D) 2nd Destroyer Flotilla in HMS *Spenser* (in which flotilla *Verulam* had been), wrote to his immediate superior, Commodore (D) Atlantic Fleet, Hugh Justin Tweedie, in support of Warren. 'I had no previous knowledge that Sir Walter Cowan had taken that point of view of the matter' he wrote with regard to the censure handed down by Their Lordships.

> I was never shown the finding of the court of enquiry, neither did Sir Walter intimate to me his views on the matter,

[*] Now Styrsudd Point Cemetary.

otherwise I should have taken steps before. I therefore deplore, from a Captain D's point of view, the decision arrived at in regard to the loss of HMS *Verulam* and ask, with great respect, that it be ameliorated.[22]

It took no little courage to write such a letter and Maclean must have felt strongly that Cowan was making an example of Warren unfairly.* Nothing was changed, however, and the reprimand stood.

Both *Vittoria* and *Verulam* were given to the state of Finland on 12 December 1919. However, when salvage efforts commenced in 1925, it was discovered that both ships were broken in two and beyond any repair.

HMHS *Berbice*

On the day that *Verulam* was sunk, a new and very welcome vessel anchored in Biorko harbour. The arrival of HMS *Vindictive* had brought with her Surgeon Commander James McCutcheon. Given that there were some 8,000 officers and men based at Biorko, Libau and Reval, McCutcheon was immediately appalled by the standard and availability of medical care for the forces in the Baltic.

On 21 July he had written to Grace 'at Reval there are two private Estonian hospitals which can accommodate acute surgical cases if they have vacancies. At Biorko there is no hospital; at Libau there is a small hospital which is insanitary. As a consequence, ships will have to carry their wounded around with them ... [which] would not give them a fair chance of recovery.'[23] He pleaded with his captain to ask Cowan to request a hospital ship, which he did.

The Admiralty agreed with the surgeon commander and HMHS *Berbice* was promptly despatched to Biorko. She had been launched as a luxury liner on 6 May 1909 by Harland & Wolff of Belfast for the Royal Mail Steam Packet Co Ltd of London. On 4 December 1915 the Admiralty had requisitioned her as a hospital ship, in which capacity she had served throughout the remainder of the war. Now, on 4 September, she dropped anchor in Biorko Sound and soon accepted her first patients, Lieutenant Payne RN and Lieutenant

---

* But it did Maclean's career no harm; he was mentioned in despatches on 8 March 1920 for 'valuable services rendered in the Gulf of Finland in command of the Second Destroyer Flotilla'. Cowan eulogised 'I find it hard to express the value of this officer's services and example' (CAB 24/96/69, NA). Maclean eventually reached the rank of Vice Admiral.

Warne RAF from *Vindictive*. It was perhaps ironic that the only death on board her whilst in the Baltic should be one of her own crewmen. On 4 October, Sick Berth Attendant Thomas H Handel was discharged dead and buried in Koivisto Cemetery.

Wear and Tear

The Baltic duty told heavily on the ships that served there. Admiral Cowan himself noted that,

> This patrolling of Petrograd Bay, though generally in smooth water, was arduous and anxious always, because there was no room to manoeuvre East or West – there were mines in each direction – much foul ground, unindicated by the charts, and the charting of the Southern Shore disagreed by a mile of longitude with that of the Northern – also for that small space, (six by twenty miles), bounded on the West by Seskar, and on the East by the minefields, three charts had to be in use.
>
> In the whole of that area no shoals (and there are many), were marked by anything better than a spar buoy. When the winter came on, with incessant snow and fog throughout the long sixteen-hour nights, I scarcely hoped that the destroyers could succeed in maintaining their stations without frequent and serious groundings or collisions.[24]

Between September and October HMS *Vimiera* bent her shafts badly on the mail trip to Copenhagen, *Wolfhound* ripped her propellers off in Kaporia Bay and had to dock in Reval for repairs and *Westcott*'s shafts were so badly distorted that she was only fit to serve as a guard ship at Helsingfors.

And mines were a perennial problem, even for the minesweepers. In October, *Banbury*, already bruised from her grounding in May, struck a mine whilst sweeping in the Hogland area. It blew a 12ft square hole in her side, flooded the engine room and damaged her paddle. Only the timely and effective action of Engineer Lieutenant William Davidson RNR saved her from sinking, for which action he was awarded the DSC.[25] Nor were the aircraft faring any better. Sub Lieutenant Conder noted that 'our seaplanes are the oldest and most obsolete we have and have been running since 1914 and [were] condemned years ago. The aeroplanes also are all old and worn out machines and mostly old types, most of them having been condemned in France years ago. Three pilots have been killed thanks to neglect.'[26] And Cowan reported on 8 September that he had 'bombed Kronstadt as often as there have been pilots and machines available; but both are now showing distinct signs of wear and our operations are therefore becoming more restricted'.[27]

This latter comment was indeed true. The little air force at Koivisto had been worked hard after Operation 'RK'. On 22 August they mounted another bombing raid on Kronstadt. Eric Bremerton's 1½ Strutter suffered engine damage and on landing the undercarriage collapsed. He was concerned that the anti-aircraft fire was becoming a real threat. 'Must fly higher', he noted.[28] The following day there were only two operational land machines; luckily, the aircraft carrier HMS *Argus** arrived with a fresh load of Camels.

As August ended, Cowan kept up the pressure from the air. On the 30th there was a further air raid on the Russian base, this time with a sea escort in case of any forced landing; there were too few pilots to risk losing one. The following day another attack was planned but bad weather forced the planes to turn back and they had to drop their bombs in the sea before landing. And on the first day of September, Cowan ordered an acrobatics display to please visiting dignitaries; this seems rather uncaring, not to say stupid, given the risks the pilots were already taking. Lieutenant Bremerton was beginning to feel a little trepidation. '[It's] apt to effect one's nerves flying over water in an aeroplane with unreliable engines and knowing the sort of reception the Reds would give one if you had to land amongst them.'[29] The Bolshevik defences were improving (or just becoming more practised) all the while. On 3 September the anti-aircraft fire was too accurate and the intended bombing attack was largely ineffective as the aircraft were forced to fly at 14,000ft for safety. Nonetheless there was another raid on the 13th.

The relentless activity led to mistakes and to health issues. One tired and sleepy officer on the airfield hoisted the morning Union Jack upside down[§] in error. The flagship saw it and thought it was a distress signal, sending a heavily-armed landing party of marines at the double. Cue embarrassed RAF personnel. Constant flying led to

---

* Originally an Italian liner, *Conte Rosso*, purchased in August 1916 and renamed, she was converted to the world's first flat-topped aircraft carrier of 14,150 tons armed with four 4in guns.
§ Flying an ensign upside down was a universal distress signal at sea.

other issues too. Lieutenant Bremerton's health suffered. 'Boils very trying, also have haemorrhoids through sitting on cushions saturated with petrol from filling up which gets icy when flying high.'[30] He was ordered not to fly for a while. It was just as well that fifteen new pilots arrived on 15 September.

And they were soon to be needed, for 17 September was a black day for the RAF. There was yet another big raid on Kronstadt. Lieutenant F J Unwin RAF took Bremerton's 1½ Strutter, as the latter was medically unable to fly it, and did not return. He was believed to have force-landed on water and drowned. That same day Lieutenant Samuel Dawson DFC, RAF was lost in another 1½ Strutter. It appeared that he was killed when his plane crashed into the sea. His body was recovered and buried at Koivisto. Dawson had come a long way to die in an undeclared and largely disowned war. He was a New Zealander, who had won his DFC for his courage during a bombing raid off the coast of Schleswig in 1918. His citation for the action read that 'Lieutenant Samuel Dawson was engaged in long distance bombing raid on an enemy aircraft station under very difficult circumstances and carried out a successful attack from a low height in the face of severe enemy fire'.[31] Another brave man lost.

The Dorpat Peace Conference
The Bolsheviks were fighting on many fronts; not just to maintain control of government in Russia but to defend themselves against the White forces in Siberia in North Russia, the North Western Army based in or near Estonia, the armies of the Baltic States and the Royal Navy. On 31 August the Soviet Government made the first move, trying to narrow down the list of enemies it had to fight, by offering peace on conditions which the Estonian Government decided were worth considering. A conference of the Baltic States and Finland was therefore convened at Dorpat, meeting between 29 September and 1 October. There it was agreed that the Baltic States should act together in any peace process and that Finland should be invited to join up if she could. There was also some agreement around Soviet recognition of the sovereign independence of the Estonia, Latvia and Lithuania and the formation of a neutral zone between the Bolsheviks and the newly independent nations.

Britain's view had been sought before the event and on 25 September the government replied to the effect that it wasn't their problem. 'As Great Britain could not supply further arms or ammunition,' the Foreign Office declared, 'they must leave the Baltic States full liberty of action in this matter.'[32] But London did confirm that, when the time came that the final status of the new states was decided at the peace conference (or the League of Nations), 'His Majesty's Government will exert such influence as they may possess to secure the satisfaction of the legitimate aspirations of Estonia, Latvia, and Lithuania, so far as may be consistent with a final and peaceful settlement in North East Europe.'[33]

So far so good; but any potential movement towards a peace treaty was derailed on the 12 October.

The Advance on Petrograd

The White Russian armies had long intended, and occasionally attempted, to advance along the southern shore of the Gulf of Finland and take Petrograd. Such a success was seen by most parties as potentially ending Bolshevik rule and the war. But the Whites had been fought to a standstill by the end of June and had retired out of Estonian territory.

Moreover, Cowan believed that the Estonian troops were 'war weary and discontented and there have been cases of units going over to the Bolsheviks'.[34] And he believed that the Reds were pressing the Estonians to make peace and to arrange a frontier, with Estonia's independence recognised by Soviet Russia. He was, however, still unimpressed by the White Russians who, he thought, 'are proving themselves quite unworthy of further support, by reason of their disobedience and disregard of General Sir Hubert Gough's suggestions … their perpetual quarrelling with each other and intrigue both amongst themselves and with the Germans'.[35] This low opinion of Britain's ally was widely shared.

Surveying the situation in early September, in a report to the Admiralty, Cowan thought that 'Estonia, White Russia and Finland are now relying on my force to protect them from the Bolsheviks but of which not one is now taking any active offensive measures to protect themselves – it might be of value to point out that this position cannot obtain indefinitely. This might possibly bring matters to a head and spur them on to combine and take Petrograd before the weather renders campaigning by land and sea out of the question.'[36]

Cowan's entreaties were answered on 12 October when the Estonians and Yudenitch's White Russian army, on the right flank of the Estonian army, once more began to advance on Petrograd. They met with immediate success, and by the 19th had reached the Tsar's summer palace of Tsarskoye Selo, just 15 miles south of their intended destination. However, the advance was checked by the failure to capture the fortresses of Krasnaya Gorka and Grey Horse, which Cowan had urged ought to be the first objective, rather than a headlong plunge towards their ultimate goal.

Cowan's ships were heavily involved in providing floating artillery support to the advance. On 14 October, for example, *Delhi*, *Dauntless, Spenser* and *Mackay* all shelled Bolshevik positions to the east of Kaporia Bay whilst aircraft bombed Krasnaya Gorka and Grey Horse batteries. Some long-range 12in fire was directed back at the ships, without effect. The Estonians advanced for as long as the guns of the light cruisers and destroyers of the Biorko Force could support them. But four miles from Fort Krasnaya Gorka they met with strong resistance and barbed-wire defences and suffered heavy losses, equal to nearly a third of their 2,000 men deployed.

Meanwhile, Trotsky had rushed back to Petrograd, arriving on the 17th, in order to put some spirit back into his forces (and execute a few commanders). A more aggressive defence of the city resulted and the White army found itself unable to resupply due to the downing of a railway bridge.

The Royal Navy bombardments from the sea, in support of the advancing Whites and Estonians, were a severe trial for the Bolsheviks and under Trotsky's urging they determined to do something about it. The Red navy was tasked to lay a minefield off Cape Dolgy Nos (in Kaporia Bay), right in the area where Cowan's ships were operating. Early in the morning of 21 October, four minelaying destroyers left Kronstadt, *Gavriil* (at one time thought by the British to have been sunk in the 18 August raid), *Svoboda*, *Konstantin* and the British Baltic Squadron's old friend *Azard*. At 0545 the first three named ships blew up in a British minefield. Some 485 men were lost with only twenty-five being saved, six of whom were picked up by an Estonian destroyer. Only the *Azard*, which had been at the rear of the line of destroyers, survived to extract itself from danger and return to harbour.

Augustus Agar believed that this was in part his doing. Before he left for London, he had undertaken one last mission for Cowan.

With Russell MacBean as his number two, and with another boat in company, he took a 55ft CMB to lay a small minefield off Kronstadt in the main south channel, an exercise designed to complete the strategy of sealing in the Soviet ships by way of mines. He asserted that it was these mines which had sunk the Soviet ships. Agar also claimed that the Bolshevik vessels had sortied in order to surrender to the RN.[37] Whatever the reasons, the Red navy was depleted by a further three ships and Cowan's mining tactics were vindicated.

Despite these Soviet losses, the White's progress had been checked. But on 24 October, Cowan finally received a ship with which he could feel more confident in tackling the forts which barred the way, a type of vessel which he had first applied for in the spring. HMS *Erebus,* under Captain John Alfred Moreton, was a monitor specifically designed for bombardment of land targets and of shallow draught to allow her to operate in littoral waters. *Erebus* (and her sister-ship *Terror*) were named for two bomb ketches sent to investigate the North-west Passage and subsequently lost in 1845. She was armed with two 15in guns, similar to the *Queen Elizabeth*-class battleships then in commission, and could deliver a 1,938lb shell from each barrel to a range of nearly 40,000 yards. She was as ungainly as a waddling duck but had a reasonable turn of speed and the class were very effective as shore bombardment platforms. She had been serving at Murmansk and Archangel as part of the British forces in the White Sea. When Murmansk was finally evacuated on 12 October, she was ordered to Copenhagen and thence to Biorko.

On 27 October, *Erebus* began the bombardment of Krasnaya Gorka, while *Delhi*, *Dunedin* and destroyers attacked the Grey Horse battery. Destroyers and some P-boats circled around the bombarding ships to provide an anti-submarine screen. *Erebus*'s shooting was not all that it might be, with some overs missing by 10 miles. The following day the monitor targeted Grey Horse, firing for four hours, but the battery responded vigorously and no damage was seen to be done.

But it was too little too late. By this time the weather had broken, with wind, rain and low cloud prevalent, making it very difficult to provide the air observation necessary to direct the firing of the monitor's guns. Additionally, the shortcomings of both planes and pilots after so long a service told heavily on their effectiveness, the Short 184 seaplanes being unable to obtain sufficient altitude to avoid the heavy and accurate anti-aircraft fire from the defenders of the two forts.

The arrival of this big ship had convinced Admiral Pitka, in charge of the Estonian attacking forces, that he should try again. But the Whites had started to fall back, firstly unnerved by the fire of the battleship *Sebastopol* from the harbour of Kronstadt supported by the guns of the moored-up destroyers *Vsadnik* and *Gaidamak*, and secondly by an extra 11,000 troops combed out from the sailors of Petrograd. This uncovered the Estonian right flank and exposed them to further losses and harassment. A furious Pitka wrote to Cowan that 'the North Russian army advanced without regard for the fact that they could not be supplied via railway ... They advanced as long as the enemy fled but retreated when they stood, leaving the Estonian right flank "in the air".'[38]

On 2 November, a high-level meeting convened between General Yudenitch, Laidoner, Pitka and General Sir Richard Cyril Byrne Haking of the British Military Mission. Here Yudenitch announced that it was impossible to continue his advance on Petrograd 'owing to increased pressure on his right flank and the consequent necessity of withdrawing troops to support it'.[39] According to Cowan, Laidoner responded by stating that he could no longer entertain any hope of taking Krasnaya Gorka 'even with all the assistance our ships can give'.[40] The White Russians and the Estonians then fell back with considerable rapidity as far west as a line between Narva and Peipus Lake, and Cowan 'devoted myself to endeavouring to ensure that, from the sea, no further attempt was made to further harass these very war-weary and dispirited troops'.[41] Out of ammunition, *Erebus* was despatched to Libau, in what would later prove to be a propitious piece of anticipation. The attempt on Petrograd was given up. As the White North Russian army limped back onto Estonian soil, they were disarmed and interned; the Estonians wanted to ensure that White territorial ambitions would not be satisfied in their country.

Cowan was disappointed at this turn of events, although it was not entirely unexpected by him. 'This therefore ends the hope of relieving Petrograd this year, to prevent which has been one of von der Goltz's aims' he wrote to the Admiralty on 4 November. And he knew where he thought the blame lay, continuing in ironic style 'and it must be a source of deep satisfaction to him that the forbearance of the Allies to thwart his plans in any degree during the whole of this year had made his task such a simple one'.[42] Once again, the admiral was being critical of the lack of 'boots on the ground' from the Allies which he had long believed were necessary.

Additionally, Cowan was of the opinion that Yudenitch thought that the ships, plus the few tanks provided by Britain for land operations, would do his job for him. He also fulminated to the Admiralty that the Whites had refused to coordinate with the Estonians and that Yudenitch's advisors had German leanings and made his efforts half-hearted. He also believed that Yudenitch had only continued thus far in order to obtain supplies and weapons from Britain. Walter Cowan was by now clearly a very jaundiced admiral! Cowan reported that 'it would be difficult to recall any offensive effort ever conducted which has shown such utter lack on intelligent leadership, or which greater military mistakes have been made'.[43]

The October campaign by the White's North Western Army is a great 'what if?' General Mannerheim knew Yudenitch from their service together in the Imperial Russian Army and asked the president of Finland, Ståhlberg, if he could take men to join Yudenitch's force and attack Petrograd with help from the Finnish White Guards. As a *quid pro quo*, Yudenitch would have recognised Finland's independence (as the other White Russian Leaders would not). But as Admiral Kolchak (nominally the leader of the White cause) was opposed to the recognition of Finland's independence, Ståhlberg denied Mannerheim's request. If the Finns had joined in, would the result have been different?

A Minor Affair
As the battles on land and sea were fought out, there was a regular supply train of ships sailing from Britain to Copenhagen or Reval bringing supplies for Cowan's squadrons. One of them was the Royal Fleet Auxiliary (RFA) *Volturnus.* She was a 615grt coaster, completed in 1913 for the Volana Shipping Co Ltd of Liverpool by R Williamson & Son Ltd, Workington. In September 1914 she had been requisitioned by the Admiralty as a stores carrier and was still employed in that role in 1919.

On 27 October 1919, *Volturnus* sailed from Deptford for Copenhagen, still under charter to the Admiralty, with some 700 tons of naval stores, mainly provisions. Her master was Arthur William Hay. He had never before navigated the Kattegat or been to the Baltic, so could have been expected to have done a little research on what obstacles the voyage might have to face, in particular the safe routes to use, given the continued presence of old minefields in the area.

But in fact Hay had neglected to read *The Notice to Mariners for Foreign Going Ships, 1 June 1919 to 1 October 1919* before the ship had sailed. This would have given him all the information necessary for a safe trip. Not only had he not read them but in the rough weather of the passage he had allowed both copies on board his vessel to become soaked with sea water, such that they were unusable.

Thus it was that, on 1 November, the course Hay had set on entering the Kattegat took him into a wartime minefield. The Skaw light vessel observed this and signalled to the coaster that she was standing into danger. A more prudent captain might have stopped his ship and enquired as to the safe route. But Hay was seemingly not on the bridge and Chief Officer Peter Fearn did not either stop the vessel or call the master.

The vessel struck a mine, which exploded and sank the store carrier six miles off the Skaw light. All sixteen men aboard escaped and were later picked up by a pilot vessel; Hay himself was slightly injured. It was a minor affair compared to the battles just concluding before Petrograd: but possibly indicative of something. Why did the master and chief officer behave in such a cavalier fashion? They had been working for the navy for five years, mainly in Scapa Flow; were they just sick of it? Did they too want to return to a normal life and trade, coasting around the British Isles?

There was no indication of their motives at the formal investigation held in Liverpool on 10 February 1920. Stipendiary Magistrate Stuart Deacon, assisted by Commander A S Houston RNR and Captain W A Fausset, had no hesitation in finding that Captain Hay was guilty of a wrongful act. They suspended his certificate for three months. Chief Officer Fearn was severely censured for his part in the loss. The court found that when he had received the signals referring to minefields from the lightship, he should have at once stopped the ship and called the master. Their reputations had fallen victim to the Baltic battle; and perhaps the weariness it increasingly invoked.

CHAPTER 14

A New Enemy in Old Clothes, Latvia, August – October 1919

While Cowan was engaged in neutralising the Soviet Baltic fleet and supporting the ultimately abortive advance on Petrograd, Duff and Brisson had problems of their own to deal with in Latvia. Unsurprisingly, General von der Goltz was the foremost of them.

As was seen in Chapter 11, despite the requirement placed on Germany that Goltz be recalled he had stayed, notwithstanding the fall of his Latvian puppet government. He told General Gough that 'his men had been promised land in Latvia and they considered themselves citizens of Latvia and he could not answer for the consequences if those who wanted to remain in Latvia were not allowed to do so'.[1] But Goltz did order all his men to move east across the 'Courish River'.

The British Foreign Office recognised the problem of these land-hungry men in an assessment prepared for the War Cabinet.

> For the majority of the troops employed, officers as well as men, colonisation is the main end in view. They have already taken root in the country where they have been engaged, and have become more colonists than fighting troops. For instance, they have taken over and have become shareholders in many of the Lettish sawmills, and are sending into Germany large quantities of milk and food of all descriptions, for which they receive no payment actually in the Baltic States, but for which they or their families receive payment in Germany. As much as thirty-seven million marks' worth of goods are stated to have been thus imported into Germany last

month without payment going out ... all they ask is to be left alone and become harmless settlers in a fairly hospitable land.[2]

But regardless of Goltz's threat and the FO's warnings, on 1 August the government in Berlin was ordered by Marshal Foch and the Armistice Commission to recall their truculent general. Evacuation of Latvia was to commence at once by both land and sea, under the supervision of General Gough, and was to be complete by 30 August. The entry of fresh German troops into the Baltic States was forbidden.

There were two problems with this edict. Firstly, such a plan did not suit the Latvians. They didn't want any German troops back on their territory, whether or not they were embarking for home; and Goltz himself wanted to leave by train. Secondly, he refused to submit a plan for evacuation until Estonia signed a peace treaty with his forces. So, despite the huffing and puffing, he stayed, and hence the existential threat to Latvia in particular and the Baltic states in general remained; Bolsheviks on the one hand, Germans on the other.

The reaction amongst the German *Freikorps* to the recall order issued in the name of *Reichspräsident* Friedrich Ebert was both unfavourable and hardly a surprise to those on the ground. They had come for land, and land it was that they wanted, as Goltz had informed Gough in July. On 24 August, the *Eiserne* Division revolted in Mitau and refused to return to Germany. The next day, various *Freikorps* leaders gathered in the city and established the *Deutsche Legion*, avowedly independent of any German government control.

Von der Goltz now played another masterstroke, not dissimilar to the one which had temporarily put his army under Latvian control. Among the plethora of adventurers, primarily Russian, who had obtained position in the White Russian armies, was one Colonel Prince Pavel Mikhailovich Bermondt-Avalov.[*] He commanded the White Russian forces in Courland in which position he had succeeded Prince Anatolii Pavlovich Liven, who had departed in late June 1919 to join the North Western White Army in Estonia for the push on Petrograd.

---

[*] Bermondt had seemingly awarded himself the rank of colonel and would shortly make himself a major general.

Bermondt, an ardent Tsarist supporter and an Ussuri Cossack, was a larger-than-life character, a quondam orchestra leader who had fought with the Russian armies and been made a POW by the Germans during the last war. He always appeared dressed in a spectacular white uniform which was hung about with various forms of weaponry. On 21 September Goltz officially handed over control of the German volunteers to him. The new formation, which combined 10,000 of Bermondt's original forces (mostly Russian former prisoners of war released from German camps) with 40,000 German volunteers, was named the West Russian Volunteer Army and declared itself in favour of a pro-German Western Central Government in Latvia.

By transferring the German volunteer units to Russian command, Goltz believed that he could continue his efforts to carve out a new German colony in the Baltic while at the same time obeying the letter, if not the spirit, of the instructions he had received from both the Allies and his own political masters. Indeed, the German government, anxious to be off the hook, immediately averred that it could have no authority over a private Russian-controlled army.

Tactical direction of the forces was exercised by German officers and von der Goltz remained its driving force and master. Finance was a problem, for the Berlin government stopped paying for the troops; but money came from German industrialists who had interests, or potential interests, in the Baltic. These included the *Deutsche Schwerer Industrie*[*] and the *Schilde* consortium in Berlin, while the Krupp company also played a considerable role in the supply of armaments. Indeed Krupp's had bought back from the German Government large quantities of surplus war material. Much of this was to keep his plants working by converting it into agricultural implements and the like. But in the middle of September 1919, Krupp's still found itself with a good deal of surplus material which they needed to get rid of as a result of the peace agreement. Much of this was handed over to Bermondt together with money in return for future concessions in the Baltic and in Russia. There was also backing from quasi-religious sects which supported Russian monarchical rule, such as the Sovereign Order of Saint John of Jerusalem; and in the end the Army simply printed its own money.

Furthermore, the edict of 1 August that no more soldiers should

---

[*] A consortium of German heavy industry manufacturers.

be sent from Germany to the region was honoured only in the breach. Although the Weimar Republic's *Reichswehrminister* (Minister of Defence), Gustave Noske,* was trying to carry out the peace agreements, much was going on behind his back. According to the British Foreign Office,

> he has had to employ many of the officials of the old regime in the departments under him, and there are a large number of them in the German War Office who are signing their names and putting the War Office stamp on orders and secret instructions of which Noske knows nothing, e.g. the movement orders to the various reinforcements, German and Russian, which have been leaving Berlin for the Baltic at midnight two or three times a week.[3]

Troops were still arriving to swell German numbers. These reinforcements were largely composed of men who had lost their homes or their living in the war, of dispossessed Alsace-Lorrainers and of soldiers of fortune who had severed all ties with a weakened Germany and wanted to make their futures abroad.

In mid-August, von der Goltz did return to Berlin and the German government replaced him with Lieutenant General Magnus von Eberhardt, holder of the *Pour le Mérite* with Oakleaves and, perhaps not coincidently, a Knight of Justice of the Order of St John. But Goltz was back in Mitau by 24 August and continued to direct affairs, using Eberhardt as his mouthpiece, an *eminence gris* behind the scenes. Commodore Duff felt that this was a serious issue. 'Those who know this man's character and his openly expressed views,' he wrote to the Admiralty at the end of August, 'find it hard to believe that the German government have any intention of carrying out the peace terms with regard to the Baltic provinces, so long as they persist in employing him in Latvia.'[4]

The problem of Graf von der Goltz and his ambitions in the Baltic simply would not go away. In the opinion of Lord Curzon at the Foreign Office in London, the aim of the pro-Baltic Germans was clear. 'There can be little doubt that for them the ultimate goal is the

---

* British army Lieutenant Colonel W L D Twiss described him thus in 1920; 'Herr Noske is a big man, rather of the warrant officer type, with a good appetite.... He was at first rather inclined to be difficult and ill at ease, but gradually thawed under the influence of wine, beer and brandy' (CAB 24/95, NA).

Germanisation of Russia, which will be brought about by utilising every force, every motive, every need of the German who is seeking fresh fields for migration or expansion.'[5] A Germanised Latvia was a convenient jumping-off point for the fulfilment of this ambition.

Not that Britain was seen as guiltless by Berlin in wishing to gain influence in Latvia. One General von Seeckt of the Army command at Kolberg, writing an intelligence appreciation in July, noted that 'in the Baltic the increase in English influence is undeniable … England wants in this way to make the Baltic provinces into an English colony and to destroy at any price the bridge between Germany and Russia'.[6] This opinion was also held by Britain's allies. When the first Royal Navy squadron had been despatched to the Baltic in 1918, the French responded in mid-December by sending the cruiser *Montcalm* to the area and Brisson was then despatched in April 1919; they feared an unopposed British presence might turn the area into a British lake for trade purposes.

And it was undeniable that the Allied missions sent to supervise the German withdrawal were exploring commercial opportunities by which money and military equipment might be once more supplied to Latvia in return for payment in flax and timber. There were commercial as well as political and territorial ambitions at play.

Riga
Despite the armistice which Colonel Tallents had arranged, his writ and role as 'protector', and that of the Ulmanis government, ran only as far as Riga, Libau and Windau. The remainder of the fledgling state remained under Goltz's and Bermondt's control. Duff, powerless on land, at least exercised control at sea and tightened the blockade of German shipping attempting to reach Latvia.

In Riga, the situation was tense. The Latvian troops were fighting the Bolsheviks on one front whilst on another the West Russian Volunteer Army was living off the land, spreading pillage and rapine far and wide. Ulmanis was moved to write to Lloyd George complaining about the uncontrolled Russo-German forces and asking for military help. Clashes between Bermondt's men and Latvians became commonplace.

On 28 September, Duff was recalled to Britain. Seven days later, Bermondt's forces began an offensive against both Latvia and Lithuania. They met with initial success, taking most of Courland

and Zemgale, whilst also driving towards Riga. By 8 October, the attacking army was advancing through the western suburbs of Riga while three German aircraft dropped bombs on the city's outer defences. Whilst Riga was now seriously threatened, a subsidiary effect of the attack was to cause the Latvians to break off their action with the Bolsheviks, allowing the latter to free up men to be sent to support the defence of Petrograd. As Cowan later noted, '[von der Goltz's] stroke against Riga just at the critical time [had] the effect of withholding reinforcements for the north-west Russian and Estonian fronts where they might have turned the scale against the Bolshevik defence of Petrograd'.[7] The Latvians defending Riga were compelled to fall back towards the River Dvina whilst Bermondt with 5,000 men tried to force his way to the river and take the only two bridges spanning it. By the 9th, the Latvians had retreated to within two miles of the bridgeheads. German planes circled over the destroyer *Abdiel* and the French *Aisne* and dropped bombs into the river near where the ships were moored. And the following morning, West Russian Volunteer Army troops arrived at the west end of the bridges and spread out down river, now directly facing *Abdiel*.

Desperate Latvian engineers removed sections from the crossings to prevent their enemy passing over and a battle of machine gun and rifle fire began to rage across the river, with the British and French ships caught in the middle. *Aisne*, moored 500 yards downstream of *Abdiel*, came under heavy fire from three directions and moved off down towards the sea. But Bermondt's force brought up field guns and began to fire shrapnel over the Royal Navy ships, especially *Abdiel*. At 1115 Captain Berwick Curtis moved half a mile down river and at 1240 was forced to move again. That night, Curtis sent a motorboat, manned by volunteers only, back upstream to contact the military and diplomatic missions still in Riga and ascertain whether or not Bermondt had actually entered the city.

By the 11th, the Russo-German army had occupied the whole of the west river bank as far as Fort Dunamunde, guarding the entrance to the channel, which they took and occupied. That night the Germans extinguished all the harbour lights and fired on some neutral vessels and tugs there. Curtis sent the French *Marne* back to watch over the neutrals and try to exert a degree of protection.

Meanwhile, Cowan was formulating his response. The naval forces at Riga when the attack commenced were the French *La Marne*, *Francis Garnier* and *Aisne* and the destroyers HMS *Vanoc* and *Abdiel*. Firstly Cowan ordered that all German vessels sighted in the Baltic should be taken in order to prevent the landing of reinforcements or extra supplies; eight were swiftly boarded and sent into Libau under prize crews. *Princess Margaret* at Copenhagen was ordered to Riga with immediate effect as was HMS *Vanquisher*. *Dragon* (at Sheerness), *Cleopatra* and *Windsor* were also directed to go to Riga as soon as possible. Finally, unable or unwilling to leave Estonia and the direction of the naval forces supporting the combined Estonian/White Russian advance on Petrograd, Cowan requested Commodore Brisson to take command of the forces in Riga, with Curtis as his chief of staff, effective upon the Frenchman's arrival.

However, before the commodore could take control, on 12 October Curtis received a visit from Baron von Roenne,[*] representing Bermondt, who informed Curtis that the attacking army could not guarantee the safety of the French or British ships and asked them to move downstream and anchor off Fort Dunamunde. All the warships complied and moved to the mouth of the Dvina but at 2100 Curtis sent boats back to bring off the members of the various missions in Riga for eventual transfer to *Princess Margaret*. She had arrived that same day at 1940 having met with *Vanquisher* on passage and both ships paused to the north of the minefields guarding the port entrance. The destroyer advised the minelayer's captain not to enter the river as fighting was taking place so Captain Smyth anchored two miles from the river entrance.

Brisson reached Riga the following day in *Mécanicien Principal Lestin* and called a council of war on board *Princess Margaret*. Twenty-three members of the military mission and nine of the political mission (together with eighteen refugees) were taken on board and HMS *Dragon* arrived, anchoring next to the big minelayer. Two French ships left for home.

At the requested meeting, Brisson, Curtis and members of both delegations took little time to come to the conclusion that 'a bombardment of the German positions by ships would be desirable'.[8] The gunnery officer of *Dragon* was instructed to confer with General Burt, in charge of the military mission, as to which positions to bombard. Meanwhile, Brisson asked Cowan for permission to put the resultant plan into action.

[*] A member of an ancient Baltic German family.

Cowan, of course, needed to seek authority himself and contacted Wemyss. Wemyss again demonstrated his lack of confidence in his political masters, telling Cowan that it would take too long to get approval from the Foreign Office and mandating him to go ahead with the bombardment on his own say-so as First Sea Lord.

Walter Cowan had never needed much urging to go on the offensive. He told Brisson to push ahead and prepared in his own name an ultimatum to Bermondt. Cowan addressed it to 'The Officer Commanding German troops whose headquarters are at Mitau and Dunamunde. I require you to withdraw your forces immediately from positions near Dunamunde,' he thundered, 'which are now a threat to Allied naval vessels in the River Dvina by noon on 15 October, after which I shall take what action I think fit.'[9] Meanwhile, at 2130 *Princess Margaret* took on yet more refugees, thirteen taken off from Riga by *Dragon*'s motorboat: so ended an eventful day.

On the 14th Bermondt and Goltz attempted the dissemblance which their re-naming of the German armies had presaged, denying the presence of any German soldiers and asserting that Dunamunde was occupied by the 1st Russian Regiment of the army of which Bermondt was the head.[*] Cowan was having none of it and simply noted that he awaited news of their withdrawal. As he wrote in a later report:

> Bermondt ... in reply to my ultimatum, stated that he was friendly to the Allies and was only resisting Bolshevism and disowned all connection with the Germans ... whose forces were in position and with little shelter, in some places less than one thousand yards from ours and the French ships, Bermondt having evidently assumed that his statements and arguments were sufficient to hoodwink me and delay our offensive action.[10]

The battle for Riga was in the balance. In the morning, a Latvian

---

[*] By now Yudenitch had repudiated Bermondt as a traitor to the White Russian cause, sending Cowan a note stating 'as Bermondt has not fulfilled any of my orders and information has been received that he has even started military action against the Lettish troops, I declare him a traitor to his country and exclude himself [sic] and any of his army troops from the lists of forces on the German front' (ADM 137/1668, NA).

force had got across the Dvina bridge but was compelled to retire, while at 1800 an artillery duel across the river was observed. At 2100 *Princess Margaret* embarked three more refugees while on board all the Allied warships preparations were put in hand for a bombardment. But some of the officers were less than sanguine about their ability to effect the outcome. Sub Lieutenant Arthur Denis Guy Bagot of *Princess Margaret* confided to his diary that 'we can do very little with the forces we have except to make possible the Lettish advance across the Dvina'.[11]

Bombardment

The sound of the fire-gong was such a tinny noise, small and insignificant against the violence it could unleash. At 1114 they sounded throughout the flotilla. *Abdiel, Vanquisher, Vanoc, Verdun* and *Dragon* opened fire together and a rain of 6in and 4in shell fell on the enemy positions. Machine-gun fire was directed back at the destroyers but was ineffective.

The primary targets were the fortress at Dunamunde (Daugavgrīva), occupied by the Russo-German forces, and the lines of troops along the river. Whilst the destroyers fired at the fort, *Dragon* had taken a position to the west of the river mouth and shot with a view to enfilade the enemy at the Bolderaa (Bolderāja) forti-fication.

At 1145 *Cleopatra* hove into view, obtained Brisson's orders from *Princess Margaret* and joined with *Dragon* in bombarding around Bolderaa at 1347. Then *Windsor* arrived half an hour later, again received her orders from the minelayer and proceeded into the Dvina to join the other destroyers attacking Dunamunde.

After spending nearly two hours attacking the Dunamunde fort, the destroyers moved up river, firing on enemy positions as they went, before anchoring again and firing at the now retreating West Russian Volunteer Army. *Dragon* and *Cleopatra* now targeted the Mitau railway, Pupe (Babite) railway station and the roads around it. Meanwhile, Latvians troops were able to recapture Dunamunde and shortly afterwards took Bolderaa. Ammunition dumps on the west side of the river were set alight by the retreating troops, their explosions adding to the noise of shellfire, whilst the beacon at the mouth of the estuary, which had been armed with machine guns by the Germans, was hit and caught ablaze, eventually falling into the sea.

The Latvians' solitary aeroplane had been operating over Dunamunde while the shelling took place and had fired a white rocket to tell the flotilla that the fortress was in Latvian hands; and at 1720, *Abdiel* signalled to *Princess Margaret* that the Latvians now held the west bank and were advancing further westwards.

It appeared that the counter-attack had been a resounding success. Latvian forces had taken 300 prisoners, captured twenty machine guns and one 3in artillery piece with ammunition. The Russo-German forces, who had, interrogation revealed, been told they were attacking the Bolsheviks, were in retreat. They were a combination of Russian ex-prisoners of war in German uniforms and Germans newly arrived from Germany in the last few days. The Russians stated that German troops were stationed to their rear with instructions to kill them if they wavered.

The local *New York Times* reporter was exultant at the victory; 'in this way some four miles of river bank have been cleared of the enemy. On traversing the captured ground the Letts were delighted to find total division casualties were one man and one woman slightly injured, remarkable testimony to the accuracy of the naval gunnery.'[12] It had been a triumph of arms but, importantly, one that would have been impossible without the concentrated fire of the British warships. As Arthur Bagot noted in his diary, 'the Letts not having heavy guns, it is obvious that the attack could not have been carried out without the assistance of the navy'.[13] The British ships had sustained no casualties and only minor damage – the shock of the gunfire had broken *Dragon*'s mercurial barometer!

The harassment of the retreating forces continued the following day. *Dragon* shifted her position further west and at 0655 began a bombardment of the Mitau – Riga railway and roads in the vicinity of the Gut of Thueringhof, firing four rounds of high explosive and Lyddite every fifteen minutes at the railway and stations. Twenty-five minutes later the destroyer flotilla in the river began an intermittent shelling of positions to the west of the Dvina.

But the situation was largely quiet. Latvian troops now held the city perimeter and *Dragon* took the opportunity to replenish with ammunition from *Cleopatra*. Guns were cleaned and sponged out. *Princess Margaret* took on provisions from *Vanquisher* and transferred the members of the two missions to the destroyer, bar two officers, for return to Britain.

With nightfall, the Germans fired gas shells into Riga, causing 'women and girls to fall in agony'[14] but, according to General Burt and as reported in the press, 'Latvia may well be proud of her young army with two months training, which has defeated the traitorous attacks by superior number of Germans of the Iron, Jaeger and Guards divisions'.[15] Such a statement somewhat gilds the lily in a number of ways, but probably went down well locally.

It is noteworthy that, in line with his initial comments to Cowan, none of Brisson's French ships took part in the bombardment; he himself directed operations from two cargo vessels, the *Bilderingshof* and *ERPJ Sosnowy*. The *Ministère de la Marine* had despatched reinforcements in the shape of the old armoured cruiser *Gueydon*, launched in 1899, but she grounded on her way to Riga and had to return to Copenhagen. The French wanted influence, but found it hard to fight.

HMS *Dragon*

HMS *Dragon* was a *Danae*-class light cruiser launched at the very end of 1917. She had a main armament of six 6in guns and carried four triple 21in torpedo tubes at a top speed of 29 knots. In August she had undertaken a very pleasant cruise around Canada and Newfoundland, where *Dragon* (in company with the battlecruiser HMS *Renown*) had carried the Prince of Wales (the future King Edward VIII) at the beginning of a royal tour of North America. From there she had returned to England only to be rushed to Riga at Cowan's request.

Her captain was forty-year-old Francis Arthur Marten. He was what might in later times be called a 'people person'. In December 1912 he had been commended by Admiral Madden for having the lowest punishment returns in his ship of anywhere in the fleet;[16] and when he subsequently left *Dragon* he was appointed firstly Captain of Royal Naval College, Osborne, and then Captain of Royal Naval College, Dartmouth, positions he held for a total of three years. He would have been a good foil for the handsome but rather feckless 25-year-old Prince of Wales who he had to nursemaid on his tour. Looking after the prince could not have been an easy job. The historian David Cannadine described the trip as 'gruelling, exhausting and lonely, the public pressure was unending and the prince's private behaviour gave much cause for criticism and concern'.[17]

Perhaps fortunately, *Dragon*'s wardroom boasted a full complement of suitably upper-class officers including Gunnery

Lieutenant the Honourable Trevor T Parker, married to Marieka Louise Leonie Kleinwort of the banking family and the 29-year-old son of Robert John Parker, Baron Parker of Waddington, together with the splendidly named Sub Lieutenant Leofric Temple Sims Williams.

Now *Dragon* was newly in the Baltic and had already played a full part in the saving of Riga. During the night of 16th/17th both *Dragon* and *Cleopatra* continued their bombardment of positions around Pupe station and some 2,000 yards north of it, ceasing fire at day break. *Cleopatra* then departed for Copenhagen and *Dragon* remained in her bombardment position, anchored and at rest. 'Collision' and 'Abandon Ship' stations were exercised at 0930; the weather worsened, making it dangerous for the destroyers to come alongside the larger ships; hands were employed fusing the shells for future use; all seemed calm.

Suddenly, at 1710, shells were observed falling abreast of the ship and close to the shore. Initially Marten was unconcerned. Earlier in the day he had received a signal from *Abdiel* asking his position and, in conjunction with his Latvian liaison officer, had come to the conclusion that there was going to be a bombardment of shore positions between the mouth of the Dvina and his current position off the River Aa. When he saw the shell splashes, Marten thought they were 'overs' from such an attack. He ordered shortened cables anyway, just in case it was proved necessary to weigh and move clear of the area. It was a fatal mistake.

The next shells fell alongside and ahead of the ship. *Dragon* was being fired on by a hidden, and hitherto unknown, battery in a wood, about five miles inland in the direction of Pupe. Now Marten knew he had to get underway but first had to weigh anchor. It was too late; three shells plunged into his ship. One hit the front of the pedestal of a 3in anti-aircraft weapon, another detonated on the port side deck, damaging the 30ft galley and one smashed into number five 6in gun on the aft superstructure. A shell was in the process of being loaded into the gun and the explosion of the enemy shell set off the charge. It caused devastation; eight men were killed outright. Petty Officer John Stephen Stroud, Able Seaman Charles W Broad, Able Seaman Lewis T E Gillingwater, Able Seaman Percy James Almond, Able Seaman George W Lowe and Ordinary Seaman James W Sleath were all joined in death by two boys first class, seventeen-year-olds William R H Trett and Alfred J Payne. Ordinary Seaman

William Larn died of his wounds shortly afterwards. Sub Lieutenant Leofric Sims Williams had been the quarters officer for the gun; now he lay dangerously wounded. Two able seamen, Walter J Norman and William J Andrews were severely injured in the blast and another boy first class, Herbert J Gilbert, together with Petty Officer John W Pearce, were slightly wounded.

The Gunner (T), Charles Edward Coles, ran from his station at the after control and dragged the wounded away from the cordite fire, extinguishing their burning clothing as he did so[*]. He was joined by Petty Officer Alfred Joseph Davis[§] who 'showed great coolness in assisting to extinguish the fire and remove the wounded'.[18] But it was already too late. Nine men were dead and five others badly hurt; not killed by Bolsheviks but by Germans and Russians. It must have seemed the war had never ended. The ship returned fire and the battery ceased shooting at them at 1735. But by then it was all over. The state of the weather prevented *Princess Margaret* from sending over her doctor to join Surgeon Lieutenant Commander Gerald R McCowen, the cruiser's own medic.

The following day, Saturday 18 October, *Dragon* briefly put out to sea and proceeded down the swept channel to open water. Here, with due solemnity, she buried her dead in the navy's traditional way. Nine British sailors were committed to the cold waters of the Baltic Sea; a little piece of England in a foreign sea.

Marten was heartbroken and believed the deaths to be his fault. 'I regret very much,' he wrote to Smyth on *Princess Margaret*, who was British SNO at Riga, 'to think that an error of judgement on my part in thinking at first that these were shells fired by the Letts, and so shortening the cable instead of immediately slipping, may have caused a delay which incurred the ship being hit and wish to take all the blame for this.'[19]

Smyth was more forgiving; in forwarding Marten's report to Cowan he noted 'I am of the opinion that, by the time it was realised that the ship was actually under fire, it is doubtful whether any steps could have been taken that would have saved the ship from being hit'.[20]

---

[*] Mr Coles received the DSC for his actions, 'for distinguished services in HMS *Dragon*' (*London Gazette* 31748, 20 January 1920).
[§] Davis received the DSM (*London Gazette* 31811, 5 March 1920). He had 'form', having performed the same sort of act in July 1918 when HMS *Conquest* was mined under No 3 gun; Davis threw the charges overboard and rescued wounded men.

Marten wrote to the relatives of each of *Dragon*'s nine dead. His letter to the mother of Percy Almond, Ellen, is representative of all of them;

Dear Madam,

I regret very much that owing to the many calls on my time and due to the arduous conditions under which we are now serving that I have been unable to write to you before to express my very deepest sympathy with you for the loss of your son Percy Almond, and to tell you that he died gallantly performing his duty on board this ship on 17th October.

The *Dragon* was hit by three shells fired from a battery onshore whilst taking part in operations against the German Forces attacking Riga, and one of these shells bursting amongst the crew of a 6in gun to which your son belonged, killing eight of them instantaneously, him among them and wounding four others.

He was buried at sea next day with his comrades in the Gulf of Riga.

I cannot tell you how much we all deplore the loss of such a gallant seaman and good shipmate, or how much we feel for you. I know that it is hard to offer any consolation. I can only say that your son lived and died up to the best traditions of the great service to which we belong, no man can do more.

Believe me, yours sincerely

FA Marten, Captain RN.[21]

On board *Princess Margaret*, where *Dragon*'s injured had been transferred, the refugees sheltering there 'raised £100 for the benefit of the relatives of those killed and wounded'.[22] And from now on, when anchoring on patrol, the cable was 'always broken at the sixth shackle, ready for slipping'.[23]

CHAPTER 15

The Saving of Riga and Libau,
October – November 1919

The battle around Riga continued in a desultory fashion for the rest of October. On the 20th, *Dragon* and the destroyer flotilla were once again bombarding Russo-German positions, this time in support of a Latvian attack on trenches near Sekar; they carried out two separate shoots and at night observed some enemy artillery fire over the city itself. The next day followed a similar pattern, although life for the matelots was somewhat improved by the appearance of HMS *Venturous* from Libau with fresh provisions. Smyth and Curtis met with Brisson, who came out to them in HMS *Vanoc*, as the 20th Destroyer Flotilla was shortly to be relieved and Captain Curtis would at last head home, while the flotilla refuelled from oilers.

On the 23rd the Germans mounted a heavy artillery bombardment on Riga and the destroyers moved downriver to avoid damage. *Venturous* was hit and suffered one man injured. On board *Princess Margaret*, Smyth observed more heavy shelling of the city just after 2100; the railway station and bridges were hit, with the former set ablaze and a large fire was seen at midnight in the centre of Riga. The following day, *Dragon* shelled German artillery positions in retaliation.

But the much-anticipated day of relief for the 20th Destroyer Flotilla was at hand. On 25 October, HMS *Voyager* arrived from Libau, joining her flotilla-mates *Versatile*, *Vortigern* and *Velox* and the handover of stores and responsibilities commenced. The next day, Berwick Curtis and his ships sailed for Copenhagen. Captain Harry Hesketh Smyth turned over his duties as SNO to Captain Marten of *Dragon* and at 0400 the following day *Princess Margaret* left Riga too, headed for Libau and then Copenhagen. Smyth was not particularly sanguine about the position he left behind. 'I consider that the general situation at present is not entirely satisfactory in as much as the general attack [by the Latvians] had been postponed indefinitely, principally owing to the lack of equipment, guns, ammunition etc; without a considerable supply of this necessary material and increasing support from neighbouring states it is doubtful whether a successful offensive can be undertaken.'[1] Furthermore he considered that the success that had been achieved was mainly due to the cooperation of the Allied ships and that when ice caused their withdrawal it would 'probably result in the Letts being thrown on their own resources, which appear to be insufficient to bring matters to a decisive issue'.[2]

The 1st Destroyer Flotilla in Riga
A new destroyer flotilla, the 1st, had arrived but the duties were just the same and they were soon immersed in the task of artillery support for the Latvian troops. On the 28th *Voyager* fired twenty rounds at German infantry positions which were said to house at least two machine guns and a radio station. But they soon received intimations that their time in Riga might be uncomfortable. On 3 November the temperature failed to rise above minus 10° Fahrenheit.* The big freeze was surely coming soon. Nonetheless and despite the cold, *Voyager* was ordered to a position about six miles west of the river mouth in order to cover a small landing party of around fifty Latvian soldiers who were attempting to destroy two German guns. The attack kicked off at 0630 and all the flotilla plus HMS *Dragon* laid down covering fire. *Voyager* fired 101 rounds at various targets – a village on the south bank of the River Aa, a crossroads and a cement factory which was being used as a strongpoint. At 1425 she was relieved of her exposed positon by *Velox* and returned to the River Dvina. Her captain, Lieutenant Commander Charles Gage Stuart, had been on the bridge since 0430, as had Sub Lieutenant Charles Fraser Harrington Churchill, who later recalled that 'unfreezing in the wardroom was a very painful operation'.[3]

And their day wasn't yet over, for in the late afternoon they fired another eighteen rounds of 4in, this time from the river, again at the cement plant and at the German GHQ. Nonetheless, the much shot-

---

* Minus 23° Centigrade.

at factory remained in enemy hands. It didn't fall until the 10th when *Voyager* once more targeted it with 151 rounds of high explosive. The Germans were driven back and now were out of range of gunnery from Riga. Charles Churchill was told that the Germans were retreating so fast that the Latvians couldn't keep up with them.

On the first anniversary of the Armistice which had ended the World War, the destroyers were anchored in the Dvina off the town. At 1100, the whole flotilla and all other British ships observed two minutes' silence to meditate on their victory. It was so cold that night that on the 12th they found themselves partially iced in. Some sailors did a little ice-skating next to their vessels and it wasn't until the afternoon that icebreakers were able to crack the destroyers free such that they could moor alongside the jetty.

Despite Captain Smyth's pessimism, Riga was fully occupied by the Latvians on 11 November; and during the rest of the month the Latvian army managed to drive Bermondt's forces out of Mitau and Windau and south into Lithuanian territory. Here the West Russian Volunteer Army suffered heavy defeat at the hands of the Lithuanians in a battle near Radviliškis, a major railway junction. This was effectively the end of their campaign and the remaining elements withdrew from the Baltic back into Germany, Bermondt amongst them; by December he was in Berlin.

But there were also problems in Libau to be addressed. On 15 November, without the aid of any dock crane, *Voyager* took on board two 77mm field guns and 2,000 rounds of ammunition together with 7,000 boxes of .303 ammunition and some sheepskin coats, all destined for the Latvian army at Libau. The following day they weighed anchor at 0730 and, despite difficulties caused by ice in the river, secured at Libau at 1830, where once again, all the equipment had to be handballed from the ship. It certainly kept the crew warm.

Meanwhile at Riga, with no more bombardments necessary and ice threatening the Dvina, *Dragon* recouped, oiled, re-ammunitioned and waited peacefully offshore until sailing for Reval on the 26th. Riga had been saved.

Libau

While the Royal Navy was helping Latvia regain control of Riga and its environs, trouble had flared up again in the west around Libau. The Iron Division was encamped around the port and the threat from them was considered to be serious. Royal Navy forces at Libau comprised *Phaeton*, Captain Lawrence Leopold Dundas in command, double-hatted as SNO Libau, together with four destroyers – *Valorous*, *Whitely*, *Winchester* and *Wryneck*. All possessed 4in guns and *Phaeton* had in addition two 6in. By the 30th October, Cowan was concerned enough to order Dundas 'with the help of the British Military Mission, get into co-operation with the Lettish Defence Forces, establish communications and observation posts and plot targets'.[4] He also despatched the light cruiser *Dauntless* from Biorko, under Captain Cecil Horace Pilcher, to add her six 6in guns to the defences. As the admiral wrote to the Admiralty, 'the Germans are now attacking the Lettish outposts on the outskirts of Libau and Windau and everything points to their intention of re-occupying both places shortly. I have ordered our ships to hinder this as much as possible without indiscriminate destruction but with no adequate land forces to hold these places, the situation could scarcely be more unsatisfactory.'[5]

The anticipated attack arrived at 1040 on 4 November. The Germans had advanced right up to the edge of the town and their troops, supported by heavy and light artillery and an armoured train, attacked Libau in the morning. They were met with Latvian defensive fire and a barrage of 4in and 6in shells from the bevy of warships in the port, which did not yet include *Dauntless*. *Winchester*, *Phaeton*, *Valorous* and *Wryneck* were anchored in a single line with 'springs on buoy or kedges out'.[6] Under the overall command of Captain Dundas in *Phaeton* (and as instructed by Cowan), squared charts had already been prepared and a communications and observation post established, and this made shooting more accurate.

All the British ships fired at timed intervals with rapid fire being ordered during the two German assaults, both of which were beaten off. The German batteries, aided by their armoured train, which was equipped with two 4in guns, were firing into the Latvian defences and the bulk of the Royal Navy reply was directed at them. The attack was driven off and, in the afternoon, a German aircraft flew over the town dropping leaflets advising the citizenry to surrender. There then followed a prolonged and heavy artillery bombardment before the Germans launched a second attack. Again it was repulsed by British shellfire and Latvian soldiery. According to the *New York Times* 'the enemy suffered heavily'.[7] Firing finally ceased at 1802, whereupon *Winchester* was despatched to Windau and the Allied Mission in Libau embarked upon *Watchman* for safety.

All was quiet on the 5th while the German artillerymen selected new battery positions. However, the RN ships continued to fire at the enemy 'whenever he presented a target'.[8] The light cruiser *Dauntless* arrived during the day and immediately exercised 'action stations'. The ships now divided into two divisions for the night, one headed by *Phaeton* and the other by *Dauntless*. This allowed for one division to be on watch while the other rested. During the hours of darkness, *Dauntless*, *Valorous* and *Wryneck* were called into action to see off a Russo-German raid. This was not without incident, for No 5 gun on *Dauntless* burst when she engaged enemy positions at 0440 on the 6th; fortunately, there were no casualties.

All ships were heavily engaged throughout the day but the 7th saw a very welcome reinforcement of the naval presence as HMS *Erebus* arrived, having been sent by Cowan from Biorko as she was out of ammunition for her big guns and, in any case, Yudenitch was falling back from before Petrograd and therefore the need for bombarding Fort Krasnaya Gorka had ceased (*vide supra*, Chapter 13).

On the arrival of *Erebus*, Captain Moreton took over as SNO Libau, but based himself on Dundas's ship, which had better communications equipment than the monitor. At the same time, he quickly readied his own ship and the following day *Erebus* took on ammunition from *Querida* and fuelled from RFA *Mixol*.

On 9 November, at 0900, a German 6in battery began shelling Libau and *Erebus* replied, firing 15in shells with half charges. Her aim was extremely accurate and the battery was silenced. Throughout the day, the monitor was kept busy replying to artillery attack. She discharged twenty-two rounds of 15in high explosive, half on 50 per cent charge and half on full charge.

There was now a period of relative calm as the Germans received reinforcements and planned their next steps. The British ships fired off the occasional shell in the general direction of the enemy but everyone was waiting for the major attack which all thought must come soon. The 10th was quiet, for example, but two trains full of German troops arrived at 'Schkudy' (Skuodas) on the Latvian/Lithuanian border. And in readiness for a new attack on Libau a German armoured train began operations around 'Dubben' (Dubeṇi) railway station. The next day, *Erebus*, *Dauntless* and *Winchester* all targeted the German HQ and on the 12th, *Erebus* fired at a building containing four companies of German troops; the third round hit the corner of the building, causing many casualties.

The renewal of the expected Russo-German offensive finally came in the morning of 14 November. The Iron Division launched a new attack, again supported by artillery, and by 0835 had driven the Latvians back into the town itself. Germans now occupied a significant part of Libau and the fighting was intense. All the Royal Navy ships in harbour fired off a continuous bombardment of the German positions, having received an urgent request for all ships to fire on the advancing army. *Erebus*, *Phaeton*, *Dauntless*, *Valorous*, *Winchester* and even ('eventually' states the official report)[9] the French destroyer *L'Ancre* all joined in. The initial German attack had captured the Latvian defences but the Latvian fight back, supported by the artillery of the Royal Navy, drove the enemy into retreat.

When the Latvians put in their counter-attack, *Erebus*, in a tactic reminiscent of the trench warfare which had recently ended on the Western Front, shot off a lifting shrapnel barrage from her twin 15in barrels. The range was very short, barely over a mile, so the ships fired over open sights using half charges. The huge guns of the monitor and their deadly shells must have been terrifying to the attacking and defending troops and, indeed, the barrage was so devastating that by early afternoon the Germans had been driven out of range. Between 0550 and 1340, *Erebus* fired 101 rounds of 15in and over 432 shells from her eight 4in guns, expending nearly all of her available ammunition.

The battle was prolonged and fierce; *Dauntless,* for example, supported the Latvian riposte by firing full salvoes, which almost exhausted her ammunition fit. Indeed, by 1400 most ships were running low on ammunition, and *Valorous* was completely out of shells.

Cowan hastily ordered the *Arethusa*-class light cruiser *Galatea*, on passage from Riga to England with two destroyers in company, to divert to Libau and replenish the ships there. She came into number seven berth at 2240 and immediately began to offload her ammunition. This took all night and it was not until 0400 that she weighed and resumed her voyage home. *Whitely* arrived with Latvian troop reinforcements on the 16th and *Voyager* arrived at 1830 the same day with the guns and ammunition loaded in Riga (*vide supra*).

The defensive action had been a complete success; the Germans were driven off and did not attack again and the Latvians were able to advance 20 miles in less than forty-eight hours. Most people thought that it was the guns of the Royal Navy that had helped see the job through, but there were other opinions. Some Latvian soldiers told Sub Lieutenant Churchill that 'the Germans had been in possession of part of the town for about three hours during which time most of them got dead drunk so that they were easily driven out'.[10]

In Admiral Cowan's view, the German purpose in the attacks on Riga and Libau was clear. 'With regard to these two attacks on Riga and Libau, it is unquestionable that the German intention was to frustrate by every means in their power any successful attack on Petrograd and Kronstadt, and to gain this footing for the winter in the Baltic Provinces with a view to overwhelming them, and then to drive on to Petrograd'.[11] Libau too had been saved by the Royal Navy.

CHAPTER 16
Life in the Baltic

The Baltic theatre was a demanding, and largely resented, assignment for most of the British sailors who served there. Conditions were spartan and few knew why they were there; they were at war but no war had been declared; many were desperate to return to civilian life; and the usual niggles of life afloat were magnified by the location and the privations that it brought with it. These issues would eventually lead to dissent and mutiny; but before examining such disobedience in the next chapter, it is important to consider the background to it, particularly with regard to the conditions of service in the Baltic in 1918 and 1919.

The nature of the war was unlike the one the navy had just finished. One ship's officer, who had served at Jutland, thought 'it really is funny getting back to war again like this; and yet so completely different to the war at home. Very much more like the peacetime conception of it with nothing much worked out beforehand and not knowing very much about your enemy's forces and where they are.'[1]

Sub Lieutenant Conder also found the contrast strange. 'This is really a remarkably nice little war,' he told his diary, 'as although we are up to war complement and in war conditions, it is not so strenuous as the last one. Fancy patrolling 12,000 yards off Heligoland and anchoring at night!'[2]

But many of the ordinary British sailors were quite surly over the fact that the war they had joined up to fight was now over yet they were still being ordered to risk their lives on behalf of foreign nations, of which they knew little and cared less, and as the campaign wore on, the threat to life posed by Soviet submarines and the hundreds, nay thousands, of mines in the area meant many ratings were left to wonder if their ship would suddenly blow up underneath them and send them to an icy grave. Moreover, as Lieutenant Agar wrote, the Baltic work was 'a thankless task for which they received little encouragement or recognition from England. Indeed, in some sections of the British press it was sometimes regarded as a duty to be ashamed of.'[3]

And, having survived a world war, the thought of being killed in some sideshow hung heavily. Sub Lieutenant John Brass had been mined and sunk during the war and fought at Jutland. In September 1919 he was assigned to HMS *Venturous* for Baltic duty. Brass was less than pleased. 'I was not enthusiastic,' he confided, 'I had seen enough of war.'[4] Twenty-five-year-old Lieutenant Roger Prideaux Selby was engaged to be married. He wondered 'how it would hit May [his fiancée] if I were to be killed'.[5] It was an understandable question. In 1916, his elder brother Gerald, a doctor, had been killed in action with the RAMC in France; and his younger sibling Cuthbert lost an arm and was made a POW serving with the RFC. He answered his own rhetorical question; 'quite badly I believe'. Marriage, Selby thought, was a worry for a naval officer, 'but worth it for the sake of the pleasure and comfort of having you,'[6] he told his wife to be.[*]

The Environment

The Baltic was inhospitably cold. On passage from Libau to Riga in December 1918, Stoker PO Fred Smith in HMS *Ceres* saw 'our superstructure covered with ice, even our boats were frozen to their davits and the rails and guns were draped with ice like lace ... I hated it, especially as the temperature fell to 20 degrees below zero'.[7] ERA Harry Boyd on HMS *Windsor*, returning to Reval from shelling the Bolsheviks at Narva, thought the sea 'very rough and freezing hard and our forecastle was a mess of ice due to the spray freezing'.[8] Men had to take care of each other to avoid frostbite. Smith remembered that 'as darkness came down so did the thermometer and a sharp look out was kept on each other's noses and ears. If red OK; if a bit white, a brisk massage with handfuls of snow to restart the circulation.'[9]

On 16 December 1919, HMS *Voyager sailed* from Biorko on the mail trip to Libau. 'A cold trip,' noted Sub Lieutenant Churchill,

---

[*] The worry didn't put him off; they married on 5 February 1919.

'spray froze on out rigging and on the bridge ladders and hand rails'. And on the 21st, Sub Lieutenant Conder on *P-31* reported the temperature as 'forty degrees of frost'; ice formed inside the ship about an eighth of an inch thick. 'Everything is kept shut and all the stoves going. At night this produces four inches of water in the mess decks.'[10] The paint above his cot was flaking off onto his clothes with the cold.

The weather and sea could turn nasty; on the destroyers and light cruisers this made for an uncomfortable existence. CPO ERA John Foster recalled that 'life on *Cassandra* in rough weather was vile, [and] I shuddered when I got a glimpse of smaller craft ... When *Cassandra* took a roll over I've seen men go white with fear, wondering if she would right herself ... we got used to it and she could take it.'[11] Midshipman Renfrew Gotto of HMS *Venomous** recalled that on 26 November 1919 a heavy sea came over the destroyer and went down the engine-room hatches soaking him to the skin; for the remainder of the patrol there were several inches of water sluicing around the engine-room platform.[12]

Probably the worst conditions were endured by the crews of the submarines during the long Baltic winter. When patrolling on the surface, spray would freeze into a mass of ice upon hitting the boat. When the watchkeepers went below their first task was to take a hammer to their overcoats to chip away frozen water which had rendered them solid. Another hammer and a chisel were kept on hand by the conning tower hatch as icing could prevent it from closing when a rapid dive was called for.

But if winter was cruel, summer brought little relief. The temperature could rise sharply. On 4 July, Lieutenant Commander Willis of *Wallace* noted that 'it is very hot now and with no awnings or side screens it is stifling below. Some of the men's messes are very bad.'[13]

These climatic conditions exacerbated the natural hazards of the Baltic Sea itself. Riddled with shoals and wrecks, and heavily mined, it made for a challenging physical environment for commanders to manoeuvre their vessels. The fact that no fewer than fifty-seven ships, thirty-eight warships and nineteen auxiliaries were damaged during the campaign by grounding, going alongside or collision,[14] testifies to this difficulty.

---

* *Venom* until April 1919.

Food and Leave

The standard of food served up whilst the ships were on Baltic duty was a constant complaint. On Christmas Day 1918, the crew of *Ceres* raised a grievance with their officers, who they accused of getting better rations, especially meat, whereas their own supply was of extremely poor quality. Everyone seemed annoyed and frustrated; in the POs' mess they played and sang the Red Flag. Extra food from on-shore was sent for and the men regarded it with great suspicion, not recognising what it was; but it turned out to be venison and was much enjoyed!

On 27 December, the ratings on HMS *Windsor* had only bully beef and biscuits for dinner; the limited diet was effecting their health, Harry Boyd noted that 'a lot of us are all pimples and boils'.[15] And the following day there were just four days' provisions left on the ship, and those only peas, bully beef and biscuits. Boyd was so desperate for food that he ate horsemeat on shore; it made him sick. Eight months later little had changed and the food situation was still poor. In August 1919, on board the destroyer *Wakeful*, it was dire. She 'has been out here with nothing but bully beef and ship's biscuit for two and a half months – not even any soap and only 10,000 cigarettes, which she stole!'[16] As Edward Conder noted that 'the provisioning up here is not at all good … It makes the men grumble which is not a good sign.'[17]

A T Wilkinson, working in a flour mill in south London, had been desperate to join the navy. He first applied, aged seventeen, to enlist as a boy seaman but was rejected because of flat feet and told to return when he was a year older. Meanwhile, the war had ended, but in July 1919 he presented himself again for service and was accepted to train as a stoker, second class; flat feet were, apparently, no handicap in the stokehold. Having qualified, by October he was still waiting to be assigned to a ship and very much wanted to go to sea. In the drafting office, he saw a notice asking for volunteers for MCS (mine clearing service) and applied, but was told that it was only for first class stokers. However, a week later he was accepted anyway as 'not sufficient numbers of volunteers had been forthcoming'.[18]

He was sent to the minesweeper HMS *Holderness* which, together with her sisters *Heythorp* and *Cattistock*, sailed for the Baltic in November. They were *Belvoir* group 'Hunt'-class Fleet Minesweeping Sloops, ships intended to clear open water. They passed through the Kiel Canal, coaled at Copenhagen and finally arrived in Reval where 'we were based and returned after every sweep until we were frozen in'.[19]

By late December 1919, the privations of Baltic service were taking their toll, and the attraction of a life on the ocean wave perhaps beginning to pall. On Christmas Eve they had to coal ship and clean down, which took until 0500 on Christmas Day. Food was in short supply; 'we were living on salt pork and bully beef supplemented by ship's biscuits with no extras of any kind. The few potatoes we had in the "spud locker" had frozen and turned black weeks before. We were also out of soap and tobacco.'[20] The fresh water tank froze every night and 'being young I never seemed to get enough food'.[21] Wilkinson thought that 'there was plenty of hard work, very little food and hardly any discipline'.[22]

And the effects of the conditions of service persisted even after returning home. Sub Lieutenant Brass complained of being 'troubled by severe bilious attacks' and arrived back home feeling very low. 'Due, I think, to the lack of fresh food and exercise in my last month in the Baltic,' he reported in January 1920, 'I was feeling pretty rotten. Almost immediately after my arrival at Rosyth I found myself in doctor's hands with an abscess in my side ... and had to endure a week of considerable pain and discomfort.'[23]

Going ashore for recreation or food did not appear to improve things. Midshipman Renfrew Gotto first saw Reval in October 1919. The town had once been the Russian Baltic Fleet's main dockyard but was now in disrepair; 'the harbour of Reval is at present uncompleted,' Gotto observed, 'and it looks as if it will remain so, as the Estonians are taking no steps in the matter'.[24] As for the town itself it 'gives the impression of desolation, the people seeming to take no interest in life at all'.[25] Lieutenant Commander Willis thought that Reval 'seems more or less derelict'.[26] And Lieutenant Eric Bremerton, newly arrived at Reval, went to a 'small café' for lunch. 'Kidney soup and donkey's ears. Not nice,' he recalled.[27] His boils and haemorrhoids, first suffered in September, later reoccurred with monotonous regularity.

Even in Finland, relief was difficult to find. Algernon Willis found that 'inferior ginger beer stuff and a piece of cake' in a Helsingfors' café cost three shillings and sixpence*.[28] Leave-

---

* About £9.45 in today's money.

breaking was also becoming a problem when the ships were back in port. In *Ceres*, Roger Selby thought that 'the main trouble about the ship is that it is ten months since they [the crew] got a night ashore or any leave and all the leave breaking is merely the outcome of that'.[29]

Mail is always important to sailors serving away from home and Cowan's staff went to great lengths to ensure its safe despatch and arrival. A regular mail run was established whereby a destroyer left Biorko for Reval, picking up post there, before calling at Libau and then Copenhagen, where it would wait for a day or two to catch the incoming mail. The trip was then made back to Biorko in reverse order 'all at 25 knots'.[30]

The Germans

Throughout the period covered by this book, and particularly the first half of 1919, the Allies were uncertain as to whether or not the Germans would both comply with the terms of the Armistice and sign the peace treaty. There was always the possibility that Germany would recommence warfare, given the opinion expressed by Field Marshal Hindenburg at the time of the Armistice, when he stated that 'the Armistice is militarily necessary to us. We shall soon be at the end of our strength. If peace does not follow we have ... rested ourselves and won time. Then we shall be more fit to fight than now, if that is necessary.'[31] Also, there were many in Germany who opposed the terms of the treaty, as has been noted above, up to and including Chancellor of Germany Philipp Scheidemann, who declared in March 1919 that the treaty was a murderous plan, trying to put Germany in chains.

Frustrated by the lack of progress in getting German agreement to the peace treaty, in June 1919 the Allies declared that war would resume if the German government did not assent and sign. To try to force the situation, the Admiralty sent the 4th Light Cruiser Squadron and half the 3rd Destroyer Flotilla to the Southern Baltic, strengthening the blockade of the German coast down to Kiel. Admiral Madden told Cowan that he had asked to bring the whole Atlantic fleet out to the German coastal blockade but the Council of Four turned him down.[32] And for Lieutenant Commander Willis, 'it appears to be touch and go as to whether or not it's to be war with Germany viz whether or not she will sign the peace terms'.[33] He did not relish the prospect for 'if it comes to war again we shall be in a rather tight place'.[34] Thus it was that before HMS *Vindictive* sailed for the Baltic, she was being held at Rosyth again the possibility that she would have to patrol in the North Sea in case of renewed hostilities.[35]

And renewed war was becoming an ever-greater possibility. The Armistice would expire on 23 June; Scheidemann's government was unable to agree on a common position and Scheidemann himself resigned rather than sign the treaty. Gustav Bauer, the new Chancellor, sent a telegram stating his intention to sign the treaty if certain articles were withdrawn but the Allies once more demanded that Germany would have to accept the peace treaty as it stood or face an invasion across the Rhine within twenty-four hours. On 23 June, Bauer conceded and sent a second telegram stating that Germany was prepared to 'sign under compulsion a totally dishonourable peace'[36] together with a confirmation that a German delegation would indeed arrive with authorisation to sign the final document.

It is therefore hardly surprising that British and French sailors and commanders were deeply suspicious of Germany's motives generally and specifically in the Baltic – and in the case of the latter with due cause. And both Cowan and Alexander-Sinclair had been ordered to have nothing to do with them, wherever possible.

Unsurprisingly, the British sailors' attitudes to, and opinions of, the Germans and Baltic *Landeswehr* were not favourable. In Riga, on 23 December 1918, Roger Selby in *Ceres* confided to his diary that 'I never thought that one could be so disgusted by the sight of a Hun and have never really had what they'd call "a hate" against them before but to see them walking about this place – I don't know what it is but one can somehow see all those beastly horrors we only read about in their eyes.' They worried him more that he liked to admit to himself; 'they look absolutely hateful, one sort of feels frightened of them'.[37] He recognised the powerlessness that the Royal Navy's mission involved too. 'They're absolute conquerors and in charge of everything so that our arrival has upset them rather, although we haven't got sufficient power to assert authority over them.'[38]

As for the Baltic Barons, they 'are really full blooded Huns themselves,' thought Lieutenant Commander Willis.[39] Furthermore, Willis believed that trying to negotiate with the Germans was a waste of time. 'Personally, I don't think it's the slightest use talking to the Hun,' he told his diary. 'We should use force first and explain to them what it's for afterwards.'[40]

But for ERA Harry Boyd, the Germans had 'sold us a pup. We have kept order [in Latvia during late 1918] whilst he has made off with everything of value.'[41]

The Danes

Whilst service in the Baltic was regarded as an arduous task, the base at Copenhagen was viewed very positively by officers and men alike. Selby of *Ceres* thought that Copenhagen was 'a devilish good place and a lot of amusement to be got but it is confoundedly expensive';[42] and Stoker PO 'Smudge' Smith found that 'the Danes were all smiles and greeted us as friends and it was a lovely clean city'.[43] For Stoker R F Rose it was 'our pleasure to languish in that delightful city of Copenhagen, which we affectionately called "Copes"'.[44]

Food and drink were easy to obtain. Returning from Reval, Stuart Stapleton went ashore and had tea at the Mits restaurant 'which is a very nice place and very up to date. Then did a little shopping and had dinner ... after that ... we went to a café, had some wine and listened to the band playing.'[45] Not a bad life at all.

British prestige and welcome in the city was reinforced by two favourable incidents early in 1919. The first involved personal heroics. 'Mechanician Henry David Maidment of HMS *Royalist* was awarded the Royal Danish Life Saving medal by the personal wish of His Majesty the King of Denmark, Christian X, for assisting a woman out of the water when she fell between the ship and the jetty.'[46] And then, on 22 February 1919, a Swedish fleet visited Copenhagen, closely followed by the arrival of Cowan's squadron. 'This Swedish visit did not appear to be very welcome to the Danes,' noted Cowan to the Admiralty, 'and coming in strength as they did [nine vessels] seemed to be adversely criticised. Comparisons were drawn in the Danish press between the Swedish ships and ours [and] were most complimentary to us and to the detriment of the Swedes.'[47] Perhaps there were memories still lingering in Denmark of the long history of strained relations between the two Scandinavian countries. Denmark and Sweden had originally been united in the Kalmar Union between 1397 and 1523. From 1448 to 1790 the two kingdoms were constantly at war, often because of a new king trying to prove his worth by waging war on the other country, for little or no political reason. There were eleven Danish – Swedish wars between 1521 to as late as 1814.[*] King Christian X himself was a regular visitor to the promenade and moorings; he would roar along the Langelinie (or 'Long Linnie', as it was known to the sailors) on his Harley Davidson motorbike, 'sometimes dismounting and looking down on our ships [and] give us a wave'.[48]

Outside of the capital, different views might pertain. Stoker Wilkinson found himself on the island of Bornholm when his ship, HMS *Holderness*, put in there in a storm on 31 December 1919. He had mixed opinions about the local inhabitants. 'I found that the people of Bornholm many of whom could speak English, had very divided views [about the British intervention]. Some were extra friendly and went out of their way to show it. Others were definitely anti-British and made no secret of it.'[49] He put this down to the fact that the island was halfway between the coast of Germany and Denmark and there were therefore many people of German descent living there. Before they left he saw a minor and amusing expression of such prejudice. 'One young girl, aged about twelve, [was] on the jetty looking at the ship and one of my mates, thinking he was giving her a souvenir, gave her a halfpenny. She looked at it, then flung it into the water and took a small German coin from her pocket and gave it to him!'[50]

However, as the campaign went on, some Danes perhaps began to regret certain aspects of the British presence. Whilst, as Lieutenant Arthur Bagot at Copenhagen averred in September 1919, 'the Danes don't seem to care for the Germans much; they seem to like the British but also the Americans',[51] he also noted that 'they [the Danes] say that the British sailors always seem to be drunk ... The reason this is noticeable is because they are often there from Biorko and such places passing through and naturally let fly when they get back to a civilised town.'[52] Gloomily, he added 'the papers here have also hinted that our sailors have brought a lot of venereal disease into the country'.[53]

This latter point may well have been true; the British sailors calling at Copenhagen seem to have tried to live up to the traditional tales of 'a girl in every port'. Stoker Rose recalled that 'we opened

---

[*] It might also be noted that the first verse of one of Denmark's two national anthems, *Kong Christian*, describes King Christian IV cleaving Swedish helmets and brains with his sword.

the ships to visitors each afternoon and many took advantage of the amenities we had to offer; ratings entertained "girlfriends" to tea in their respective messes and in many a dark corner one could hear the mutterings of matelots vowing undying love and promises that would never be fulfilled'.[54] And Able Seaman William Robinson, who had a girlfriend in Copenhagen (and another at home) reported that on one day, 17 January, *Royalist* had an 'open gangway' and 'hundreds of visitors, mostly girls', on board.[55]

But it was not just the sailors who were culpable, the 'working girls' were also active in pursuit of their trade. Sub Lieutenant John Brass of HMS *Voyager* recalled a night out with some fellow officers when one of their number was determined to find a girl. Eventually he found one who asked for five shillings as the price of passion. At this the officer took fright, thinking it too cheap for a safe encounter; as he hurried off she pursued him and clamped hold of his arm, yelling 'all right, for an English gentleman, two-and-sixpence'.[56]

Other Temptations

The perils of service in the Baltic could encompass all sorts of temptation and misdemeanour. On 18 October, for example, Captain Marten of HMS *Dragon* had occasion to formally reprimand three warrant officers, Gunners Richard Horne and John Shelton together with Shipwright Harry Roberts, because 'during the month of September [they] exceeded the amounts allowed by Kings Regulations for Warrant Officers Wine Bills'. This was one day after nine men had died on board in the action at Riga.

Indeed, alcohol – its presence or absence – was a recurrent issue. Sub Lieutenant Brass encountered vodka for the first time in Reval. 'The national drink I found disappointing in flavour,' he noted, 'but it fulfilled all my expectations in regard to after effects.'[57] The local cabarets too, met with his approval. 'We found the Russian dancing, the Russian music and the ladies of various nationalities on the staff of the cabaret both stimulating and inexpensive.'[58]

The strain of duty, or possibly the lack of it, sometimes made for bad behaviour. HMS *Venturous* carried the flotilla torpedo specialist, a lieutenant commander with seemingly little to do. John Brass recalled that this gentleman 'before lunch took on board a large cargo of gin, which assured a good sound sleep in the afternoon. After tea it was [a round of] bridge followed by more gin prior to dinner and after dinner more bridge.'[59]

Alcohol was unavailable in Finland*, which was a legally dry country, so drinks could be sold on shore at a significant profit to a ship's officers' mess wine bill. The duty of guard ship at Helsingfors was thus much coveted but unfortunately, because of the high numbers of damaged ships now on station, the role was 'permanently occupied by vessels partially disabled',[60] much to the chagrin of the others.

There was, however, the occasional bright spot. On three successive days, 30 October to 1 November, there was entertainment. A rugby match 'in freezing conditions with snow'[61] between HMS *Delhi* and the rest of the flotilla; *Delhi* won, as perhaps behoves the flagship. Next day, a six-a-side hockey match; and finally, *Vectis* staged a music hall show, '*Vectis* Vaudeville'.[62]

But despite such jollity, the witches brew of conditions and mission, together with societal change at home, was fermenting into a poisonous draught.

---

* Prohibition came into effect in Finland on 1 June 1919.

CHAPTER 17

Mutiny!

At the end of the 1914–18 war, most soldiers and sailors just wanted to go home; to loved ones they had hardly seen, careers they needed to restart, wages they wished to earn and lives shattered by war to rebuild.

But there were delays; men were kept in service against their wishes. The three-fold problem was firstly that the government needed to retain a standing army and navy to enforce the Armistice terms and to provide an army of occupation in the Rhineland; secondly, it was necessary to keep a force in being as a precaution until the peace treaty had been signed (and, indeed, in case it wasn't); and finally, the rising tide of nationalism in both Ireland and India seemed to indicate that armed intervention would increasingly be necessary.

Moreover, the method of demobilisation eventually adopted was considered unfair by many in the services. Instead of 'first in, first out', a process of releasing so-called 'pivotal men' (a list which included civil servants, miners, fishermen, shipbuilders, construction workers and teachers) and apprentices was used, with a view to ensuring the speedy recovery of key industries. These 'pivotal men' were often those who might well have been 'last in' as members of reserved occupations under the conscription schemes.[*]

There was thus considerable unrest. Just two days after the Armistice 7,000 soldiers in a camp at Shoreham mutinied and marched to Brighton where they met both the Mayor and the Chief Constable. A general was sent to parlay with them and days after his

[*] On 17 January 1919 the scheme was amended; priority was then also given to those who had enlisted before the introduction of conscription in 1916, men with three or more wound stripes and those over forty-one years of age.

visit thousands of them were suddenly demobilised; it thus appeared to many that mutiny worked. On 3 January 1919 when a body of soldiers at Folkestone, who had been home on leave for Christmas, were instructed to embark for France they refused to obey orders. Men from other camps hurried to join them and some 10,000 soldiers assembled outside Folkestone town hall. Speeches were made complaining about conditions and how they were being treated. Admiral Wemyss noted that 'soldiers had held the pier, picketed the boats, and [had] not allowed any soldier except colonial to embark. Eight generals in white kid gloves had come down from London to harangue the mutineers without the least effect; a battalion sent down from Canterbury was disarmed and their ammunition thrown into the sea.'[1] There were similar protests at Dover on the same morning, when about 2,000 troops turned back from Admiralty Pier. Others joined them and they marched in full uniform and with their rifles to the town hall to put their grievances. They then formed a Soldiers' Union and elected a committee comprised entirely of rank and file.

In several parts of Britain, especially in camps in and around London, mutineers commandeered lorries and drove to Whitehall to deliver their protests directly. On 9 January, 1,500 soldiers based at Park Royal in west London marched on Downing Street to confront the Cabinet, and on 8 February, some 3,000 soldiers from different encampments marched from Victoria Station to Whitehall in protest at food and sleeping arrangements. They were met at Horse Guards' Parade by a battalion of the Grenadier Guards with fixed bayonets, who halted their progress and escorted them to Wellington Barracks.

Obviously, all was not well with the soldiery: and, to a similar extent, the Royal Navy had its problems too. A former Civil Lord at the Admiralty, George Lambert, MP for South Molton, put it to the House of Commons on 12 March 1919 that 'the conditions [in the Royal Navy] were very, very serious, as the representatives of the Admiralty know, at the end of last year, and I think they would have been more serious had it not been for the tact of the officers, and I can quite understand it'.

Lambert then articulated the problem as he perceived it.

The men of the lower deck are not machines. They saw in the newspapers, and they heard of the rise in the rates of pay of civilians, and that reacted upon them in the increased price of food on their wives and families. They were not making big profits; they were risking their lives daily in their ceaseless vigil in the North Sea or the Channel, or they might have been sweeping mines in the Heligoland Bight. But undoubtedly there was at the end of last year grave unrest in the navy and that grave unrest was aggravated by the publicity. I do not want to be violent, but I think I am correct in saying that a match would have touched an explosion … It was not because of war weariness, and not because of any disloyalty to the officers, but because of pay and other grievances gradually accumulating, there was being prepared a striking act of insubordination. I am certain of that.[2]

Lambert knew whereof he spoke. On 13 January, the gunboat HMS *Kilbride* was in harbour at Milford Haven. The crew refused duty, claiming that their pay was insufficient for the job, and demanded to see their captain, who rebuffed the delegation. The men then declined to put to sea and raised a large red flag over their ship. Eight men were eventually court-martialled and sentenced to terms of hard labour ranging from ninety days to two years.

There were also frequent complaints about being sent to the Baltic and other parts of Russia, not least because, unlike the army, there was no choice. Those soldiers who were serving in Russia, defending British and Allied arms stores and acting as military advisors to the White Russian forces, were all volunteers. But the navy did not give that option. A ship was sent, and the men on it had no choice but to go with the vessel. Hence the rebellion on the river gunboat HMS *Cicala* in July; based in Archangel, she suffered a general refusal of duty. The 'strike' was only ended when Rear Admiral Green threatened that they would be shelled by his other ships if they did not return to work.

In fairness to the Admiralty, First Sea Lord Rosslyn Wemyss was well aware of the problems over pay. The weekly pay of a naval rating in 1914 was one shilling and seven pence, and 'had been for many decades' according to Admiral Fremantle.[3] It had not been raised at all during the war, whilst price inflation had run at over 200 per cent.

Wemyss had instituted a committee under Admiral Jerram to study the problem and it recommended an increase to four shillings a week. This only represented a 'real' increase of 10 per cent against the 1914 levels but was still too much for the Cabinet. On 6 May, Wemyss met with Lloyd George and Bonar Law at the House of Commons to discuss the Jerram recommendations. Both politicians cavilled. Wemyss was incensed.

That evening, Wemyss wrote to Long;:

> From reports made to me I feel assured that, should any post-ponement of an announcement that the government had accepted the pay and pensions recommendations of the Jerram Committee be made, there will be serious trouble in the Fleet. Under these circumstances I feel it my duty to say that I do not feel myself responsible for the conduct of them and that it would be my duty to ask the prime minister to relieve me of my responsibilities.[4]

Under such pressure the Cabinet gave in and the increases were agreed to on 9 May; but it took until the autumn to implement them.

Trouble in the Baltic

As noted in the previous chapter, the combination of poor pay and continued service was exacerbated in the Baltic Squadron by issues of inadequate food, restriction of leave and bad living conditions. These concerns were further worsened by a lack of knowledge over why and who they were fighting and what for. The war was over; 'Why are we still here?' thought most men. Edward Conder saw a small demonstration of the reluctance to go to the Baltic when HMS *Vectis* was preparing to leave Portsmouth to join Cowan's force on 6 August 1919. 'Only one man is absent and he probably deserted as we are going to the Baltic and he knows it,' he noted. He found it very odd as the man had appeared to be quite content on the ship until then.[5]

Cowan himself tried to address this last issue on 6 September in a typically bellicose memo (number 565) he wrote to all ships' commanding officers for onward briefing to their crews.

> I am frequently told by commanding officers that there is a perplexity as to the reason of our presence in the Baltic and Gulf of Finland. The reply to this is that we are here to keep order and police these seas until all nations bordering on it

have found a stable government and are at peace with each other, or until I receive further orders.

He went on to justify his tactics.

As we are a force of 'light' ships only, and have been threatened and attacked by 'armoured' ships, our current defence is to strike at them whenever opportunity offers, so as to preoccupy then and interfere with their plans ... I have considered it necessary to act whenever possible on the offensive ... to enable me to hold on here [Biorko] where only we can keep an effective watch on the enemy, who possesses superior forces.

This may all have been true – but it didn't answer any of the men's grievances; and his aggressive stance filled many with fear of death or injury in a cause they knew little of. And Cowan could not say that he hadn't been warned of the possible consequences. Writing to him on 8 October, First Sea Lord Rosslyn Wemyss offered a veiled criticism of Cowan, one which revealed his inner resentment that Cowan had demanded the level of force that he now possessed (and the concomitant effort that the Admiralty had to make in order to send them to him) and Wemyss's own concerns for the morale of the men so deployed. 'I very much regret that you did not find yourself able to do with less [*sic*] destroyers. Here we are, absolutely out to the clinch, and I cannot maintain your forces up to the present strength and at the same time give relief to those ships as often as I should like to and as I think should be done.' And in the letter's final paragraph, Wemyss politely made it clear that he did not endorse Cowan's lack of concern for the strain placed on his command. 'But I have no doubt that in considering the question you have taken into consideration the morale of the men and that you feel justified in your proposals.'[6]

Trouble soon came, albeit not at Biorko Sound. The 1st Destroyer Flotilla was based at the 'stone frigate' HMS *Columbine*, otherwise Port Edgar, on the Firth of Forth. The ships of the flotilla had already seen arduous service in the Baltic and had been informed by Cowan on their departure for Britain that they were to receive extended leave of twenty-one days on their return. In fact only sixteen days were granted; arguably the leave period was not, in any case, within Cowan's gift.

On 12 October they were told to prepare to sail for the Baltic once more. Between 150 and 200 sailors (the estimates vary) downed tools and left their ships instead. They came from all the effected ships – *Wryneck*, *Versatile*, *Velox*, *Voyager*, *Vancouver*, *Valorous* and *Wallace*. Urged on by three ringleaders, the sailors convened a meeting in Edinburgh at which they resolved to travel to London in order to march on the Admiralty and present their complaints; further, they decided that they would not serve again in the Baltic. Seventy-nine men did not return to their ships and forty-four of those took the first available train to London.

Urgent messages were sent to London and the Admiralty asked the police to meet the protesters' train. And so on arrival at King's Cross they came face-to-face with the unflappable Inspector Henry Stowell. Firstly, he asked if they had travel warrants; only one of them did, and that was out of date. Then, given that it was around midnight, he advised them that it was too late to go to Whitehall and that he would accommodate them at Somers Town Police Station. Placing himself at the head of the sailors, he ordered them to form up on him and then marched them out of the terminus, a modern-day Pied Piper, leading his band of malcontents away. The following day warrants were issued for the arrest of all seventy-nine men, now listed as deserters, and the protest died away. But the Admiralty was badly shocked.

Commodore (D) Hugh Justin Tweedie, in charge of all the Atlantic Fleet destroyers at Port Edgar, was strongly of the opinion that 'although service in the Baltic is greatly disliked by officers and men ... these are only handles to ferment mutiny by a revolutionary organisation, the Soldiers', Sailors' and Airmen's Union'.[7] In fact this organisation was in the process of being absorbed into the National Union of Ex-Servicemen, run by one A E Mander, described by the Director of Naval Intelligence as 'a scoundrel of the first water'.[8] A rather more informed view was taken by the captain and first lieutenant of HMS *Versatile*, Commander Gerald Charles Wynter and Lieutenant Francis R Baxter. In a memo prepared for Tweedie they made nine telling points:

- the men do not know why they are going out.
- if they are going on active service, against whom and on whose behalf.
- during the last service, food was reduced for the greater part

of the time below the base ration allowed and frequently not all [of even that] was available.

- the Army allow for volunteers, sailors were ordered to go.
- no recognition [was] granted in the press.
- the burden was falling on certain vessels unevenly.
- the active service bonus had been stopped in July for no reason.
- in the event of a rating being killed, his dependents should get the same benefits as when on active service.[9]

The officers of the affected ships handled things delicately. In spite of the desertions, normal night leave was given as a sign that the men were trusted by their officers. And the day after the mutiny, Monday 13th, Tweedie assembled all ships' companies ashore to address them. He did it very informally; the men were not fallen in but were just a 'muddled up collection with the officers all in amongst them'.[10] Commodore Tweedie 'expressed sympathy with the men, explaining what he had done, and was doing, everything in his power to better the conditions of service in the Baltic. At the same time he appealed to them to uphold the traditions of the service.'[11] Sub Lieutenant Charles Fraser Harrington Churchill had just joined HMS *Voyager*. He thought that 'the conduct of the men at this meeting was far from all that could be desired. Remarks and questions were shouted out by a few hot heads and a general feeling of discontent prevailed.'[12] But he believed Tweedie handled the situation with tact. A court of enquiry into the incident, held on 21 October, echoed all of these points, adding 'ships' companies do not understand the political situation which renders it necessary for the flotillas to be kept on active service in the Baltic against the Bolsheviks and others with whom the country is not at war'.[13] But the Admiralty merely sent a message to Cowan on the 19th that the 1st Destroyer Flotilla was on its way 'but there is insubordination' and he should 'prevent them mixing with other ships' companies'.[14] That would not stem the tide.

Nor did it satisfy those in Parliament who followed naval matters. That eternal burr under the saddle of the Admiralty, Lieutenant Commander Kenworthy, rose to put a question on 29 October. He asked the First Lord of the Admiralty, Walter Long, 'whether he has considered the desirability of only sending volunteers to take part in naval operations against the Russian

Soviet Government; and whether he is aware that certain naval ratings are dissatisfied with the different treatment meted out to His Majesty's Army as compared with the Royal Navy in this respect?'

Long tried to downplay the situation.

The navy is manned by volunteers for service throughout the world, and therefore all officers and men are required to proceed wherever the Government may direct. It may be that this fact has created a sense of grievance in a few cases; but I am quite sure that the vast majority of officers and men of the navy fully appreciate their duty in this respect.

The point regarding 'volunteers' was, of course, untrue.

Now Colonel Wilfrid William Ashley, MP for Fylde and a former leading light in the Navy League, joined in the fun; 'While fully agreeing with the answer of the Right Hon Gentleman,' he intoned, 'might I press him to see that men, when they get back from the Baltic, are given proper leave?'

Long again tried a sidestep; 'My Hon and gallant friend asks a totally different question. I think I can say without reserve that the men who have been returned from the Baltic have been given leave … ' Here he was interrupted by Ashley's shout of 'No! No!' But Long ploughed on; 'I beg my Hon and gallant friend's pardon. I think he includes two different things. They have had their proper leave. But there are demands for special leave. These demands are now being considered, and the Admiralty have every desire to try and meet them.'[15]

Despite these honeyed words trouble continued to wrack the Baltic squadron. On 11 November 1919, exactly a year after the Armistice, the aircraft carrier HMS *Vindictive* was at Copenhagen loading stores and preparing to return to Biorko. The working routine was disrupted by a party of about forty sailors who appeared on the quarterdeck and demanded to see the Commander. He replied that he would see four of them 'in the usual way'. The men left but then returned in greater number shouting 'We want some leave'. The Commander ordered them to disperse, which they declined to do and the Master-at-Arms was similarly ignored. Eventually they were persuaded to leave but on reaching their messes began to sing and shout, including revolutionary songs and slogans.

Given worsening weather, Captain Grace decided to shove off

and hands were ordered to their sailing stations. But in the stokehold, the Senior Engineering Officer, Mate (E) H C Curtis, experienced difficulties with some disaffected men. Somebody shut off the oil supply to the engines; going aft, Curtis caught two stokers in the act of stopping the fans. As he tried to prevent them from so doing, somebody kicked him. The disobedience was eventually supressed; two ringleaders were identified, both of whom had been seen tampering with the fans. They were stokers. Stoker First Class Henry Charles Makeum Moore had joined up for twelve years in 1912. Twenty-seven years old, he had regularly been awarded, and then been stripped of, good conduct badges. His partner in crime was twenty-year-old Stoker First Class Percy Horseman, initially a 'hostilities only' man who had entered the navy in January 1918, only to sign up for twelve years four months later.

Both men were arraigned before a court marital. But that did not end the trouble. The following morning virtually no one turned up for duty. This provoked Captain Grace to arrest five more alleged 'ringleaders'. They were condemned to ninety days' hard labour before a dishonourable discharge. Another six were arrested, but resistance continued. The next morning fourteen crewmen were still refusing duty and were arrested.

The court martial of Moore and Horseman was held aboard the brand-new light cruiser HMS *Dunedin* in Biorko Sound on 18 November. They faced three charges; that they 'did make a mutinous assembly; 'did wilfully disobey the lawful command of a superior officer; and 'did join in a mutiny accompanied by violence'.[16] Both men pleaded guilty to the second charge, but denied mutiny, which carried a much heavier punishment.

Captain Grace himself acted as the prosecutor, before a court whose President was the captain of *Dunedin*, Charles Nicholas, and a panel which included Captain Mackworth and, representing the Judge Advocate's office, Paymaster Lieutenant Commander Cecil Hugh de Denne, both from HMS *Delhi*. Commander Somerville Peregrine Brownlow Russell of *Venomous* was also of the party but nearly failed to make the trial as 'a tug had to be sent for him as the harbour ice was too thick for his boats'.[17] Grace detailed the insub-ordinate behaviour and also identified that they had 'traitorously tampered with the fan engine, thereby endangering the lives of the men in "A" stokehold and the safety of the ship which was under way at the time and on active service'.[18]

In their defence, the two accused stated the reason for their protest was their 'not understanding the reason for the stoppage of our leave at Copenhagen, after long and arduous service in the Great War and ... still continued in the Baltic'.[19] It cut no ice. Both were found guilty and sentenced to five years' penal servitude[*]. It was a sentence intended to be exemplary.

Word soon got round the fleet. Sub Lieutenant Conder recorded in his diary on 23 November that '*Vindictive* had more of less of a mutiny at Copenhagen as the captain refused leave (she had been up here five months without any)'.[20] The resentment and sedition continued. In November, the minesweeper crews complained of the conditions and the danger and declared they had had enough. They were mainly 'hostilities only' men and had reached the end of the extra years' service that they had volunteered for after the Armistice; they claimed that it had been expressly stated at the time that they would not be involved in any further warfare.[§] On the flagship *Delhi*, there was unrest too. By late December the crew had a long list of grievances which were not properly addressed. Apart from the ongoing problems of poor food and conditions and a lack of understanding why they were there, they were concerned that the ship would not sail back to England before ice locked them in to Biorko Sound; there was no arctic clothing and the ship was not fitted with any heating equipment. The prospect of a bleak and very cold Christmas away from home did not appeal to them. But spirits were lifted when Cowan ordered the *Delhi* to Reval, where he went to see Pitka.

On his return, as he came over the side, he announced a return to Biorko straight away. The men, who had been looking forward to a run ashore in the city, were unimpressed. When both watches were ordered to prepare to sea, only 25 per cent of them reported for duty. For the next few hours, divisions' officers tried to work with the senior ratings to change opinion around. There were lower-deck deputations, interviews and a 'general feeling of malaise and uncertainty'[21] before the ship could put to sea, some hours later. A more emotionally intelligent top team than Cowan and Mackworth might, perhaps, have been able to avoid such problems.

---

[*]The sentences were reviewed in late December and reduced to two years for Moore and one year for Horseman.
[§] The men had been deliberately retained as there was a pressing need to clear all the mines which littered the North Sea and other British waters.

Some captains were able to manage such issues, however. HMS *P-31* had spent many weeks conducting anti-submarine patrols out of Biorko. On 19 December, the ice became too thick to operate from there and they moved to Reval where, because of overcrowding in the harbour, she was instructed to lie outside in the roadstead with orders to conduct A/S operations off Kronstadt itself, a dangerous occupation at any time. 'Many and varied and utterly useless were our unrestrained comments,' according to Sub Lieutenant Edward Conder. The following day, some of the seamen, 'fortified by "Dutch courage" came aft and made a row, knowing that the captain would hear'.[22] The captain himself came on deck, identified the two ringleaders and told them to turn in.

The next day, the lower deck was ordered cleared at 0900 and the captain spoke to the men and then told all those who had demonstrated the evening before to fall in aft. In solidarity, all of the crew did so excepting four. He told them to elect a spokesperson and later met with that man and listened to the issues raised. 'Everyone was very reasonable and the affair ended.'[23]

By the end of December, both Biorko and Reval were completely frozen in. Most ships now gathered in Reval were ordered home. The minesweeper HMS *Holderness* was instructed to sail for Copenhagen, towing a Motor Launch. On the first night out, a boiler clean at sea was decided upon, which would mean four hours' cleaning before four hours' stoking for each of the four watches. As this was a difficult and demanding evolution usually performed in harbour – and one which even then took three whole days – there was considerable resentment amongst the stokers over the demand. They decided that they would refuse point blank to do the work and the seamen, with whom they shared a mess, agreed to back them. There could thus be expected to be three officers and five petty officers opposed to forty ratings.

When the Stoker Petty Officer appeared and ordered the cleaning to commence nobody moved. 'We're not turning to,' someone said. 'All right, get up on the quarterdeck,' the PO ordered.[24] Again nobody moved. The petty officer left and returned with the coxswain. The stokers were given a lecture about mutiny and veiled threats of a firing squad and then the PO and coxswain left.

They returned to say that the captain would meet them on deck and discuss their grievance; he spoke to each man and then asked them collectively to give him a solution to the problem. It was suggested that if they moved to three stoking watches, with the fourth watch permanently assigned to cleaning, it would work much better. The skipper accepted the point, common sense prevailed and the ship went back to work. A potential mutiny had been avoided by a practical commander.

The House of Commons, or to be more exact the monomaniacal Lieutenant Commander Kenworthy, returned to the subject of morale in the Baltic on 3 December. He asked Long 'if he is aware of the complaints made by the crews of certain of His Majesty's ships in the Baltic owing to the lack of fresh provisions and of canteen supplies; and whether any steps have been taken to improve matters?' Long replied that the answer to both questions 'was in the affirmative'.

Major Gerald Hurst now intervened to ask Long 'whether he is aware that many seamen now serving in the Baltic are ill-informed as to the objects of their service; whether he will consider the expediency of having the men enlightened as to the vital national interests involved ... ?' Long once more was economical with the truth. 'The necessary steps have already been taken in regard to this matter,' he answered. Kenworthy pounced, knowing the untruth, and ironically asked if 'the House be informed what are the vital national interests involved in this matter, seeing that the seamen of the Baltic fleet have been given full information [while] the House has been told nothing?' Long gave him the Parliamentary equivalent of a brush-off. 'I have dealt with the question on the Paper, and if the Hon Member wants other information I suggest he had better apply to those who framed the question.'[25]

In fairness to Long, his continual evasion was not altogether his fault. The Cabinet of which he was a member had, with the exception of Churchill, been continuously tepid towards the Russian intervention as a whole and desperately wanted a way out of it. He was just the unfortunate dummy in the target range.

And neither Cowan nor the Royal Navy never really overcame the basic issue; most of the men were sick of war and didn't understand, or – if they understood – agree with, the reasons why they were still there. And the half-hearted commitment of the politicians meant that the operation was not treated with either the respect or support that it deserved by the press or many of the public.

The Home Front

The harsh and unsympathetic conditions of service in the Baltic undoubtedly influenced the mutinies that took place. But in some respects they were merely a reflection of what was happening at home in Britain.

The year 1919 saw Britain edge as near to mob rule as it had ever done. Men returning from the war found there were no jobs for them and that those who had stayed behind had often profited from their apparent lack of patriotism. They discovered that black and Asian workers had been imported to fill their places and showed no signs of wanting to leave – this being a particular issue in the port cities of Liverpool and Cardiff.

Colonial troops, trapped in camps in Britain, wanted only to go back to their own countries and could not understand why this was not allowed. Their frustration boiled over into violence, such as that at Epsom on 17 June, where a police sergeant was killed, or at Kinmel in Wales where an entire Canadian camp went on the rampage in March, leading to fifty courts martial. And on Peace Day, 19 July, a mob attacked and burned down Luton Town Hall where a celebration of the peace was planned.

A police strike on 1 August was generally poorly supported but in Liverpool half the police force did not turn up for work and riots and public disorder were not far behind. Racially-motivated white on black attacks, widespread looting and burning, and a complete breakdown in civil control ensued and the government sent in troops. They also despatched HMS *Valiant*, a 29,000-ton battleship armed with 15in guns, to moor in the River Mersey, her huge presence a reminder of the nemesis that the rioters might bring down on themselves; her marines went ashore and secured the vital docks area.

A railway strike starting on 26 September offered more chaos; how would essentials like food and coal get to where they were needed? The government ordered the formation of a civil guard, the 'Citizens Guards'; 70,000 signed up for it and committed to help preserve law and order. Looking at the state of the country at the time, the *Manchester Guardian* of 27 September commented 'What will happen? Among many people there is the same sense of apprehension as there was in August 1914.'

Of course, it would be a mistake to assume that there was universal support for the rise of militancy. In many quarters there was very little backing for the growing tide of socialism, nor was violence the sole preserve of the left. Sub Lieutenant John Ernest Padwick Brass had been taken from Royal Naval College Dartmouth (Britannia) at the outbreak of the war, having completed only three months of the intended year-long cadet course. He had endured an eventful war, serving on HMS *King Edward VII* when that pre-dreadnought battleship struck a mine and sank in January 1916 and was at Jutland with the battleship HMS *Orion* in 1916, seeing out the war with her. In common with other young officers whose education had been interrupted, he was sent in 1919 to Cambridge University and attended courses at Queen's College for six months. The university boasted a flourishing socialist society, which was not to Brass's taste, nor that of his fellow naval students. When the socialists announced a meeting in a local hall 'the navy got to hear of this and attended in force'. Brass reported that:

The meeting, and the attendant speakers, proceeded in a perfectly orderly manner until the end when the navy and the anti-socialist graduates demanded the National Anthem.

This request the platform refused to comply with ... a party of particularly hefty men immediately raided the platform and informed the two male members of it (the rest were women) that they would be beaten on the buttocks until they did sing 'God Save the King' ... then decided to duck them in the Cam.

The evening finished with a general attack upon the offices of a certain varsity newspaper suspected of socialist, if not Bolshevik, tendencies. Their offices were completely wrecked.[26]

Furthermore, in July Lieutenant Commander Willis noted that he had 'read in the papers that the Labour Party Conference have voted for Direct Action (i.e. a General Strike) to coerce the government into abandoning operations in Russia. What a lamentable state of affairs.'[27]

But Britain was on the rocks, ruined by the Great War, bankrupted and indebted and utterly changed. Threats to the pre-existing order were manifold; deference and respect for authority, societal expectations, the workplace and the electorate, had all altered substantially. To some in power, even demobilisation was a threat, for without jobs and homes for them to go to, returning soldiers would look like nothing more than the 'masterless men' who plagued post-Napoleonic Britain, or the wandering bands of the Thirty and Hundred Years Wars. Britain needed to be rebuilt. She did not need to be at war in Russia.

CHAPTER 18

End Game, November – December 1919

In the end, most things in national governance come down to money. Britain did not have enough to rebuild the country, restore economic stability and provide the standard of living that the government had been elected to deliver. Lloyd George knew this and also understood that an unwelcome, unnecessary and costly war was not enhancing his political position. Moreover, his Secretary of State for War and Air was not helping him. As Cabinet Secretary Sir Maurice Hankey noted, 'Churchill obviously does not care to be War Minister without a war in prospect and finds the task of curtailing expenditure distasteful'.[1]

It was against this background that Lloyd George had written to Winston Churchill on 22 September 1919 stating that he had 'repeatedly urged Churchill to concentrate on reduction of War Office expenditure' but that 'Churchill is obsessed by Russia to the exclusion of all else'. He reiterated the occasions on which the Cabinet had supported Churchill in Russian policies 'which have failed' and stated that they could do no more.[2]

In a final plea in the same letter, the Prime Minister wrote:

I wonder whether it is any use making one last effort to induce you to throw off this obsession which, if you will forgive me for saying so, is upsetting your balance. I again ask you to let Russia be, at any rate for a few days, and to concentrate your mind on the quite unjustifiable expenditure in France and at home and in the east, incurred by both the War Office and the Air Department. Some of the items could not possibly have been tolerated by you if you had given one-fifth of the thought to these matters which you have devoted to Russia.[3]

It was the voice and tone of a very frustrated man. Lloyd George had had enough.

So too had the Admiralty; on 23 October, Wemyss wrote a memorandum for the War Cabinet entitled 'Baltic – policy during the coming winter'.[4] 'In view of the near approach of the time when, through weather conditions, our forces will be obliged to evacuate the Gulf of Finland, the Admiralty are anxious to obtain from the Cabinet a decision as to the line of action to be adopted in the Baltic during the winter months,' he began. After praising the navy's role there he trailed out a baited line; 'it is needless to point out that the withdrawal of our naval forces would not only considerably lessen the Admiralty's difficulties but save vast sums of money.' That sentence certainly got the attention of Lloyd George and his Chancellor Austen Chamberlain.

'Although no arbitrary date can be fixed as to when the ice conditions will make it impossible for our ships to remain in the Gulf of Finland without being frozen in,' Wemyss continued, 'it is assumed that this will be any time after 12 November'.

> The object of our forces in the Gulf of Finland has been to guard our friends from attack by sea by the Bolsheviks, and this has so far been achieved. It was hoped that the *pourparlers* between the Baltic States and the Bolsheviks which were to have begun on 29 September[*] would have cleared the political horizon, but owing to recent events we are at present no nearer any conclusion than we were. It is not likely, therefore, that any decision as to the withdrawal of our forces can be arrived at on this basis.

Thus his arguments so far were that he could save money; but this should not be taken to indicate that the overall area was in any way safe from the Bolsheviks.

Wemyss's next line of reasoning followed:

> Although climatic reasons will enforce the withdrawal of our ships from the Gulf of Finland, it will not be necessary on those grounds to withdraw them from the Baltic – though such procedure is most desirable. The climatic reasons which

---

[*] i.e. the Dorpat conference.

will drive our ships out of the Gulf of Finland will probably –
but not with certainty – prevent the Bolsheviks from taking
that action which, up to the present, we have prevented; for
although they might, with the use of icebreakers, break
through the ice if we have nothing there to prevent them, it is
improbable that they will have either the energy or the morale
to do so. Riga will be closed by ice but Libau may be
considered an ice-free port.

It is therefore for consideration whether, on some date after
12 November, the whole of our forces should be withdrawn
from the Baltic, or whether a section of them should remain at
Copenhagen for the winter.

Now he deployed the money argument again.

This latter step would entail the maintenance of this force,
whatever its size, at a considerable distance from its base, and
the expenditure of a large sum of money.

Unless, therefore, any objection is raised, the Admiralty
propose to instruct the Senior Naval Officer, Baltic, to
withdraw the whole of his forces and return to England when
forced by climatic reasons to evacuate the Gulf of Finland.

He was offering the Cabinet a choice. Save money and bring home a
force whose role he had long seen little point in, given his inability
to obtain clear direction for its use. Or keep the squadron on station
in Copenhagen, for no logical reason, and incur expenditure.

A Decision at Last
Wemyss's memorandum was considered during a conference held
at 10 Downing Street at noon on 31 October. With Wemyss present,
the meeting considered the action which had been taken to date by
the British ships in the Baltic, during which 'the Prime Minister
expressed the opinion that the bombardment at long range of forts
on shore was doing more harm than good to British interests'.[5]
Unsurprisingly Churchill cavilled. He 'deprecated any proposal to
issue instructions for the immediate cessation of these bombardments until such time as it was practicable to ascertain the exact
situation at the moment'.[6]

Lloyd George brushed these objections aside and Churchill

found no supporters in the Cabinet. The conference decided that Cowan should be ordered to evacuate the Gulf of Finland 'when forced to by climatic conditions'.[7] The Admiralty was also asked that a small force be maintained somewhere in the area to show the flag, a deployment which should be as small as possible. It was required to submit proposals to this end.

Finally, and no doubt as a sop to Churchill, he was requested to report to Lloyd George as to the 'the exact situation at the moment on the left flank of the forces operating against Petrograd, and the extent to which any order for the immediate cessation of the co-operation of the British Fleet might affect this situation'.[8]

The 23 October memorandum was to be Wemyss's last contribution to the debate. On 1 November, David Beatty, made the youngest-ever Admiral of the Fleet in April and ennobled as the 1st Earl Beatty, Baron Beatty of the North Sea and Brooksby in August, gained the prize he had sought all year and became First Sea Lord.

It fell to him to reply to the Cabinet's request for a face-saving small force to be maintained in the Baltic, but the memo that was presented over his signature sang exactly the same song as had Wemyss's last missive.

On 4 November Beatty wrote

It is understood that the main reason advanced in support of this proposal is to show the flag … Experience has, however, shown that the presence of an odd light cruiser or destroyer in the various ports has [had] little or no stabilising effect on local affairs since the German aggression became pronounced. The inability of HM Ships to do more than advise and the necessity for removing themselves when matters became threatening have tended still further to emphasise the fact that a weak naval force is only effective as long as the other side chooses to allow it to be so – in short, 'the bluff has been called'.

In this statement, Beatty was echoing the complaints of Cowan, Duff and others that, without a force on land, the naval mission was largely impotent in the face of non-maritime aggression.

He then dealt with the question of what exactly the mission of a minor naval presence was in the Baltic:

If a British force, however small, remains in Baltic waters during the winter months it appears certain that there will be calls on this force from the various Baltic States for protection and assistance. Refusal of such requests would inevitably lessen British prestige in these States; acquiescence would equally inevitably lead to operations on an ever increasing scale culminating eventually in the presence of a force similar to that now employed.

Beatty next addressed the issue of the conditions of service.

All light cruisers and destroyers have had a particularly arduous period of service in the Baltic during the past eight months. The conditions, which are unavoidable, are described as far worse than war. Further service there would be extremely unpopular and would expose the men to the various political elements which obtain in those ports. As an instance of this danger, Bolshevik propaganda had already been found in the possession of some British seamen, which would obviously have had its effect on the weaker elements. It would be necessary to limit the period of service to one month, bearing in mind the considerations outlined and the unsuitability of light cruisers and destroyers to very cold weather.

It could not be the work of one or two ships:

It is considered that the minimum force that it would be worthwhile retaining there would be two light cruisers and five destroyers, based at Copenhagen.

The destroyers are necessary on account of the danger from mines; it is not fair under peace conditions to ask cruisers to run the risk of being mined without some escorting force in attendance.

It would be necessary for a force equal to the above to proceed to the Baltic and return at frequent intervals for relief purposes, involving great expense. This expense would be added to by the necessary provision of fuel at the base; canteen stores, provisions, etc., would also be required should one of the ships have to proceed to Libau, etc.

And then there was the elephant in the room; the cost. 'It is estimated that the cost for three months would amount approximately to £140,000* for fuel alone. There would undoubtedly be other expenses, but these are so vague that anything nearer than the merest guess is impossible. £50,000 soon slips away in these indefinite expeditions.'

Beatty then made his, and the Admiralty's, position as clear as possible.

> In conclusion the Admiralty desire to point out that they are unable to see that the maintenance in these waters of what is really, in view of its size and combination, a non-fighting force, would result in any gain which is not more than counter-balanced by the objections set forth above. In consideration of the considerable cost involved and the pressing need for economy, the Admiralty recommend that the entire force be withdrawn.[9]

The need to reduce costs everywhere was very clear to all members of government; but why were the Admiralty so keen to eschew this expenditure? On 1 December, three weeks from the date of Beatty's memo, First Lord Walter Long was to present the Admiralty's financial estimates for the year 1919/1920. The figures would show a budget reduction against the previous year of £167.5 million; and against the run rate it was an even greater fall – nearly £200 million. They did not want to fritter their limited resources away on pointless political wars; they wanted to spend it on new battleships and cruisers (see also Appendix 3).

*   *   *

Whether it was Beatty's memo, his pressing need to reduce all non-essential government expenditure, or merely a combination of the many factors at play in Russia and the Baltic, Lloyd George decided enough was enough. He went public with the Cabinet's decision to withdraw, and before Churchill had submitted the report requested at the 31 October meeting.

On 8 November the Prime Minister made a speech at the

---

* Perhaps £7.6 million in today's money.

Guildhall in which he cut the ground away from beneath his Secretary of State for War's feet. 'We cannot, of course, afford to continue so costly an intervention in an interminable civil war,' he intoned. 'Our troops are out of Russia. Frankly I am glad. Russia is a quicksand.'[10] Churchill, who was present, looked visibly shocked and shaken. A decision had finally been taken – and made public.

And on 20 November, in the House of Commons, Lloyd George elaborated on his remarks of twelve days earlier. Questioned by the ever persistent Lieutenant Commander Kenworthy about the blockade of Russian ports which Alexander-Sinclair and Cowan had both been encouraged to engage in, and which Kenworthy averred was 'causing intense suffering to innocent women and children in Soviet Russia', the Prime Minister replied:

> The maritime policy in the Baltic is that of the Allied and Associated Powers, not of this country alone. There has been, in the strict sense of the term, no blockade of Russian ports. We have been engaged in helping the Baltic Provinces in the struggle against Bolshevik Russia which involved the use of the naval forces of the Allied and Associated Powers, to prevent the Bolshevik ships of war from bombarding Baltic ports and assisting Bolshevik troops, and to hinder supplies useful to those troops from entering Bolshevik ports. But this problem is being solved by natural courses as with the formation of ice, both the ships which might have traded with Petrograd and the Allied war ships which might have turned them back, must go elsewhere. It is not proposed that the British Fleet should undertake the patrol of the Baltic in the spring.[11]

This was a somewhat disingenuous answer at best; but the last sentence of it was confirmation of his Guildhall speech. Beatty's recommendation had been heard.

Kenworthy wanted to make sure he had nailed the point and asked a second question. 'Can the Right Hon Gentleman say whether, in case of arrangements between the Baltic States and Soviet Russia, any hindrances will be put in the way of traffic between the ice-free ports and Soviet Russia by our Navy?' The Prime Minister waspishly replied 'if the Hon Member will take note of what I said he will see that it is not proposed that our Fleet should patrol the Baltic'.[12]

Lloyd George's speech succeeded in quietening the criticism from his political left which had been reaching hysterical proportions. A report dated 26 November from Sir Robert Stevenson Horne,* the Minister of Labour, assured him that the newspaper *Labour Leader* had reiterated its advice to the Labour movement not to be content with any 'merely negative policy towards Russia, but to insist upon a positive peace with the Moscow Government', while Philip Snowden, chair of the Independent Labour Party (ILP), 'follows a similar line of argument, but is much less sceptical than he was last week of the sincerity of the Prime Ministers policy'. The report concluded that Lloyd George had probably doused that particular fire as 'it would appear that the failure of Yudenitch's attempt on Petrograd, together with the Prime Minister's speeches, has prevented an ILP and British Socialist Party campaign, of which hints appeared last week, to secure a more important place for the Russian issue at the forthcoming special Trades Union Congress than it seems likely to receive'.[13]

Not unnaturally, the Prime Minister's repudiation of intervention in Russia was welcomed by the Bolsheviks, who nonetheless gave out the impression that he had been driven to it by a fear of revolutionary socialism at home. In an interview with a reporter from the *Daily Express*, People's Commissar for Foreign Affairs Georgy Chicherin stated that 'we all know that this conduct of Mr Lloyd George is due to a large extent to the influence of the British working class who are demanding ... the British government should cease to support counter-revolution in Russia'. But he also slyly mentioned the commercial reasons that made détente desirable. 'We do see in the present declaration of Mr Lloyd George a step taken under the direct influence of the British business world who understand their real interests and do not wish them to be sacrificed for enigmatical and incomprehensible purposes.'[14]

Meanwhile, during renewed talks at Dorpat in eastern Estonia, Latvian, Estonian and Bolshevik delegations were trying to agree a Baltic peace, even while fighting persisted on the Estonian and Latvian fronts. The American commissioner at Riga summed up the position on 26 November in a telegram to the US Secretary of State:

---

* Who had served at the Admiralty during the war as Assistant Inspector-General of Transportation (1917), then Director of Materials and Priority in 1918 and Director of Labour and Third Civil Lord later that year.

Bolsheviks [are] hoping that disputed points, especially possession of city of Walk, causing difficulties between Estonia and Latvia, may lead to separate peace with the former, and with Yudenitch eliminated, allow strong Bolshevik attack on Latvian eastern front... . I am reliably informed that Estonia has for a month been secretly and separately negotiating in Moscow. Bolshevik demands now stiffened including free passage merchandise and agents through the port of Reval which was refused by Estonia. England believed to be apathetic. French policy especially desired.[15]

It could certainly be believed that England was apathetic from Lloyd George's reply to a question in Parliament. Asked by Colonel Josiah Wedgewood* if 'His Majesty's Government are being kept informed as to the negotiations for Peace at Dorpat; and whether he can give the House any information as to how the negotiations are proceeding', Wedgewood received the dead bat reply that 'a conference is actually taking place at Dorpat, attended by representatives of the Provisional Governments of the Baltic States to decide on their attitude with regard to the peace proposals of the Soviet government. The British High Commissioner will keep His Majesty's government informed of the progress of the negotiations, but no information has yet been received.'[16] The 'and I don't care' was left unsaid!

In Britain, in the Baltic and in Russia, everyone was sick of war.

---

* Wedgewood had joined the RNVR at the outbreak of war and won a DSO at Gallipoli. Changing uniform, he was sent with the rank of colonel to Siberia to stiffen anti-German and anti-Bolshevik resistance. He joined the ILP in 1919.

CHAPTER 19
Withdrawal, November – December 1919

The daily grind of work and patrol in the Baltic was seemingly unaffected by the political decisions and debates at home. On 2 November 1919, the anti-submarine sloop *P-38* rammed HMS *Vectis*, flooding the seamen's lower mess deck and number one oil tank. Sub Lieutenant Conder noted that that 'a P-boat is much harder to see in the dark. It also had no lights. They apparently did not know that we patrolled at night.'[1] One would have thought by now that such patrolling would be well known. The rapid interchange of ships from Biorko to Britain must have made briefing less effective.* Two days later, *Winchester* lost her propeller whilst on patrol in Kaporia Bay. The constant duty was daily eroding the force.

Going back home was a persistent dream for most of the men. On 6 November *Vectis* was finally sent back to Britain. But Conder's luck was out; that same day he had been sent to the hospital ship *Berbice* with an illness. When he was finally discharged on the 23rd, he was assigned instead to the coastal sloop *P-31*. Fortune was not with him.

But despite Edward Conder's mischance, a slow withdrawal was being put into effect. *Princess Margaret* left for Copenhagen on the 19th, taking some of the crew of HMS *Banbury* with her together with three special passengers; Maxim Litvinov and two female secretaries. Litvinov was a member of the People's Commissariat for Foreign Affairs, charged with trying to open negotiations with the British government for prisoner exchange and peace (see also Appendix 5).

---

* And indeed, on 2 December, Cowan asked the Admiralty not to replace 1DF as new ships' commanders arriving at that time would find the conditions difficult and mistakes would be made as an inevitable part of their learning process (2 December, ADM 137/1668, NA).

On the 24th, *P-31* was sent to Biorko with the destroyer *Wanderer* to tow two CMBs back to Reval. But the weather was now firmly against continued operations; the following day *P-31*'s tow, *CMB-86BD* (Francis Howard's boat in the Kronstadt raid), sank in a gale and the destroyer wrapped the tow wire of her motor boat around her propeller.

Withdrawal or not, the artillery support for the Estonians continued. At their request, on the 24th HMS *Voyager* and *Wallace* had fired 100 rounds each of 4in shell at Bolshevik positions six miles northward of the Narva River and then anchored up for the night. The following day they were due to resume their attack but the same weather that had disrupted the towing of the MLs was so bad that the plan was called off. Cowan was less than sanguine about the merits of such actions by now, telling the Admiralty that 'there is little permanent value in these bombardments as a consequent infantry advance seldom results'.[2]

On the 26th, the paddle minesweepers were sent home. *Banbury*, *Chelmsford*, *Cheltenham*, *Harpenden*, *Lanark*, *Hexham* and *Lingfield* were all despatched to Chatham where they were to be demobilised. The minesweeper volunteers would finally get their release.

Duff returned to Libau in *Caledon* on the 26th, with instructions to place himself under Cowan's orders until the admiral departed for home, whereupon Duff would assume the responsibilities of SNO Baltic. He was strictly enjoined to confine himself to the defence of the Baltic States whilst SNO and to engage in no offensive actions outside that remit. And at the end of November, the seaplane stations were dismantled and all the leftover gear burnt.

December

It was nearly all over. But there were losses yet to be sustained and men would still die in a cause already abandoned by all but the Royal Navy sailors in the Baltic.

Flying the land planes had not been possible since 10 November as 'it is too cold at high altitudes without electrically heated clothing',[3] and the aerodrome had been evacuated on 27 November. By mid-November the seaplane patrol too had to be given up. 'They couldn't get the engines started in this weather,' noted Lieutenant Commander Willis.[4]

With no further operations possible for her aircraft, *Vindictive* prepared to leave Biorko on 8 December. Cowan went on board and addressed the ship's company before she departed for Reval and then Libau, where she joined *Dauntless* and *Caledon*. By the 12th ice was forming in Libau harbour, too thick for *Vindictive*'s boats to work in. Whilst in harbour, Captain Grace landed two RAF working parties together with four Sopwith Camels[*] and two 1½ Strutters, leaving them at Libau for use as trainers with the nascent Latvian air force. *Vindictive* finally left on the 21st headed for Portsmouth via Copenhagen after six months' continuous and arduous Baltic duty.

But the patrols continued still, and so did Cowan's lack of sympathy for his toiling matelots. On 15 December, *P-31* left Biorko for patrol but her circulation inlets became choked with ice, which rendered her unable to proceed. Cowan was furious with what he took to be a lack of zeal. He berated her captain, Lieutenant Commander Thomas Gilbert Carter, and 'accused us of crying out before we were bitten and made rude signals. He might have learnt a lesson in tact by coming aboard and keeping his ears open,' fumed Conder.[5] One of the ships inconvenienced by the breakdown was *Venomous*, on the Stirs Point patrol, surrounded by floating ice and due to be replaced by *P-31*. Not only did she have to continue with her duty, *Venomous* also had to tow the stricken P-boat to safety.

Problems continued to beset the run-down ships. In late December, *CMB-72A*, Edward Bodley's command in the Kronstadt adventure, was deemed in too poor a condition to warrant towing or shipping home and was stripped down and scuttled off Reval. *ML-156* became a casualty of the evacuation at the same time. Whilst she was being hoisted out of the water at Reval for inspection and repair after being mined and prior to being towed home, she was dropped from the crane and badly damaged. Her condition was judged to be beyond the dockyard's ability to repair and she was left where she was to be sold off locally.

On 19 December, Cowan in *Delhi* left Biorko for the last time, in company with HMS *Dragon*, six destroyers, colliers, an oiler and the store ship *Volo*. Just before leaving, a note and a bouquet of flowers were handed on board, addressed to Cowan, from an unusual source – the 'Ladies of Koivisto', the town near to the makeshift airstrip and

---

[*] The four Camel 2F.1 planes donated to Latvia at this time were serial numbers 8136, 8137, 8185 and 8187. They became Latvian air force numbers 7, 6, 8 and 9 respectively. Three of them participated in the first Latvian national aviation festival, held in Spilve, Riga on 25 July 1920.

where some of the British dead were interred. 'Dear Admiral Cowan,' it read, 'The ladies of Koivisto are very grateful to you, sir, and to your brave fleet and flyers, for that you have guarded us [*sic*] and the shores of our dear Finland. We should be very pleased if you would accept these flowers. Ladies of Koivisto.'[6] Clearly, the officers and men of the RN had made an impression and possibly not spent all of their time at sea or asleep in their ships! Cowan had previously also received a letter of thanks from the 'Representatives of the Province of Viborg, Finland'.[7]

But the patrolling was unrelenting still, now based out of Reval. The previously separate Stirs Point, Kaporia Bay and Seskar patrol areas were now combined into one, named 'B' patrol, and the destroyers continued to plod around their beat.

The 4th Destroyer Flotilla ships *Bruce* (flotilla leader), *Torbay*, *Shamrock*, *Sesame*, *Strenuous* and *Serene* arrived in Libau on the 19th, replacing the 1DF, whose ships *Versatile*, *Vortigern*, *Valorous*, *Whitley* and *Wryneck* departed the following day, the Admiralty choosing to ignore Cowan's request not to send out ships and crews unfamiliar with the conditions.

Fellow 1DF destroyer *Voyager* arrived at Copenhagen on her way home, carrying 'some commercial travellers and other gents'[8] they had picked up in Reval and Libau. She left for England on the 23rd, with the crew hoping to be home for Christmas. However, the destroyer encountered a severe gale that reduced the vessel's speed to only 4 knots. Their festive dinner was instead held at sea and comprised corned beef and ship's biscuit.

The same day that *Voyager* departed Copenhagen, *Venomous* sailed from Biorko. She too met with awful weather on passage and arrived in Copenhagen on Christmas Day in snow. Midshipman Renfrew Gotto recorded that they spent a 'pretty miserable Christmas'.[9] Even then their trials were not over, for on Boxing Day they departed for Chatham into a very strong gale, such that they were forced to anchor outside Copenhagen harbour and wait for the weather to moderate. Eventually, the captain lost patience and sailed but 'the weather was so bad that no one was allowed on the upper deck for two days and the watchkeeping officers slept and lived in the chart house'.[10] Their cabins were flooded to a depth of 2ft.

Finally came the great departure. *Delhi* and *Dragon* patrolled in the Gulf until the 21st and then put into Reval. On 28 December, the rest of 1st Destroyer Flotilla left Reval for Britain at 0700 (HMS *Wallace*,

Warwick, Vanessa and *Walker*). The depot ships HMS *Maidstone* and HMS *Turquoise*, with their associated submarine flotillas, also sailed for home, as did the 'S'-class destroyers HMS *Seawolf, Sardonyx* and *Tenedos*. Lastly, at about half past six in the evening, Cowan in *Delhi*, together with *Dragon*, left Reval for good.* 'Out paravanes' was ordered as usual; mines were still a constant worry. On passage, they called at Copenhagen one last time and Cowan was given the privilege of a private audience with King Christian X.

The day after Cowan's departure, the minesweepers *Cattistock, Holderness* and *Heythorp* set out from Reval, each towing a motor launch. They also headed into a great storm. On HMS *Holderness*'s second night at sea, the 30th, sailing for Copenhagen from Reval the weather turned very nasty. They were towing *ML-124* which, in the freezing cold, 'looked like a miniature iceberg'.[11] *Holderness* was shipping water on deck and then the tow rope parted. A party was sent to board the motor launch, now adrift, which given the ice that covered it proved very trying, until a seaman on a lifeline manged to attach another towing hawser. The following night the tow snapped again and this time the hawser wound itself around the starboard propeller. Short of coal, with only one propeller, and in the teeth of what was now a violent storm, there was nothing for it but to run for the tiny port on Rønne on Danish Bornholm Island, whereupon the locals, taking pity on their plight, invited the crew to their New Year's Eve party. The ML washed ashore on the southern side of the island of Öland and was abandoned there.

Heythorp was towing *ML-98* and experienced similar issues with the weather. In snow squalls and gale-force winds the tow parted several times, being reconnected only with the upmost difficulty. Eventually, the tow broke for the final time at 0630 and the launch disappeared behind snow and gale-driven waves in which she foundered. Following her sister, and similarly low on coal, *Heythorp* ran for the shelter of Bornholm Island. Only *Cattistock* made it safely to Copenhagen, with *ML-125* in tow; and she was practically out of fuel.§

---

* *Dragon* arrived at Chatham on 3 January and her crew received a welcome three weeks' leave. *Delhi* came into Plymouth where Admiral Sir Montague Browning, port CinC, sent out Cowan's wife and daughter in his barge to greet the returnee.
§ It was MLs *98* and *124* that were lost that night according to the Admiralty record, not *98* and *125* as stated in some reference volumes.

But the saddest loss of the ships that sailed at the end of December was the Admiralty steel drifter *Catspaw*, pennant number 3988. She had been a popular sight in Reval and Biorko, acting as a general maid of all work, tender to the flagship, a despatch vessel transporting people, orders, supplies, mail and everything else between the warships she served. Under the command of 21-year-old Acting Lieutenant Rowland Reynolds she left Reval on 28 December, bound for Copenhagen and then home. On passage she picked up two sub-lieutenants, Geoffrey Williams and Frederick Vallings, and some ratings all of whom had been manning a forward signalling station on the coast opposite Kaporia Bay.

All three young officers were on the books of HMS *Delhi*, although Reynolds had never actually joined her. Having been at Cambridge University for ten months until 2 November, to further an education at Royal Naval College, Dartmouth cut short by the onset of war, he had been assigned to *Delhi* three days later but instead took command of *Catspaw*. Despite this, he had somehow managed to get into Captain Mackworth's bad books, for on 22 November, Mackworth wrote to the Admiralty that Reynolds had 'not yet joined *Delhi*, it would appear that this officer is not suitable or likely to be satisfactory in a flagship, request that his appointment be cancelled'.[12]

During the night of the 30th, in the midst of dreadful weather, *Catspaw* disappeared. All fourteen men on board, three officers and eleven ratings, were lost. They died when the war was effectively over, returning to the home they desperately wanted to see and in a campaign the reason for which they probably did not comprehend. Fourteen lives snuffed out in a cause that the politicians had mostly never wanted and had now deserted, leaving the navy to die at their whim.

Soon, at St John's Rectory in Perth, the Reverend Canon George Ross Vallings, DSO MA would learn that his twenty-year-old son, Sub Lieutenant Frederick Francis Orr Vallings,* was not coming home. Petty Officer George Hicks Bennett left a wife and three small children in Kemsing, Kent. And in Beaumont Road, Plymouth, the

---

* Like Reynolds, Vallings had attended Peterhouse College, Cambridge, for two terms commencing in January 1919 as part of a select group of junior officers chosen by the Admiralty to further their education, which had been interrupted by the war. He was posthumously Mentioned in Despatches in March 1920, as was Acting Lieutenant Geoffrey Hugh Coleman Williams, also lost with the *Catspaw*. Reynolds was not so remembered.

widow Elizabeth Bowerman would discover that her son Thomas John, an ERA fifth class and nineteen years of age, was lost to her as much as her husband was.

The Swedes found the bodies washed ashore and gave them a decent burial at Kviberg Cemetery, Gothenburg, where they still lie. They keep company with the dead of an earlier battle, Jutland, from which sailors in HMS *Ardent*, *Shark* and *Black Prince,* among others, found their last resting place in Sweden. The wreck of the *Catspaw* was eventually discovered lying in 27ft of water to the east of Segerstade lighthouse; her bell, two machine guns and other weapons were recovered.

P-31 was luckier. She had left Estonia on Boxing Day and arrived at Portsmouth on New Year's Day 1920. Edward Reignier Conder was granted a whole six weeks' leave.

Concerns

Whilst the Royal Navy withdrawal was being carried out, there were those who expressed concerns as for the future defence of the area and particularly the Finnish/ Soviet border. On 17 November, Major J D Scale, the British Assistant Military Attaché at Helsingfors (and who had been Agar's 'boss' for his courier activities) wrote a note to London.

He was worried that it seemed necessary to strengthen the Finnish frontier against possible Soviet attack, particularly on Lake Ladoga (Finnish; Laatokka).[*]

> It is almost certain, should hostilities continue that in the spring the Soviets will concentrate forces against Finland … the narrow peninsula between the Baltic and Lake Ladoga is too well defended to break through but with destroyers and transports from the eastern shore of Ladoga, a considerable force could be landed on the western [Finnish] shore, as the Finns have no naval force to oppose it.[13]

Naval forces were necessary to prevent this possibility; but where would they come from?

Scale consulted with Agar who advised that four CMBs, equipped with torpedoes, wireless sets, mines and Lewis guns would be ideal.

---

[*] The largest lake entirely in Europe and the fourteenth largest freshwater lake by area in the world.

Such vessels were available at Biorko or could be sent out from England. At the Foreign Office, Lord Curzon wanted to be assured that, if supplied, the CMBs couldn't be re-exported. He wrote to his ambassador in Helsingfors that he would permit the Finns to have CMBs 'on condition that they undertake to adhere, when initiated, to the International Committee for the Control of Arms Traffic'.[14]

Unsurprisingly, given the budget reductions being demanded of it, the Admiralty was worried about the cost; two CMBs plus eight torpedoes would amount to £61,000, Walter Long told Curzon; who would pay? And the Deputy Director of Military Intelligence agreed to the principle of the handover of the boats but insisted that it should be clearly understood that there would be no British personnel to man them included in the deal. Britain wanted out, and to stay out, of this Baltic conflict.

It had not been quite a full evacuation of the region by the Royal Navy. Commodore Duff with *Caledon* and *Dunedin* and part of the 4th Destroyer Flotilla remained at Copenhagen together with three small French escorts. Duff sent his ships, as climatic conditions permitted, to visit Reval and Libau and kept watch over an iced-in Red fleet. Such an operation, with the need for relief every six weeks, occupied a goodly part of the available light cruisers and was unpopular at the Admiralty, and especially with Admiral Madden, in charge of the Atlantic Fleet, who had to provide the necessary vessels. He wanted to add some capital ships to the mix, to even out the odds should the Russians come out in the spring, and to release some of his cruisers. His request was denied.

Treaties

While the Royal Navy began to plan, and then action, its withdrawal from the Baltic and the politicians in London washed their hands of the whole affair, the Bolshevik-Estonian war played out its last acts.

With the collapse of the White Russian North Western Army's assault on Petrograd, and subsequent retreat into Estonia, the Bolsheviks were once more able to press an attack against the Estonian borders. Commencing on 16 November, the Seventh and Fifteenth Soviet Armies attacked the fortified positions at the border near Narva, with 120,000 men facing 40,000 Estonian fighters. After repeated attacks, the Seventh Army achieved some limited success but by end of November the fighting on the front calmed down, as the Soviets needed to resupply their forces.

Meanwhile, on 18 November, Jaan Tõnisson replaced Konstantin Päts as Estonian Prime Minister and the following day offered to restart the Dorpat peace talks, this time without the complicating presence of the other Baltic States. The talks began on 5 December, with territorial issues the main bones of contention. In order to pressure Estonia over the peace talks, the Soviets launched a new wave of intensive attacks on 7 December and their forward units crossed the River Narva, only to be beaten back by a counter-attack the following day. It became a war of attrition and by the end of December the Red Army had suffered 35,000 casualties and had been fought to a standstill.

Consequently, progress was finally made at the peace conference and a treaty was concluded on 31 December, with a ceasefire coming into effect on 3 January 1920. This accord, known as the Treaty of Tartu (Dorpat), was signed by both parties on 2 February 1920 and established the border between Estonia and Russia, affirmed the right of Estonian people to return to Estonia and Russian people to return to Russia and required that Estonian movable property evacuated to Russia in the World War be returned to Estonia. Most importantly, it recognised Estonian independence *de jure*, which had never been on offer from the White Army and Kolchak 'government'.

The treaty also provided for the write-off of all Estonian debt from Tsarist times and the payment to Estonia of fifteen million roubles, being their 'share' of the gold reserves of the former Russian empire. Additionally, the Soviets agreed to grant concessions for the exploitation of one million hectares of Russian forest land and to build a railway line from the Estonian border to Moscow. In return, Estonia undertook to allow the Reds to build a free port at Tallinn, or another agreed harbour, and to erect a power station on the River Narva. Estonia had survived and had become a free and independent state, an unthinkable achievement without the support of the Royal Navy.

Poor benighted Latvia took longer to reach its much desired independence. On 3 January 1920, united Latvian and Polish forces launched an attack on the Soviet army in Latgale, an area ruled by the Bolsheviks but culturally Latvian. By February, the territory had been conquered, thus completing the union of ethnically Latvian lands, and an armistice was signed between Latvia and the Reds. However, it took until 11 August for the participants to sign a peace agreement, the Treaty of Riga, which officially ended the Latvian war of independence. In Article II of this concord, Soviet Russia recognised the independence of Latvia as inviolable 'for all future time'. Latvia too had finally attained its freedom; and it would never have reached that Elysian place had the guns of the Royal Navy not been so decisive a factor in Latvian self-defence. While the treaty included provisions for reparations, Latvia had, in fact, no practical industrial infrastructure, much of which had been taken to Russia during the retreat of 1917. Agriculture and land reform became the focus for economic development in the new state.

For both Estonia and Latvia however, their independence would be short-lived. The infamous Molotov-Ribbentrop Pact of 1939 and subsequent Soviet annexations of the Baltic States demonstrated the bad faith in which the hard-won agreements of 1920 had been reached.

Britain too sought normalisation of relations with the Soviets. In December 1919 the Allied Supreme Council, at the urging of Lloyd George and in the teeth of resistance from France, formally withdrew its support from the White Russians and from January 1920 lifted the blockade of Soviet ports. Negotiations for a reciprocal trade treaty began in the May. Britain's interest was more than trade, however; the government wanted to exact an agreement that Russia would not meddle in its Imperial possessions (particularly India,* but also the related countries of Afghanistan and Persia), or in Britain itself, spreading insurrection and communist doctrine.

As Lord Curzon put it:

> We know from a great variety of sources that the Russian Government is threatened with complete economic disaster and that it is ready to pay almost any price for the assistance which we, more than anyone else, are in a position to give. We can hardly contemplate coming to its rescue without exacting our own price for it and it seems to me that that price can better be paid in a cessation of Bolshevik hostility in parts of

---

* Lenin himself had stated in 1920 that 'England is our greatest enemy, it is in India we must strike them hardest' (Hopkirk, *Setting the East Ablaze*, p 1).

the world of importance to us, than in the ostensible interchange of commodities, the existence of which on any considerable scale in Russia there is grave reason to doubt.[15]

It was a good example of post-war realpolitik in action.

In May 1920, the brand new 15in-gunned battlecruiser HMS *Hood*, the pride of the British fleet and flying the flag of Admiral Sir Roger Keyes, with the 13.5in-armed HMS *Tiger* and a flotilla of nine destroyers had been ordered to sail for Copenhagen and then Reval as a way of placing a little more pressure on the Soviet side in the peace negotiations and to alert the Soviet fleet at Kronstadt as to the consequences of any sort of offensive activity that summer. With the Reds driven out of Latvia and Estonia and armistices in place, these orders were countermanded. Instead *Hood* completed an agreeable shakedown cruise in Scandinavian waters, a plan which had been the original 'cover story' for her Baltic mission. And Duff was told by the Admiralty that offensive action against Russia was very definitely not to be undertaken.

The Anglo-Soviet Trade Agreement was finally signed on 16 March 1921;* Britain was the first Allied country to accept Lenin's offer of a trade deal and both sides agreed to refrain from hostile propaganda. An undeclared war was finally at an end.

---

* The lifetime of the trade agreement would be chequered and short. The Soviets increased, rather than reduced, their activities against British interests in Asia and elsewhere, despite their undertakings. On 8 May 1923, Curzon sent an ultimatum telling them to cease and desist or the trade agreement would be terminated. Russia could not afford such a rupture at this point and eventually backed down, giving several commitments that it would cease trying to undermine the British Empire. Perhaps foolishly, these were believed. When the Labour leader Ramsay MacDonald became Prime Minister in 1924, he immediately accorded full diplomatic recognition to Soviet Russia, Britain being the first major power to do so. But this, and the trade agreements, were revoked on 26 May 1927 by Stanley Baldwin's government in protest at continued Soviet intriguing against British interests.

CHAPTER 20

In Memoriam

'The Allied fleet rendered irreplaceable help to the fighters for freedom.'[1]

The Estonians and Latvians did not forget the aid that the Royal Navy provided in the fight for their independence. But the most formal recognition of that aid was late in coming and only then at the urging of an English peer. Nonetheless, there are memorials in both countries which are lovingly cared for, with some remembered annually.

Latvia

Latvia celebrates 11 November 1919, the day that Riga was liberated from the Russo-German forces of the West Russian Volunteer Army, as Lāčplēsis Day. Since 1988, a popular tradition has developed of placing candles on and by the walls of Riga Castle in honour of those who died. The naming of the celebration is taken from the Order of Lāčplēsis,* which in turn is named for the hero-protagonist of the Latvian national epic poem, Lāčplēsis, the 'bear-slayer' and defender against the aggression of the German Teutonic Knights.

Latvians do not forget those who came from overseas to help their national cause either. Thirty-six British servicemen, most of who died in the prisoner of war camps during the Great War, lie in the British 'Bed of Honour' in the large civil Nikolai cemetery in the town of what was known as Mitau and is now Jelgava, in Latvia, immaculately tended by the town council. The bodies were moved to Jelgava after the Armistice from other burial sites, including

---

* The highest Latvian military award.

Mitau Russian Cemetery and Libau North Cemetery. Their graves are sited to the left of the main path (to the right of which are interred Latvian soldiers killed in the war of independence) and lie in four lines, watched over by a Cross of Sacrifice, with each grave marked by a standard Commonwealth War Graves Commission headstone.

Amongst them is an anonymous seaman's grave, inscribed 'a British Seaman of the Great War, died 17 October 1919'. This was the date of the attack on HMS *Dragon* but all her dead are accounted for and why his name is not recorded, and indeed who he was, is a mystery to this day. Another sailor who lost his life in the Battle in the Baltic lies with this unknown colleague; 24-year-old Leading Signalman Edward James Cowles of the destroyer HMS *Abdiel*, who died of illness on 2 October 1919.[1]*

There is also a memorial plaque relating to HMS *Dragon* and the nine men killed on 17 October at Bolderāja, the site of the old Bolderaa fortress, in the outskirts of Riga. Here, it has become a tradition to hold a wreath-laying ceremony in October or November.

L-55

The submarine HMS *L-55* had been lost with all hands on 4 June 1919 (*vide supra* Chapter 10) and never found or recovered. In 1926, a Russian trawler snagged a wreck in the Gulf of Finland which, a year later, was confirmed by Russian minesweepers as being that of the British submarine. Desperate for more modern submarine technology, the Soviet government raised the boat from over 100ft of water, intending to learn what they could from the remains. The corpses of some of the crew were found to be still on board.

The British Conservative government of Prime Minister Stanley Baldwin formally requested the return of the bodies. Soviet Russia would not permit a British warship into Kronstadt to collect them, so thirty-nine coffins§ were taken aboard the Ellerman's Wilson Line ship SS *Truro* for transfer to Reval. At 0900 on 29 August 1928 *Truro* moored at Kronstadt and a decked-over barge came out alongside

---

* Cowles, from Plumstead, had been a labourer in a cable works before the war. After joining the navy, he received a medal from the Italian government for aid given at the time of a volcanic eruption. He died from complications following an insect bite.
§ Different sources give varying numbers of coffins; some assert thirty-four, some thirty-two. Thirty-nine is the number loaded on *Truro* as witnessed by her First Officer and reported in the *Hull Daily Mail* of 6 September 1928. Forty-two men had been on board when she was lost.

her, covered with evergreens and black crepe and with the caskets under the decking. They were made of deal, painted black; those of the officers had a small cross on them. A band played funereal music whilst the coffins were loaded aboard and all the ships in the harbour flew their flags at half-mast. And when *Truro* weighed and started to leave the harbour, the old cruiser *Aurora* fired a salute.

On anchoring at Reval at 1000 the next day the weather was typically atrocious, raining and blowing hard. Here the caskets were received onto HMS *Champion*, perhaps appropriately a 'C'-class cruiser, many of whose sisters had served in the Baltic campaign. The coffins were laid out on deck, draped with Union Jacks, while a guard party with reversed arms stood watch. It was intended to hold a memorial service on *Champion* at 1600 but the weather was so poor that the plan was abandoned. In Reval, the town band played 'Nearer My God to Thee' and the flags were flown at half-mast.

Once arrived at Portsmouth, the remains were taken to Fort Blockhouse where they lay in state until 7 September, when the bodies were interred in a communal grave at the Royal Naval Cemetery, Haslar*. A freestanding screen memorial with a stepped arched head on a shallow rectangular base was erected by the grave, on which was set a raised border and five raised panels. The central panel was flanked by the inscription '1914-1919', and inscribed onto the panel was the legend:

HERE ARE RECORDED / THE NAMES / OF THOSE OFFICERS / AND MEN OF / HM SUBMARINE L55 / SUNK / IN THE BALTIC ON / THE 4TH JUNE 1919 / WHO LIE BURIED / IN THIS GRAVE.

The outer four panels bear the names of the forty-two victims, arranged alphabetically.

The Soviet navy refitted the salved *L-55* at the cost of a million roubles and she became the class ship of a new line of submarines. Renamed *The Atheist*, she began trials in 1931 and promptly sank again, killing fifty men. Once more she was salvaged and became a training craft, until finally scrapped in 1953.

---

* Also known as Clayhall Royal Naval Cemetery.

Estonia

The Estonian Maritime Museum at 70 Pikk Street is in the heart of old Tallinn. Outside its entrance there is a memorial plaque dedicated to four British admirals in recognition of their assistance in the fight for Estonia's freedom. On black polished stone, headed by a line drawing of a warship, it records in English and in Estonian the following tribute.

IN MEMORY
Of the officers and seamen of the British Royal Navy
Who served and gave their lives in the cause of freedom
In the Baltic during the Estonian War of Independence
1918–1920
MALESTUSEKS
Briti Kuningliku Merevae ohvitseridele ja meremeestele
kes voitle sid ja andsid oma elu Balti rikide vabaduse eest
Eesti Vabqdussmas
1918–1920
The following Admirals were decorated
With the Estonian Cross of Liberty for their distinguished
services:
Merevaeohvitserid.keda silmapaistva teenistuse eest
autasustati Eesti Vabadusristiga:
Admiral Sir Edwyn Alexander-Sinclair GCB MVO VR I/1
1865–1945
Admiral Sir Walter Cowan of the Baltic Bart KCB DSO MVO,
VR I/1
1871–1956
Admiral Sir Sydney Freemantle GCB MVO VR I/1
1867–1958
Admiral Sir Bertram Thesiger KBE CB CMG VR I/1
1875–1966
On behalf of the grateful people of Estonia
Tanulik Eesti rahvas

The shade of Admiral Rosslyn Wemyss may feel a little miffed at being omitted from this list, given his exertions in the cause. Likewise Duff's could have felt somewhat hard done by. And Cowan is missing an asterisk from his DSO, which he was awarded twice. But this is to cavil too much. It is a fulsome tribute to some determined men.

The Church of the Holy Spirit* also lies at the centre of Tallinn's old town district. It dates from the thirteenth century; for centuries this simple whitewashed church has ministered to the faithful of the city. In July 2003 it witnessed a moving and heartfelt ceremony when the Royal Navy's First Sea Lord, Admiral Alan West, together with the commander of the Estonian Defence Forces, unveiled a memorial in the chancel of the church. Inscribed onto brass are the names of those British men who lost their lives in the defence of Estonian and Latvian freedom during the Baltic campaign of 1918–20. Above it hangs a White Ensign and opposite are the votive flags of the church.

The memorial is not without error, giving an incorrect date for the attack on HMS *Dragon*; and Stoker First Class John Elliott of *Verulam* is omitted from the listing. But it is nonetheless a fitting tribute to those who gave their lives in the cause.

It is not just sailors who are remembered; five RAF men died in the campaign too and are recorded on the tablet. They include Pilot Officer Fred Cardwell who was shot down by machine-gun fire from the ground on 25 October and was buried at Koivisto. He is also honoured in a family memorial at Marton Burial Ground, Blackpool. In the same Tallinn church there is additionally a small plaque recognising Admiral Rosslyn Wemyss, so justice to 'Rosy' was finally done.

Next, in 2005, the Baltic gained a memorial in Portsmouth Cathedral, very similar in design and format to the one in Tallinn. On 16 December, the Duke of York unveiled a Roll of Honour board in the choir, divided into four panels, listing the ships and crews, below which is a dedicatory tablet.

Finally, at St Saviour's Church, Riga, the 'English Church' on the banks of the River Dvina and where the Royal Navy held Christmas Day parade on 1918, the Duke of Edinburgh dedicated a third memorial in October 2006; again it is akin to that in Tallinn and is mounted in the north-east corner of the nave.

All of these three Baltic campaign remembrances owe their existence to the efforts of a determined and well-connected British earl. Eton and Balliol educated George William Beaumont Howard, 13th Earl of Carlisle (born 15 February 1949), is an academic and commentator on Baltic States' matters. He lived for some time in Tartu, Estonia, which country appointed him a Knight 1st Class of

---

* Also known as the Church of the Holy Ghost.

the Order of the Cross of Terra Mariana. It is largely due to him that these memorial plaques to the dead of the Baltic campaign have been erected in Tallinn, Riga and in Portsmouth.

Finally, in 2007 a film of the Latvian wars of independence was produced. *Rigas Sargi* ('Defenders of Riga'), directed by Aigars Grauba, focuses in particular on the battles of November 1919 against the Western Volunteer army of General Bermondt-Avalov. However, as the historian Jonathan Smele commented 'few people outside Latvia noticed'.[2]

Nine Dead Men

The dead of HMS *Dragon* have another, rather more ephemeral, memorial in the yellowed pages of old Parliamentary *Hansards*. The indefatigable and monomaniacal Lieutenant Commander the Honourable Joseph Kenworthy kept their cause alive as he pursued the government seeking retribution for their deaths.

He asked his first question on 9 December 1919, demanding to know 'whether Bermondt's forces are partly Germans; whether they have already killed nine British seamen on board His Majesty's ship *Dragon*; and whether there is any change in the declared Allied policy of compelling Bermondt and his German allies to evacuate the Baltic Provinces'?[3] Receiving no satisfactory answer, he tried again the following day. 'May we have some details about the lamentable death of nine sailors on board His Majesty's ship *Dragon*?' Kenworthy enquired.

> This vessel was fired upon by Bermondt's artillery, and we know that nine gallant men were killed, blown to pieces, and one officer and four men wounded. She was delayed in getting away from danger, and was deliberately fired upon by the Russians ... Is it a fact that His Majesty's ship *Dragon* had both anchors down, and the cables were not even on the slips, when fire was suddenly opened on her?[4]

Then on 18 December he was harassing Lloyd George on the subject, asking 'the Prime Minister whether His Majesty's Government intend to demand satisfaction for the damage done to His Majesty's ship *Dragon*, the killing of nine of her crew, and the wounding of five others by Colonel Bermondt's artillery'.[5] Receiving no answer, he repeated his question a further two times, without response.

His final attempt to get satisfaction for the dead came on 12 February 1920, when he asked the Under Secretary of State for Foreign Affairs (Lieutenant Colonel Sir Hamar Greenwood) 'whether he can state the present whereabouts and activities of the Russian Colonel Bermondt; and whether it is intended to demand satisfaction from this officer for the killing of nine seamen on board HMS *Dragon*?' Greenwood, one images rather wearily, replied that 'as regards the first part of the Hon and gallant member's question, according to the latest information, Colonel Bermondt is stated to be in a nursing home in Berlin in a semi-insane condition. As to the second part, no decision has been reached since the reply of the Prime Minister to the Hon and gallant member on December 18th.'

This did not seem enough to the dauntless commander. He pressed his point; 'are the Government taking any steps to obtain satisfaction? Is anything being done, or are these nine men to go unavenged?' Greenwood offered a soothing reply. 'Every step has been taken that can be taken in the interest of the dependents of the men who were, unfortunately, killed when on duty. We do not know what steps have been taken against an ex-colonel in a semi-insane condition in a Berlin hospital.'[6]

And there the matter rested.

A Medal

During the campaign it had been suggested that a special medal be struck for those who served. Indeed such a promise had been made in Parliament. On 3 December, Major Gerald Hurst MP asked the First Lord of the Admiralty 'whether he can hold out any hope of rewarding their service [in the Baltic] by the grant of an extra bar to the War Medal or of a gratuity?' Long replied that 'the necessary steps have been taken in regard to this matter. The grant of a clasp to the War Medal for service in the Baltic has been approved.'[7]

But such talk came to nothing. Instead, the criteria for the British War Medal was extended in 1922 to include mine clearance at sea as well as participation in operations in North and South Russia, the eastern Baltic, Siberia, the Black Sea and the Caspian between 1918 and 1920. As the British War Medal was the basic First World War British decoration (of which some 6.5 million were issued), awarded to anyone in the forces who had completed twenty-eight days' mobilised service, it was hardly much recognition for the men of the Royal Navy in the Baltic, most of whom would already have qualified for it by reason of their previous wartime service. Yet again, it appears that the powers-that-be preferred to ignore their navy's efforts.

A Flagship

In 2005, the Royal Navy minesweeper HMS *Sandown* was sold to the Estonian navy. She had been the lead ship of her class, built by Vosper Thornycroft and commissioned on 9 June 1989.

On entering the Estonian forces, *Sandown* was renamed EML *Admiral Cowan*, in honour of Walter Cowan's exploits in Estonia's cause, and became the flagship of the Estonian Navy and part of its mine sweeping flotilla. *Admiral Cowan* is the lead vessel of the Estonian Navy Mineships Division and was the first of the three modernised *Sandown*-class minehunters received from Britain.

The memory of the Royal Navy's Baltic campaign is thus even now kept alive and there are still British-built minesweepers in Estonian waters.

CHAPTER 21

Conclusions

Against what objectives should the success or otherwise of Britain's Battle in the Baltic of 1918 and 1919 be judged? If it was to protect and nurture into life the fledgling republics of Estonia and Latvia, then it succeeded, albeit only for twenty or so years. If, as Winston Churchill wished, it was to prevent the spread of communism, then it failed.

Nor did it deter German interest in the area. 'German military and patriotic circles are disappointed at the failure of the Baltic scheme, but will not abandon their hope of acquiring a predominant position in Russia, and of eventually forming an alliance with Russia,' thought Lieutenant Colonel Twiss.[1] The Germans were in fact surprised that the Allies ultimately wanted them to evacuate the area. In his memoirs, Ludendorff wrote that at the Armistice 'we did not consider any abandonment of territory in the east, thinking that the Entente would be fully conscious of the dangers threatening them, as well as ourselves, from Bolshevism'.[2]

The Allied intervention was not a bloodless exercise. The Baltic campaign cost Britain 188 casualties, with another nine taken prisoner. Twenty officers and 108 men were killed, all but five of them being Royal Navy (see Appendix 6). These are, of course, small losses compared to the millions of men killed or injured during the 1914–18 war. But they were all someone's father, brother, son; all some mother's child; and nearly all of them were men who thought their war was over and that home, and a productive and enjoyable life, awaited them. For their relatives, there was no ceremony such as had been held during the Peace Day Parade at the Cenotaph on 19 July 1919 to ease their pain of loss. There was no knowledge that their menfolk had sacrificed their lives in a glorious cause. They were merely the dead.

In terms of *materiel*, two destroyers, two sloops, one submarine, one light cruiser, an Admiralty drifter, ten light craft and a stores carrier were sunk (see also Appendix 7). A total of 238 ships were deployed on station with a daily average of eighty-eight deployed between July and December 1919 (see also Appendix 8). This was a significant commitment and expense at a time when Britain desperately needed to spend money on things other than war. On the other side, the Soviets lost five ships sunk, three surrendered and four seriously damaged; and the Reds never had command of the sea in the Baltic.

Cowan had returned to no doubt pleasing encomia. Admiral Sir Charles Madden, CinC Atlantic Fleet wrote to congratulate Cowan on his Baltic service. The fleet was absent on exercises but 'it would have given every officer and man, and me in particular, much gratification to have put to sea and welcomed you in the old naval style,' he told Cowan. Madden could not, however, resist a barb at the frocks; 'I hope that those who are greater than I will recognise how all important and successful your work has been. It has been restricted only because you lacked support from Paris*.'[3]

As for the politicians, Walter Long wrote to Cowan on receiving his final report of 31 December 1919; 'I venture to think that the report tells a story which adds to the lustre of the great service of which you are so distinguished a member.'[4] It is telling that he had not read the report when he made such comment.

Long's lack of attention was, in a sense, a general and defining feature of the Baltic adventure. As a campaign it was cursed by political disinterest and vacillation. Furthermore, the contradiction between backing a movement, the White Russians, who wished to reincorporate the Baltic States into a new Russian empire, whilst at the same time the Supreme Allied Council supported and fought for the independence of these same Baltic States, probably did not aid clarity of thought in the corridors of British and Allied political power.[§] Wemyss forced the Cabinet's hand on several occasions but there was never a clear government lead, except that of Churchill and his opinions were largely disowned by his colleagues.

Indeed, it is the case that the Russian intervention and the Baltic

---

* i.e. the Allied Supreme Council.
§ As F. Scott Fitzgerald wrote 'the test of a first-rate intelligence is the ability to hold two opposed ideas in mind at the same time and still retain the ability to function'. *The Crack Up* (New York: New Directions, 1945)

Sea battles were primarily due to Churchill's insistence during 1918 and 1919 that the Bolshevik cause should be defeated. He at least remained true to this belief throughout his life. Speaking in the House of Commons on 26 January 1949, for example, he stated that 'I think the day will come when it will be recognised without doubt, not only on one side of the House, but throughout the civilized world, that the strangling of Bolshevism at its birth would have been an untold blessing to the human race'.[5]

Nonetheless, Churchill's stance did him little short-term good. It exacerbated his reputation for military rashness and again made Lloyd George doubt his judgement and refuse him the Chancellorship, which Churchill craved. It increased the gulf between Churchill and organised labour, the trade unions and the Labour Party. Doubtless it also played some role in his losing his parliamentary seat of Dundee, by a large majority, in the November 1922 election.[*]

This was an annoyance for Churchill; but the survival of Bolshevism was a tragedy for Russians and for the world. The lowest credible estimate of the number of Russian citizens who lost their lives as a direct result of Stalin's policies, for example, is around 20 million.[6] During the 1930s, Stalin would send two million Kulaks to Siberia and murder another 30,000 in their homes. Their 'crime' was to have worked to get a cow or two, or an acre or two of land, more than their neighbours. In China, Mao Zedong killed two million of his own people between 1949 and 1951, another three million during the course of the 1950s and forty-five million in the Great Leap Forward of 1958–61, largely from starvation.[7]

Communism could have been stopped at birth, although possibly not in the manner that Churchill espoused. The historian Niall Ferguson avers that 'the only reason that Lenin was able to get from Zurich to Petrograd was that the Imperial German Government paid for his ticket', which is certainly true, adding 'an estimated $12 million was channelled from the Kaiser's coffers to Lenin and his associates'.[8] Furthermore, no one believed that the hereditary nobleman Ulynanov (Lenin's original name) was capable of mass murder, as he so willingly proved to be. Poor Russia merely

---

[*] He did not regain a seat in Parliament until October 1924, as MP for Epping, when he also was finally appointed to the coveted Chancellorship.

exchanged one form of authoritarian dictatorship for another. As the *Spectator* put it in June 1918, 'Bolshevism ... turns out to be nothing but an autocracy "by the proletariat" – and not even by the proletariat but by that part of the proletariat which believes in Bolshevism. All the bloody upheaval of the revolution has occurred in order that a kind of inverted Tsarism might be enthroned.'[9]

Marx may have been an original thinker but he was at best an idealist and at worst an utopian idiot, although to Lenin a useful one, as were (and are still) many others in the West. And Lenin's government, and those that followed in Russia and around the world, were living proof of George Orwell's comment 'the truth is that, to many people calling themselves Socialists, revolution does not mean a movement of the masses with which they hope to associate themselves; it means a set of reforms which "we", the clever ones, are going to impose upon "them", the Lower Orders'.[10] From a world viewpoint, Churchill was probably right.

But the Bolsheviks were not the only enemy. The Allies insisted that German troops stay in place in the Baltic after the Armistice to defend the area from Bolshevik incursion. But instead they found that this simply fuelled the German and Baltic Baron desire for a *Kleindeutschland* on the Baltic and potential jumping off point into Russia. As a result, and despite the fact that the war of 1914–18 was over, Germans killed Royal Navy sailors and fought British attempts to secure the freedom of the Baltic States' lawful governments at every turn. And they had the support of some, if not all, of the German national government and industrial complex, with whom the Allies were at the same time negotiating a peace treaty.

The White Russians, who Churchill insisted were the solution to the Bolshevik problem, were definitely not the answer to the Estonian and Latvian desire for independence; their aim was to re-unite Russia's lost territories. White Russian, Communist, Baltic German, German land seekers – all interested parties had their own agendas and all were just as likely to be an enemy as a friend. Cowan and his officers did well to emerge from such a mess with dignity, never mind a degree of success.

Economics and Industrial Policy

But the level of intervention that Britain committed to the fight was never going to be enough to achieve a definitive outcome. Indeed, as Napoleon had demonstrated and Hitler would learn, a land war against Russia in Russia is a desperately uncertain, and even in victory possibly Pyrrhic, exercise. Unless the Americans came in, the 'war' was probably unwinnable and certainly unaffordable; Austen Chamberlain knew this (*vide supra* Chapter 8) as did Lloyd George. But once the idealist US President Woodrow Wilson had suffered a stroke (October 1919) and the US Senate rejected his plan for a League of Nations* Mandate over Armenia (May 1920), America withdrew into a self-obsessed isolation that lasted until 1941. It is perhaps ironic that the USA would spend the second half of the twentieth century, and expend much treasure and blood, fighting a foe it might indeed 'have strangled at birth'.

Moreover, there was little public commitment to the fight in Britain. The real concern of the country was peace and a better standard of living. The industrial unrest which had characterised the workplace in the years leading up to the war, driven by increasingly powerful trade unions and the so-called 'Triple Alliance' of rail, coal and dock (and other transport) workers came back with a vengeance in 1919.§ A total of 32 million days were lost to strikes[11] involving 2.4 million workers and industrial relations were everywhere poor, particularly in the still-nationalised mines, railway and port systems. One of many victims of such action was Lieutenant Ronald Blacklock and the crew of HMS *L-12*. Returning from his Baltic assignment to Plymouth in October he found 'a railway strike in progress, so it was impossible to give leave and we were marooned there for a fortnight'.[12]

There was a constant suspicion that this unrest was being fomented by Bolshevist agents (as some undoubtedly was) and keeping Russia and British intervention in the headlines did nothing to stop the spread of such unrest. Lloyd George responded by establishing an 'Industrial Unrest Committee' under the chairmanship of Home Secretary Edward Shortt, later renamed the 'Supply and Transport Committee' and run by Sir Eric Geddes, now free of his Admiralty responsibilities.

Socialist MPs now held fifty-seven seats in Parliament, fifteen more than previously and were vocal in their opposition to the Baltic and Russian intervention, and the 'Hands off Russia

---

* Despite it being Wilson's idea, America never actually joined the League of Nations or signed the Treaty of Versailles; Republicans led by Henry Cabot Lodge insisted that only Congress could take the USA to war and Wilson refused to compromise over the issue. The enabling legislation was thus never passed by the Senate.

§ They had originally planned a grand strike for 1915 but the war supervened.

campaign' (*vide supra* Chapter 6) was dominated by those of a left-wing persuasion.

Finally, Britain had a burning need to recommence its export trade and earn revenues from abroad. Its economy was shattered and the primary budget deficit was over a billion pounds. Britain owed the USA £842 million. The war had bankrupted the country, not least because she gave so much of her precious treasure to her Allies to keep them in the war.[*] And there seemed no chance of getting back the £568 million which was owed by Russia. In 1919, British net debt was 140 per cent of GDP. Russia was a potential market and Britain needed peace to be able to trade with her; and trade was being lost through the blockade of the Soviet state.

For example, before the war the Russian market purchased 75 per cent of Scottish cured herring production. Some Scottish herring fishermen took great exception to the continued blockade of communist Russia after the war. The loss of this market brought hardship in its wake to the traditional herring fisheries of Shetland, Orkney and the north-eastern Scottish coast, 'a by-product,' noted the Shetland-based writer Donald Murray, 'of the way the likes of Winston Churchill declared war on the fledgling Soviet state, banning all trade with it. Many people emigrated from the country, their fishing nets folded as they packed up suitcases for their outward voyages to Canada and the United States.'[13] This is unfair on Churchill, for the blockade was not his responsibility, but his may have been the loudest voice in support of it. And Lloyd George, in a platform speech, spoke of the 'bulging corn bins' which were waiting for the British markets to open 'but this proved to be a Russian myth', as that benighted country was 'about to enter upon the worst famine seen in Europe since the seventeenth century'.[14]

World trade would be in competition with the USA, France and particularly Germany, post the signature of the Treaty of Versailles and the acceptance of the reparations demanded of it. Reginald McKenna, a former Home Secretary, First Lord of the Admiralty and Chancellor of the Exchequer and now Chairman of the London Joint City and Midland Bank, recognised this. In a speech to the Commercial Club of Chicago in October 1921, he gave his opinion that Germany could never repay her debts. His argument was that in

[*] The Americans insisted that Britain borrow on behalf of the other Allies because she thought that the chance of getting the money back from her continental 'friends' was small.

order to earn sufficient money to do so, Germany would have to export massively and the only way to be successful at this was to undercut the competition on price. In his view, this was a direct cause of the two million unemployed in Britain at that time, as German exports were causing great injury to British trade and underselling the UK the world over.[15] The growing consensus was that money and manpower should be devoted to modernising Britain's industrial base and restoring its balance of payments, rather than squandered in unwanted wars. The politicians were in a cleft stick.

Impact on Naval Morale

The refusal of London to provide adequate (as he saw it) support for Cowan's efforts continually frustrated him, as it did Duff and other senior officers. In one report to the Admiralty Cowan verged on insubordination:

> It is hard to understand how any collection of statesmen and soldiers in high office could, in the face of urgent recommendations and reports of those on the spot – all of them consistent and constantly reiterated – disregard and take no effective action in a matter which will lead to a fresh war or to an ignominious betrayal of the two small states, which were encouraged to rely on our effective support against German domination.[16]

Lieutenant Commander Willis of *Wallace* certainly agreed with his admiral. In June he wrote that

> one way or the other it doesn't seem that the authorities at home have been particularly bright about the business … a couple of divisions would be sufficient to clean up both the Bolsheviks and the Huns and probably could have done it a month or so ago. Later on the problem may have to be tackled and then it will take considerably more than two divisions.[17]

The constant questioning of his campaign no doubt added to Cowan's woes. He would have in mind the various points regarding the legitimacy of British actions in Russia that were now being raised in Parliament. The ever-interested, and increasingly left-leaning, Lieutenant Commander Kenworthy was in the van of this movement. For example, on 19 November he asked Walter Long 'whether, in view of the fact that no state of war exists between His Majesty and the Soviet Government of Russia, he will state why British men-of-war have been bombarding the Russian fortress of Kronstadt; and in what way this bombardment helps to protect the coasts of Esthonia [*sic*] or other friendly people?' He placed heavy emphasis on the 'undeclared war' part of his question. Long could only reply 'in order to disorganise the dockyard and naval base, and thereby prevent craft based on Kronstadt from attacking His Majesty's ships in Finnish and Esthonian waters'.[18]

Many of the sailors felt this lack of commitment deeply. As Sub Lieutenant Conder wrote in his diary, 'it is impossible to conduct a campaign of any sort when those at home are apparently endeavouring to hinder as much as possible'.[19] If it seemed like that to Conder at the bottom of the leadership chain, what must it have felt like to the more senior officers?

The court of enquiry into the events at Port Edgar makes this point well.

> The ships' companies are of the opinion that service in the Baltic is war service but they do not consider that it has ever been recognised as such. Considerable fighting and fairly heavy casualties have occurred without the country even being aware that the flotillas were on active service.
>
> Mention was made in the press that the 1st Destroyer Flotilla was at Scotland when they were in fact actually on active service in the Baltic. This may in itself appear a trivial matter but it is not considered as such by the men.[20]

As all successful leaders have known, and Frederick Hertzberg[*] was to codify, recognition is an important part of motivating people, and poor working conditions are demotivating. Cowan appeared not to recognise this, showing at times a distinct lack of empathy with the travails of his men, and thus falling short of the standards set by Jellicoe and Beatty, for example, although emulating his friend Keyes.

---

[*] The creator of the two-factor theory in the 1960s, also known as Herzberg's motivation-hygiene theory, which states that there are certain factors in the workplace that cause job satisfaction, while a separate set of factors cause dissatisfaction.

As a consequence of all of these points, mutiny disfigured the campaign and perhaps prefigured the naval mutiny at Invergordon of 1931. Apart from the problems of recognition and political indifference, the war weariness and lack of commitment to the Russian war mirrored the attitudes at home. And the temporary breakdown of the instant and unquestioning obedience which characterised naval (an indeed military) behaviour before and during the Great War again reflected the disintegration of traditional class structures and workplace behaviour which was to become evident in Britain generally.

But with the exceptions noted in this book, the Royal Navy stuck to its task despite political indifference, an ill-defined mission, uncertain allies and a hostile climate. And the poor conditions of service and its impact on morale which led to the seditious behaviour of some crews did not break the bonds of the naval community which existed between officers and men and the rather paternal, not to say feudal, relationship between the two. ERA David Taylor of the mutinous HMS *Vindictive* received a telegram (which took ten days to reach him) informing him that his wife had presented him with their first child, a boy. He revealed it to the Engineer Commander who called the wardroom orderly and ordered two double whiskies, which they drank together. The commander then told him that the captain would like to see the message and sent him to Grace's cabin. 'I knocked on the door and the captain called me in. I showed him the telegram and he pressed the bell knob, the steward lifted the shutter of the office and Captain Grace ordered another two double whiskies.'[21] *Noblesse Oblige* remained the order of the day.

* * *

The 128 British sailors and airmen who died in the campaign did not die entirely in vain. Estonia and Latvia were helped to become independent states; and the Royal Navy's command of the Baltic and the Gulf of Finland paralysed the Bolshevik response at sea, and allowed for the very useful addition of seaborne artillery to the Baltic States order of battle. On land Britain was largely impotent, but Gough and Tallents both made substantial contributions to the success of the land war fought by Estonian and Latvian volunteers.

In the Baltic campaign, the politically-driven restriction of military efforts shows a foreshadowing of the desire to fight a limited war, much evidenced in recent political history; for example, those in Iraq, Libya and Afghanistan. The fact is, as 'Jacky' Fisher recognised, there is no such thing as a limited war. 'Moderation in war is imbecility,' he proclaimed at the First Hague Peace Conference of May 1899,[22] and 'hit first, hit hard and keep on hitting'[23] was his credo. Instead soldiers and sailors (and more latterly airmen) were and are sent into harm's way with inadequate resource and with their arms tied behind their backs by political and societal constraints.

The Battle in the Baltic was, in the end, not a triumph of British arms. But it was a triumph, if only marginally, for the bloody-minded resolve of the Royal Navy.

CHAPTER 22

Envoi

The Baltic campaign produced heroes and villains, three VCs and a peerage.

Walter Cowan was created a Baronet for his Baltic service in the 1921 New Year Honours List, 'of the Baltic and Bilton, County Warwick', and the grateful Estonians awarded him the Cross of Liberty, Grade I, First Class (VR I/1). His next seagoing appointment came on 31 March 1921 when he was given command of the Battlecruiser Squadron with his flag in HMS *Hood*, not a joyous time for that ship. As his flag captain on *Hood*, Cowan had again chosen Geoffrey Mackworth. Both men had by now a reputation as strict disciplinarians, possessed of short tempers and apt to hasty judgements. One of Cowan's first duties was at Rosyth, where the ship and its crew were assigned to protect essential services in the event of a General Strike. The 'Triple Alliance' was already causing disruption in the mines and in public transport and worse was feared. Some of the disaffection which had characterised life in the Baltic spread to HMS *Hood* and several of the seamen's messes were found to be decorated with red bunting. Cowan and Mackworth took this as an incitement to mutiny and amongst those disciplined for the supposed sedition was the Master-at-Arms, who received three years' penal servitude. Such severe punishments did not make for a happy ship. Indeed, the ship's biographer defines the bad feeling engendered by Cowan and Mackworth's command as rivalling the Invergordon Mutiny and 'the most unhappy period in the *Hood*'s long career'.[1]

Following the battlecruiser posting, Cowan served as Commander-in-Chief Coast of Scotland and Admiral Superintendent of Rosyth Dockyard before being appointed

Commander-in-Chief America and West Indies Station for the two years ending 22 July 1928. He was advanced to Vice Admiral in 1923 and Admiral in 1927, served as First and Principal Aide de Camp to King George V in 1930 and was placed on the retired list in October 1931, at the age of sixty.

Family life was not of great interest to Cowan. He had married 32-year-old Catherine Eleanor Millicent Cayley, daughter of a Yorkshire-based gentleman farmer, in 1901 and they had conceived one child, a daughter. But his wife did not share his passion for hunting and for this among other reasons the marriage broke down and they separated. When Catherine died in 1934, Cowan had already devoted himself full time to the hunting field and his horses which he stabled at his house near Kineton in Warwickshire. By 1935 he had become the Assistant Hunt Secretary for the Warwickshire Hunt and in 1939 briefly held the Mastership.

But war was not done with Cowan, nor he with it. After conflict with Germany broke out again, Churchill appointed Roger Keyes as Director of Combined Operations in June 1940. Keyes immediately enlisted his old chum Walter Cowan and, accepting the rank of Commander RNR, Cowan travelled to Scotland to train the newly-formed Commando division in small boat handling. From here, Cowan managed to get himself sent to the North African theatre of operations with the Commandos and saw action at the second Battle of Mechili in April 1941. The following month, now in his seventieth year, he took part in an expedition along the North Egyptian and Cyrenaica coast aboard HMS *Aphis*, a river gunboat from the China Station. The ship was repeatedly bombed while Cowan stood on deck blazing away with a sub-machine gun at the attackers. His total disregard for his own safety led some to believe that he was actively courting death.

Subsequently, Cowan involved himself in the Battle of Bir Hakeim where, having attached himself to the Indian Army's 18th King Edward VII's Own Cavalry, he was captured on 27 May 1942, having fought an Italian tank crew single-handedly armed only with a revolver. He was repatriated in 1943, as a result of his age, under an agreement with Italy whereby 800 Italian seamen from the Red Sea Flotilla, interned in Saudi Arabia, were exchanged for a similar number of British prisoners of war. However, no parole was asked for or given and Cowan promptly re-joined the Commandos and saw action in Italy once more during 1944. Here he was awarded his second DSO, 'for gallantry, determination and undaunted devotion to duty as Liaison Officer with Commandos in the attack and capture of Mount Ornito, Italy and during attacks on the islands of Solta, Mljet and Brac in the Adriatic, all of which operations were carried out under very heavy fire from the enemy'.[2]

The war over, Cowan returned to the hunting field and died in 1956 in his eighty-fifth year. His title died with him. Admiral Sir Walter Henry Cowan, First Baronet Baltic and Bilton, KCB, DSO & Bar, MVO, RN was buried with full naval honours. On 17 February a gun carriage, with a Royal Navy escort, bore his coffin through the streets of his home village of Kineton. The Reverend Seymour Gardener conducted the burial service at St Peter's Church, where Cowan's rear admiral's flag still hangs,[*] and 'Titch' Cowan was finally laid to rest in the New Churchyard. The final line of the inscription on his gravestone reads 'A Brave Man to Be Remembered'; for surely no-one could ever say that Cowan was anything other than a courageous man and a warrior, whatever faults of leadership he may have possessed.

Admiral Rosslyn Wemyss left the Admiralty on 1 November 1919 never to return. His dismissal rankled with him, as did the fact that unlike *inter alia* Beatty, Jellicoe, Madden and Keyes, he had received no recognition or pecuniary reward for his efforts during the Great War. To King George V, with whom he had been on friendly terms for most of his life, Wemyss did not hold back his disgruntlement. 'Your Majesty will have been aware of the attacks that have been made on the Admiralty for many a month past and of the intrigues which have been going on to oust me,' he wrote after he had left office. Wemyss went on to express his disappointment that his name 'did not appear in the last War Honours list' (this despite the fact that he had been made an Admiral of the Fleet on the day he after he left office and was raised to the peerage as Baron Wester Wemyss, of Wemyss in the County of Fife, on 18 November). In conclusion he stated that he was sad 'to see my naval career terminated at the comparatively early age of fifty-five and my consequent retirement from the service to which I have wholeheartedly devoted forty years of my life'.[3] In retirement he wrote his memoirs and became a non-executive director of Cable & Wireless.

---

[*] In the north-east corner of the nave, rather incongruously above a space given over as a children's play area (in 2018).

He lived for some time in Cannes where he died in his garden on 24 May 1933 and was buried at his ancestral home, Wemyss Castle.

Augustus Agar (incidentally always, and wrongly, referred to in his Admiralty record as 'Augustine') remained in the Royal Navy after the war. Advanced to captain in 1933, at the outbreak of the new world conflict Agar was commanding a destroyer flotilla from which post he took command of the cruiser HMS *Dorsetshire*. On 5 April 1942 she was attacked by Japanese dive-bombers and sunk, south-west of Ceylon. Agar literally went down with his ship, so deep that one of his lungs was permanently damaged, but surfaced to cheer his men through a 24-hour ordeal of sun and shark attack until they were picked up. On his return to England, Agar was appointed Commodore and President, Royal Naval College, Greenwich, a position he held to the end of the war. In 1945 he stood as a Conservative candidate in the General Election but failed to gain a seat, whereupon he retired to a farm at Hartley Mauditt near Alton, Hampshire, to grow strawberries. In 1920, Agar had married Mary Petre, Baroness Furnivall, in Westminster Cathedral. They divorced in 1931 and Agar remarried the following year, taking as his bride Ina Margaret Hurst in a ceremony in Bermuda. He died at his home, Anstey Park House, on 30 December 1968. A private funeral was held on the second day of the new year at Alton Roman Catholic Church, followed by interment in Alton Cemetery.

Claude Dobson served on after the war, and from 1922 to 1925 was assigned to the Royal Australian Navy at Flinders Base, Victoria. On his return he was put on the books of HMS *Victory* for more than six months of unpaid time, while he battled health and vision problems that rendered him fit only for harbour duties. Advanced to captain at the end of 1925, Dobson eventually retired ten years later at his own request. In naval retirement he lived in Walmer and manged a lending library. Dobson married Edith MacMechan in 1920 and they had twin daughters three years later. He was advanced to rear admiral on the retired list in 1936 and died in Chatham Hospital on 26 June 1940, aged only fifty-five. Claude Dobson was buried in Woodlands Cemetery, Gillingham, where there is a memorial stone in his honour, and is also remembered at the Freemasons' Hall, London.

Gordon Charles Steele also remained in service with the Royal Navy and in 1923 was advanced to lieutenant commander. A clever man, who had excelled at his training ship school when a boy, he had an aptitude for foreign languages and became a naval interpreter in Russian. In March 1925 he was appointed to the staff of the Rear Admiral, Submarines*, at Gosport before becoming first lieutenant of the new cruiser HMS *Cornwall* on the China station. In 1929 he choose to go on half-pay, being too young to retire, in order that he might became Captain Superintendent of his *alma mater* HMS *Worcester*, a post he held from that time until 1957, and where he made a number of advanced innovations to the syllabus. After retirement, in January 1958 he found himself the subject of the TV programme *This Is Your Life*, hosted by Eamonn Andrews. He was also a Liveryman and Freeman of the City of London, a Fellow of the Institute of Navigation and a Younger Brother of Trinity House. Gordon Steele died in Exeter on 4 January 1981 in his eighty-ninth year and was buried in All Saints New Cemetery, Winkleigh, Devon, where there is a small memorial cross in his remembrance. His wife, May Mariette, who Steele had married late in life, died the following year.

Estonian Admiral Johan Pitka, who Cowan had described as having 'always shown a most correct instinct for war, both on land and sea'[4] was recognised for his cooperation with the British forces with the award of the KCMG (Knight Commander of St. Michael and St. George) in the January 1920 honours, an award entirely in the gift of the monarch. His own government also recognised him with the Cross of Liberty, First Class, and the Latvians with the Order of Lāčplēsis, Second Class. After independence had been gained, Pitka and his family emigrated to Canada and became farmers there. In 1930 he returned to Estonia and became involved in politics but when the Soviets once more invaded his homeland in 1940, Pitka fled to safety in Finland (where he tried to join the Finnish army, but was rejected owing to his age). His three sons were not so fortunate and were murdered by the communists.

In 1944, Pitka came back to Estonia to help organise military resistance and to fight once more for Estonia's independence. His death is still something of a mystery. Some sources claim he died in combat against a Soviet tank unit, others that he was lost in the Baltic attempting to gain sanctuary in Sweden. Whatever the cause, he lost his life in 1944, aged seventy-two, a warrior still, in combat which he, like Cowan, seemed unable to live without. His wife and daughters, and their families, fled first to Sweden and then re-

---

* Vice Admiral Wilmot S Nicholson.

settled in Canada, and are buried in Vancouver, British Columbia. In 2014, Estonia erected a memorial to Pitka in Tallinn.

What of the 'villains', if villains they be, von der Goltz and Bermondt-Avalov? Gustav Adolf Joachim Rüdiger Graf von der Goltz returned to Germany on 18 December to write his memoirs,[*] in which he claimed that his major strategic goal in 1919 had been to launch a campaign in cooperation with the White Russian forces to overthrow the Bolshevik regime by marching on St Petersburg and effecting the installation of a pro-German and anti-Bolshevist government in Russia. However, he did not disappear from public life. For six years from 1924 he ran the German government department for the military education of German youth and, by reason of his presidency of the United Patriotic Organisations, he participated in the Harzburg Front of 1931, a coalition of right-wing parties opposed to the Weimar government. Goltz died in 1946 aged almost eighty-one, at the Kinsegg estate in the village of Bernbeuren, Bavaria.

On reaching Germany, Bermondt was put in a mental hospital. This at least had the effect of keeping him away from the revenge wished upon him by some British politicians, led by the indefatigable Lieutenant Commander Kenworthy MP. Nevertheless, Bermondt clearly recovered sufficiently to publish his memoirs (in which he noted that he formally resigned command of his army in Berlin on 24 December 1919, having first promoted himself to the rank of major general at the beginning of the month). He lived in Germany from 1921 and, like Goltz, was involved in right-wing movements. But the Nazis imprisoned him and he was subsequently deported to Belgrade from whence he finally moved to the USA, where he died in 1974.

There were undoubtedly some less than angelic men amongst the British sailors deployed. But most ships' crews showed a sort of quotidian heroism. Despite the problems of food, climate and mission, the basic humanity which has always characterised the British sailor was never far from the surface and the compassion displayed to those he rescues and defends is one of the defining features of the Great War Royal Navy. Examples have been cited during the course of this story but one final demonstration can stand for all of those which are unreported and unknown.

Whilst based at Biorko on HMS *Vindictive*, ERA David 'Buck' Taylor remembered playing football in the snow on shore where he

---

[*] *Meine Sendung im Finland und im Baltikum* (Leipzig, 1920).

and his mates were approached by a little boy, about four or five years old and wearing only a man's waistcoat. His parents had been killed by the Bolsheviks. Without a moment's hesitation, they wrapped him in a naval greatcoat. A petty officer took charge of the lad and obtained permission from Captain Grace to bring him on board the carrier. The boy was named Jimmy, put on the ship's books, kitted out with a hammock, toothbrush and clothing and given shoes which were obtained ashore. The crew bought him a train set which he played with on the quarterdeck and Captain Grace was moved to allow him to use his straddled legs as a tunnel. Jimmy was eventually adopted by the anonymous petty officer and taken back to England with *Vindictive*.[5]

There was, of course, one other hero – inanimate and yet still immortal – which survived the battle in the Baltic. *CMB-4*, Agar's boat in the sinking of the *Oleg*, did make it back to England and was exhibited at the Motor Boat Exhibition at Olympia in 1920.[*] Unfortunately, she then lay neglected at Hampton Wick for nearly thirty years. In 1967 she was placed on display at the Shipbuilding Industry Training Board's centre at Southampton; and between November 1982 and April 1984, *CMB-4* was painstakingly restored at the International Boat Building Training Centre at Lowestoft from whence she was later removed to the Imperial War Museum, Duxford, where she can still be viewed, tucked away in a corner.[§]

But perhaps the last word on heroes should be given to the Estonian people, through the mouthpiece of their representatives. At the end of December 1919, the Foreign Office sent to Cowan and the Admiralty an official communication received from the Estonian government. 'The Estonian people,' it read, 'will never forget the bravery and gallantry shown by the British Bluejacket, who has always gone into action with the greatest dash whenever the occasion offered and has not hesitated to risk his life on behalf of our country. You may rest assured that he will always be a welcome guest in our ports.'[6]

---

[*] The 'Motor Boat and Marine and Stationary Engine Exhibition'.
[§] At the time of writing, a replica of *CMB-4* is being constructed at Boatyard No 4 in the Portsmouth Historic Dockyard. There are no extant destroyers from the period and there is only one surviving 'C'-class cruiser, the much-altered museum ship HMS *Caroline*, at the Alexandra Dock, Belfast.

Key Chronology of the Russian Revolution, 1917

Gregorian Date	Event
8 March	International Women's Day; strikes and demonstration in Petrograd, growing in force over the next days.
11 March	Fifty demonstrators killed. Tsar prorogues State Duma and orders Petrograd military district commander to quell demonstrations by force.
12 March	Troops refuse to fire on demonstrators. Prisons, courts and police attacked and looted.
15 March	Tsar Nicolas II abdicates. Provisional government under Prime Minister Prince Lvov formed.
16 April	Lenin returns to Russia.
3–4 May	'April Days'; mass demonstrations by workers, fall of first provisional government.
18 May	First coalition government forms. Kerensky made Minister for War and Navy.
16 June	All Russian Congress of Workers and Soldiers Deputies opens in Petrograd.
16–17 July	'July Days'. Mass armed demonstrations in Petrograd demanding 'all power to the Soviets'.

19 July	Major retreat by Russian army. Arrest of Bolshevik leaders ordered.
20 July	Lvov resigns, Kerensky becomes prime minister.
4 August	Trotsky arrested.
8 September	Second coalition government ends.
8–12 September	Kornilov mutiny.
13 September	Petrograd Soviet approves Bolshevik motion for an all-socialist government which excludes the bourgeoisie.
14 September	Russia declared republic.
17 September	Trotsky and others freed.
18 September	Bolshevik resolution on government wins majority vote in Moscow Soviet.
8 October	Third coalition government formed. Bolshevik majority in Petrograd Soviet elects Bolshevik Presidium and Trotsky as chairman.
23 October	Bolshevik Central Committee approves armed uprising.
2 November	First meeting of Military Revolutionary Committee (MRC) of the Petrograd Soviet.
7 November	October Revolution launched by MRC. Winter Palace attacked and captured. Kerensky flees Petrograd.
8 November	Second congress of Soviets. Walkout of Mensheviks and moderates. Congress approves formation of all-Bolshevik government with Lenin as chairman.

Article XII of the 1918 Armistice

II. Disposition Relative to the Eastern Frontiers of Germany

Twelve – All German troops at present in the territories which before belonged to Austria-Hungary, Rumania, Turkey, shall withdraw immediately within the frontiers of Germany as they existed on August First, Nineteen Fourteen. *All German troops at present in the territories which before the war belonged to Russia shall likewise withdraw within the frontiers of Germany, defined as above, as soon as the Allies, taking into account the internal situation of these territories, shall decide that the time for this has come.*

[author's italics].

Armistice signed 0500 on 11 November, to come into effect six hours later, at 1100.

Admiralty Naval Expenditure and Estimates, 1915–1920

Year

1915–16 £205,733,597 net
1916–17 £209,877,218 net
1917–18 £227,388,891 net
1918–19 £325,000,000 (estimated)
1919–20 £157,528,800 (estimated)

Run Rate November 1918

The weekly rate of expenditure on the Royal Navy at the time of the Armistice was about £6,750,000 or a rate of more than £350,000,000 a year.

(Source: statement of the First Lord of the Admiralty, 1 December 1919, HMSO)

The CMBs at Kronstadt, August 1919

Boat	Officers	Boat Fate
31BD	Cdr Claude C Dobson DSO RN Lt Russell H MacBean RN Sub Lt John C Boldero	
86BD	Sub Lt Francis W Howard RNR Sub Lt Robert Leslie Wight RN Act Sub Lt Francis Walter Howard RNR	Damaged
88BD	Lt Archibald Dayrell-Reed DSO RNR Lt Gordon C Steele RN Act Sub Lt Norman Eyre Morley RN	Damaged
72A	Sub Lt Edward R Bodley RNR Sub Lt Roland Hunter-Blair RN	
7A	Lt Augustus W S Agar RN Sub Lt Edgar Robert Sindall RNR	
79A	Lt William H Bremner DSC RN	Sunk
62BD	Acting Lt Cdr Frank T Brade DSC RNR	Sunk
24A	Lt Laurence L S Napier RN	Sunk

Litvinov in Copenhagen

Maxim Litvinov (born Meir Henoch Mojszewicz Wallach-Finkelstein) had been appointed as the Bolsheviks' unofficial representative in Britain but was arrested by the British government in 1918 on a charge of having addressed public gatherings held in opposition to the British intervention in Russia. He was later exchanged for Robert Bruce-Lockhart, who held an analogous position in Moscow, and had been imprisoned by the Russians for alleged spying.

Litvinov's mission to Denmark was not initially successful. The British representative there allegedly handed back to Litvinov unopened the letter containing the proposals he had been sent to make. Litvinov therefore made contact with James O'Grady, MP for Leeds, and General Secretary of the National Federation of General Workers since 1918.

O'Grady met with Litvinov in late November and British consul Herbert Adolphus Grant Watson in Copenhagen reported on 2 December that O'Grady had told him that 'the Soviet government definitely wants to come to an understanding with border Baltic states and that His Majesty's Government were the Chief Obstacle to making peace'.[1] Watson asked if he should make a statement to the effect that this was not so and that 'any consideration of peace is entirely one for border states and the Soviet government to decide'.[2]

Questions were raised in the House of Commons about this contact on 15 December with voices calling both for O'Grady to be banned from meeting with the Russian emissary and for Lloyd George to interest himself in the proposals.

Lloyd George ducked the issue, replying that 'if the Soviet authorities in Russia want to make peace they must make it with the people with whom they are at war – with General Denikin, General Kolchak, and others. They must make peace amongst themselves first'.[3]

Nonetheless, O'Grady was later credited with achieving some success dealing with Litvinov with regards to prisoner exchange, including Lieutenant Bremner who was released to Copenhagen on 4 February 1920.

British Casualties, Baltic Campaign

Royal Navy	Officers	Men
Killed	16	107
Wounded	8	50
Taken Prisoner	3	6

Royal Air Force		
Killed	4	1
Wounded	2	0
Total casualties	33	164

The Royal Navy lost a total of 123 officers and ratings killed in action plus a further 58 wounded.

Royal Navy Ship Losses, Baltic Campaign, 1918–1919

1 Submarine, *L-55*, mined and sunk.

1 Destroyer, *Verulam*, mined and sunk.

1 Destroyer, *Vittoria*, torpedoed and sunk by enemy submarine.

2 Minesweeping Sloops, *Gentian* and *Myrtle*, mined and sunk.

3 Coastal Motor Boats sunk during the attack on Kronstadt.

2 Coastal Motor Boats blown up; unserviceable.

2 Coastal Motor Boats and 2 Motor Launches sunk through stress of weather whilst in tow.

1 Store Carrier, *Volturnus*, mined and sunk.

1 Light Cruiser, *Curacoa*, mined and salved.

1 Light Cruiser, *Cassandra*, mined and sunk.

1 Paddle Minesweeper, *Banbury*, mined and salved.

1 Motor Launch, *ML-156*, mined and salved but written off.

1 Admiralty Oiler, *War Expert*, mined and salved.

1 Mine-layer *Princess Margaret*, damaged by mine.

A total of sixty-one destroyers, minesweepers and other ships, including the light cruiser *Calypso,* were damaged and repaired locally or sent back to England for attention.

(Sources; CAB 24/96/69, NA; Bennett, *Cowan's War*, p 228)

Royal Navy Warships and Auxiliaries deployed in the Baltic Campaign

Light Cruisers 23
Destroyers and Flotilla Leaders 85
P-Boats 3
Monitors 1
Depot Ships 4
Minelayers 2
Submarines 20
Minesweepers 18
Aircraft Carrier 1 (plus a total of 55 aircraft)
Coastal Motor Boats 10
Motor Launches 4
Despatch Vessels 1
Trawlers and Drifters 3
Tugs 3
Oilers 28
Colliers 17
Ammunition Ships 2
Store-ships, Carriers etc 9
Lighters 3
Hospital Ship 1

Total 238

(Sources; CAB 24/96/69; Bennett, *Cowan's War*, p 227)

List of Place Names

Place names used by the Royal Navy and in this book with the modern name in brackets.

Bolderaa (Bolderāja)
Biorko Sound (Björkö Sound, Korsholm; now the Russian
    Beryozovye Islands)
Brest-Litovsk (Brest)
Dorpat (Tartu)
Dunamunde (Daugavgr va)
Dvina (Daugava) River
Elsinore (Helsingør)
Goldingen (Kuldīga)
Helsingfors (Helsinki)
Kaporia (Kaporje, Koporye, Kaporskaja) Bay
Kristiania (Oslo)
Kronstadt (Kronstadt)
Kunda (Kunda)
Libau (Liepāja)
Mitau (Jelgava)
Nargen Island (Naissaar)
Narva (Narva)
Ösel Island (Saarenmaa)
Petrograd (St Petersburg)
Pupe (Babite)
Reval (Tallinn)
Riga (Riga)
Seskar (Seiskari) Island
Stirs Point (Styrsudd)
Walk (Valga)
Wenden (Cēsis)
Windau (Ventspils)
Wulf Island (Aegna)

Author's Notes

I wrote this book firstly because I thought it was important to tell a story that few people now, and indeed then, understand. But I also think it important because it prefigures a recurring motif of modern times – the tension between political judgement (or the lack of it) and the actual reality of executing political decisions on the ground and under fire.

Secondly, the tale is also interesting because the period it is set in it marks a fault line between the Britain of the nineteenth century and a more recognisably modern one; but first the country had to pass through a post-war depression which can be said to have lasted nearly twenty years.

The Royal Navy also had to change, or perhaps more accurately, was forced to change. The Washington Naval Treaty of 1922, gave away forever Britain's naval leadership to the USA. In the words of one historian, 'few in Britain suspected that the Royal Navy's overwhelming lead in both numbers, expertise and war experience, coupled with age-old tradition, would be ever eroded ... The British had not banked on the fickleness and short-sightedness of their own politicians, coupled with the burning ambition of the United States, to wrest the trident away.'[1] It was an implicit recognition of at least two verities; Britain no longer had the economic supremacy that she had before the war; and the USA had gained massively in terms of finance and power projection from the world conflict.

Lastly, I wrote the book because it is easy to forget the sacrifices which ordinary men made in the campaign and the lives lost or blighted. It is not fashionable to talk about Britain's post-1918 wars. But men died to serve their country and help protect or create new nationhood and, in common with the Earl of Carlisle, I think it is important that they are not overlooked in the greater loss of the hecatombs of the First World War. Out of common courtesy, and because they have the euphony and flavour of the times, I have given the participants in the story their full names when first met.

The story has been told from a largely British prospective and mainly (but not solely, see bibliography) using Anglophone sources;

278

however, it is informed by wide reading of academic books on Russia and the Baltic. It was not an easy book to write but I bless the memory of the nameless member of the Admiralty Historical Section who decided to arrange the Baltic telegrams into sequential files, now held at the National Archives; that gave me somewhere to start.

The writer of historical works in the UK is helped considerably by both the quality and the availability of archives and by the skill of the archivists who manage them. To the staff and trustees of the following institutions I owe a continued debt of thanks. The National Archives, Kew; the Imperial War Museum, London; the Churchill Archive, Churchill College, Cambridge; and the Liddle Collection, University of Leeds Library (Special Collections). In addition, those who maintain on-line resources, such as the incomparable http://www.naval-history.net deserve my gratitude. And a special word of thanks is merited to the tribe of second-hand booksellers, who provide out-of-print editions of all sorts of valuable source volumes.

This is my fifth book with Seaforth Publishing and I thank Julian Mannering of that esteemed house for his continued support and sage advice. The book's index was once again prepared by the indefatigable Dave Cradduck, with his usual skill and promptitude. Peter Wilkinson drew the maps with artistry and Ernest Bondarenko took some excellent photographs in Tallinn. Dr Vaughan Michell, chairman of the Britannia Naval Research Association, kindly allowed me to reproduce two fascinating pictures of a restored 40ft CMB. And from the USA, Tony Lovell helped with a fire-control question.

Most books contain errors of commission or omission. If there are errors or solecisms in this volume the fault is mine and I should like to hear of them; to err is human.

My friends in both Britain and France support me in my peculiar fascination for the Royal Navy of the early twentieth century, without necessarily understanding it. And to Vivienne I offer my undying thanks for the help, support and belief in me and my books which makes them possible.

Notes

The following abbreviations will be used.

Institutions

IWM   Imperial War Museum, London.

NA   National Archives, Kew.

CAC   Churchill Archive, Churchill College, Cambridge.

LC   Liddle Collection, Brotherton Library, University of Leeds.

Books

BNAE Hiden and Salmon, *The Baltic Nations and Europe.*

FDTSF Marder, *From the Dreadnought to Scapa Flow.*

TTF   Lieven, *Towards The Flame.*

It is the convention that page numbers be given for citations. This is not always possible in the modern world. Some digitised documents lack page numbering and some archives hold unnumbered single or multiple sheets in bundles under one reference or none at all. Thus, page numbers will be given where possible but the reader will understand that they are not always available or, indeed, necessary.

Chapter 1

1. *TTF*, p 83.
2. *BNAE*, p 14.
3. Ibid, p 17.
4. Ibid, p 21.
5. *TTF*, p 190.
6. Ibid.
7. *TTF*, p 103.
8. Ibid, p 350.
9. Churchill, *The Aftermath*, p 284.
10. CAB 23/16/2, NA.

Chapter 2

1. *Daily Telegraph*, 28 December 1917.
2. Figes, *People's Tragedy*, p 538.

3. *TTF*, p 2.
4. Kinvig, *Churchill's Crusade*, p 5.
5. CAB/23/4, NA.
6. Spinney, *Pale Rider*, p 67.
7. Kasekamp, *A History of the Baltic States*, p 90.
8. 18 October 1918, CAB 24/70, NA.
9. *Baltic Times*, 15 December 2004.
10. CAB 24/87, NA.
11. Gerwarth, *The Vanquished*, p 69.

Chapter 3
1. CAB 23/8/8, NA.
2. Ibid.
3. Ibid.
4. Hattersley, *David Lloyd George*, p 500.
5. CAB 23/8/8, NA.
6. Ibid.
7. Ibid.
8. Beatty to Wemyss 12 November 1918, ADM 116/1825, NA.
9. Docs 13776, IWM.
10. Docs 11909, IWM.
11. ADM116/1772, NA.
12. FO 371/3361, NA.
13. FO 371/3361 and ADM 137/1663, NA.
14. The Diary of Ove Rode.
15. ADM 116/1772, NA.
16. CAB 23/42/10, NA.
17. Ibid.
18. Balfour to Wemyss, 28 November 1918, ADM 116/1602, NA.
19. ADM 137/1949.
20. Roskill, *Naval Policy*, p 145.
21. ADM 137/1663, NA.
22. 29 November 1918, ADM 116/1602, NA.
23. Bonar Law to Geddes, 23 November 1918, ADM116/1809, NA.
24. 22 November 1918, ADM 116/1605, NA.
25. Copy of will in private collection.
26. *FDTSF*, vol 2, p 16.
27. ADM 203/99, ADM 203/100, NA.
28. Bennett, *Cowan's War*, p 35.
29. Docs 13776, IWM.
30. Docs 23738, IWM.
31. Docs 13776, IWM.
32. Ibid.

Chapter 4
1. Docs 11909, IWM.
2. Ibid.
3. Docs 23738, IWM.
4. Ibid.
5. Ibid.
6. Docs 11909, IWM.
7. 6 December 1918, docs 5609, IWM.
8. Docs 23738, IWM.
9. Liddle/WW1/RMNM276, LC.
10. ADM 137/3810, NA.
11. Ibid.
12. Ibid.
13. Docs 13776, IWM.
14. Dunn, *Securing the Narrow Sea*, p 64.
15. Bennett, *Cowan's War*, p 38.
16. Docs 13776, IWM.
17. Ibid.
18. Ibid.
19. Ibid.

20. Ibid.
21. Ibid.
22. Ibid.
23. Docs 11909, IWM.
24. Ibid.

Chapter 5
1. *Baltic Times*, 15 December 2004.
2. Bennett, *Cowan's War*, p 39.
3. Ibid, p 41.
4. Docs 13776, IWM.
5. CAB 23/42, NA.
6. Ibid.
7. Liddle/WW1/RNMN276, LC.
8. Ibid.

Chapter 6
1. CHAR 2/105/2, CAC.
2. Speech in Wolverhampton, 24 November 1918.
3. RECO 1/775, NA.
4. Speech 24 November 1918, Gilbert, *The Stricken World*, p 227.
5. Kinvig, *Churchill's Crusade*, p 164.
6. Gilbert, *Stricken World*, p 278.
7. Hattersley, *David Lloyd George*, p 502.
8. Ibid.
9. Somervell, *British Politics since 1900*, p 134.
10. Ullman, *Britain and the Russian Civil War*, p 153.
11. CAB 23/42, NA.
12. *New York Times* Current History, https://novaonline.nvcc.edu/eli/evans/HIS242/Documents/Prinkipo.pdf

13. *Spectator*, 1 February 1919.
14. *New York Times* Current History, https://novaonline.nvcc.edu/eli/evans/HIS242/Documents/Prinkipo.pdf
15. Ibid.
16. CAB 23/9/18, NA.
17. Ibid.
18. Ibid.
19. CAB 23/15/2, NA.
20. Ibid.
21. Ibid.
22. Ibid.
23. Ibid.
24. Ibid.
25. Ibid.
26. Roskill, *Hankey*, vol 2, p 62.

Chapter 7
1. *FDTSF*, vol 2, p 9.
2. Ibid, p 18.
3. Smith, *A Yellow Admiral Remembers*, p 272.
4. Bennett, *Cowan's War*, p 59.
5. Ibid, p 66.
6. Oglander, *Roger Keyes*, p 71.
7. Keyes, *Adventures Ashore and Afloat*, p 331.
8. Cunningham, *A Sailor's Odyssey*, p 137.
9. ADM 137/1664, NA.
10. Ibid.
11. Dawson, *Sound of the Guns*, p 151.
12. ADM 137/1664, NA.
13. Ibid.
14. de Courcy-Ireland, *A Naval Life*, pp 60–1.
15. ADM 137/1664, NA.

16. Ibid.
17. Bennett, *Cowan's War*, p 77.
18. CAB 24/96/69, NA.
19. ADM 137/1665, NA.

Chapter 8
1. Quoted in Gerwarth, *The Vanquished*, pp 70–1.
2. CAB 24/97, NA.
3. CAB 24/87, NA.
4. Gerwarth, *The Vanquished*, p 72.
5. Bennett, *Cowan's War*, pp 80–1.
6. Office of the Historian papers relating to the foreign relations of the United States, the Paris Peace Conference, 1919, volume XII.
7. CAB 23/15/7, NA.
8. Ibid.
9. Ibid.
10. Ibid.
11. Ibid.
12. Ibid.
13. Ibid.
14. United States Department of State; Papers relating to the foreign relations of the United States, 1919. Russia (1919) Chapter IV. The Baltic provinces, p 673.
15. CAB 23/15/7, NA.
16. Ibid.
17. Wemyss, *Life and Letters*, p 443.
18. Hansard HC Deb 16 April 1919 vol 114 cc2944-6.
19. Ibid.
20. Cunningham, *A Sailor's Odyssey*, p 100.
21. Ibid.
22. Wilson, *Empire of the Deep*, p 463.
23. Cunningham, *A Sailor's Odyssey*, p 100.
24. ADM 137/1665, NA.
25. Docs 7433, IWM.
26. Ibid.
27. Ibid.
28. Cunningham, *A Sailor's Odyssey*, p 102.
29. Ibid, p 103.
30. Ibid, p 104.
31. CAB 24/96/69, NA.

Chapter 9
1. United States Department of State/Papers relating to the foreign relations of the United States, 1919. Russia; Chapter IV: The Baltic provinces, p 676.
2. Ibid.
3. ADM 137/1665, NA.
4. Dawson, *Sound of the Guns*, p 155.
5. Ibid, p 156.
6. Docs 4865, IWM
7. Ibid.
8. Ibid.
9. Ibid.
10. ADM 196/45/53, NA.
11. ADM 116/2062, NA.
12. Dukes, *Red Dusk*, p 189.
13. Ibid.
14. Diary 22 May, WLLS 3/1, CAC.
15. Ibid, 23 May.
16. Ibid.
17. Ibid, 27 May.
18. Ibid, 31 May.

19. Ibid.
20. Docs 6898, IWM.
21. Docs 16636, IWM.
22. Docs 7433, IWM.
23. United States Department of State/Papers relating to the foreign relations of the United States, 1919. Russia Chapter IV: The Baltic provinces, p 679.
24. ADM 203/99, 203/100, NA.
25. CAB 24/96/69, NA.
26. Dawson, *Sound of the Guns*, p 162.
27. CAB 24/96/69, NA.
28. Agar, *Baltic Episode*, p 104.

Chapter 10
1. Liddle/WW1/029.
2. Diary 6 June, WLLS 3/1, CAC.
3. Ibid, 8 June.
4. ADM 196/52/301, NA.
5. Evans, *Keeping the Seas*, p 187.
6. Crawford, *Fallen Glory*, p 84.
7. Agar, *Baltic Episode*, p 3.
8. Ibid, p 25.
9. Ibid.
10. Diary 4 June, WLLS 3/1, CAC.
11. Agar, *Baltic Episode*, p 49.
12. Diary 4 June, WLLS 3/1, CAC.
13. Agar, *Baltic Episode*, p 50.
14. Agar, *Footsteps in the Sea*, p 97.
15. Ibid, p 99.
16. Agar, *Baltic Episode*, p 75.
17. Docs 16636, IWM.
18. Agar, *Baltic Episode*, p 82.
19. Ibid.
20. Agar, *Footprints in the Sea*, p 112.

21. Ibid.
22. Agar, *Baltic Episode*, p 87.
23. Ibid, p 93.
24. Hansard, HC Deb 13 August 1919 vol 119 cc1278-9.
25. Agar, *Baltic Episode*, p 108.
26. ADM 137/1679, NA.

Chapter 11
1. Diary 13 June, WLLS 3/1, CAC.
2. Ibid.
3. Webb, *1919*, p 104.
4. CAB 24/82/13, NA.
5. Ibid.
6. Ibid.
7. Ibid.
8. Docs 17490, IWM.
9. 8 July, ADM 37/1667, NA.
10. CAB 224/5/66, NA.
11. Ibid.
12. Ibid.
13. FO 608/192, NA.
14. CAB 24/5/66, NA.
15. ADM 137/1667.
16. Ibid.
17. *Spectator*, 7 June 1919.
18. hmshood.com.
19. Taffrail, *Endless Story*, p 317.
20. Dawson, *Sound of the Guns*, p 165.
21. ADM196/144/82, NA.
22. ADM 116/2062, NA.
23. ADM 137/1667, NA.
24. ADM 116/2062, NA.
25. Docs 5609, IWM.
26. ADM 137/3818, NA.
27. ADM 137/1667, NA.
28. Ibid.
29. *London Gazette* 31748 – 20 January 1920.

30. 23 July, ADM 137/1667, NA.
31. Docs 7433, IWM.
32. Dawson, *Sound of the Guns*, p 164.
33. Docs 8535, IWM.
34. Diary 12 July, WLLS 3/1, CAC.
35. Docs 8535, IWM.
36. 5 August 1919, ADM137/1667, NA.
37. CAB 24/88/93, NA.
38. 5 August 1919, ADM137/1667, NA.
39. Docs 8535, IWM.
40. Docs 7433, IWM.
41. CAB 24/88/93, NA.
42. Ibid.
43. Ibid.
44. 5 August 1919, ADM137/1667, NA.
45. ADM 196/45/170, NA.
46. Hansard, HC Deb 23 July 1919 vol 118 cc1331-2.

Chapter 12

1. Agar, *Baltic Episode*, p 105.
2. Ibid.
3. Cannadine, *Decline and Fall of the British Aristocracy*, p 277.
4. Lake, *The Zeebrugge and Ostend Raids 1918*, p 20.
5. Fremantle, *My Naval Career*, p 237.
6. Marder, *Fear God and Dread Nought*, vol III, p 497.
7. Roskill, *Earl Beatty*, p 285.
8. Letter to King George V post resignation WMYSS 5/3, CAC.
9. Wemyss, *Letters*, p 443.
10. Ibid, p 444.
11. Diary 8 August, WLLS 3/1, CAC.
12. ADM 196/50/15, NA.
13. Agar, *Footprints in the Sea*, p 324.
14. Docs 8535, IWM.
15. CAB 24/88/93, NA.
16. Ibid.
17. Ibid.
18. Ibid.
19. Ibid.
20. Docs 8535, IWM.
21. 31 August 1919, ADM 137/1679, NA.
22. Wemyss, *Letters*, p 444.
23. Ibid.
24. *The Times*, 11 October 1919.
25. Agar, *Footprints in the Sea*, p 142.

Chapter 13

1. Docs 16636, IWM.
2. Ibid.
3. Ibid.
4. Ibid.
5. CAB 24/88/93, NA.
6. Docs 16636, IWM.
7. Ibid.
8. Ibid.
9. Ibid.
10. ADM 137/3824, NA.
11. Ibid.
12. CAB 24/88/93, NA.
13. Docs 16636, IWM.
14. ADM 156/178, NA.
15. Docs 16636, IWM.
16. Ibid.
17. de Courcy Ireland, *A Naval Life*, p 75.
18. Ibid.
19. ADM 156/178, NA.
20. CAB 24/88/93.

21. Docs 16636, IWM.
22. ADM 156/178, NA.
23. 5 August 1919, ADM 137/1667, NA.
24. CAB 24/88/93, NA.
25. *London Gazette* 31748, 20 January 1920.
26. Docs 16636, IWM.
27. CAB 24/88/93, NA.
28. Docs 8535, IWM.
29. Ibid.
30. Ibid.
31. *London Gazette* 30913, 20 September 1918.
32. CAB 24/94, NA.
33. Ibid.
34. CAB 24/88/93, NA.
35. Ibid.
36. Ibid.
37. Agar, *Baltic Episode*, p 199.
38. Docs 16636, IWM.
39. 4 November, ADM 137/1668, NA.
40. Ibid.
41. CAB 24/88/93, NA.
42. 4 November, ADM 137/1668, NA.
43. 15 November, ADM 137/1668, NA.

Chapter 14
1. FO 608/192, NA.
2. CAB 24/94, NA.
3. Ibid.
4. Duff 28 August 1919, ADM 137/1667, NA.
5. CAB 23/94, NA.
6. *BNAE*, p 37.
7. 4 November, ADM 137/1668, NA.

8. 28 October 1919, ADM 137/1664, NA.
9. Bennett, *Cowan's War*, pp 176–7.
10. CAB 24/96/69, NA.
11. Docs 4632, IWM.
12. *New York Times*, 20 October 1919.
13. Docs 4632, IWM.
14. *New York Times*, 20 October 1919.
15. Ibid.
16. ADM 196/90/85, NA.
17. Cannadine, *George V*, p 79.
18. ADM 137/1668, NA.
19. 18 October 1919, ADM 134/1667, NA.
20. Ibid.
21. http://www.hmsdragon1919.co.uk/16280.html
22. Docs 4632, IWM.
23. Docs 4312, IWM.

Chapter 15
1. 28 October, ADM 137/1664, NA.
2. Ibid.
3. Liddle/WW1/RNMN/050, LC.
4. CAB 24/96/69, NA.
5. 4 November, ADM 137/1668, NA.
6. 8 November, ADM 137/1668, NA.
7. *New York Times*, 6 November 1919.
8. 8 November, ADM 137/1668, NA.
9. ADM 137/1668, NA.
10. Liddle/WW1/RNMN/050, LC.
11. CAB 24/96/69, NA.

Chapter 16

1. 2 December 1918, docs 5609, IWM.
2. Docs 16636, IWM.
3. Agar, *Footprints in the Sea*, p 230.
4. Docs 7309, IWM.
5. Docs 5609, IWM.
6. Ibid.
7. Docs 11909, IWM.
8. Docs 13776, IWM.
9. Docs 11909, IWM.
10. Docs 16636, IWM.
11. Docs 23738, IWM.
12. Docs 4312, IWM.
13. Diary 4 July, WLLS 3/1, CAC.
14. CAB 24/96/69, NA.
15. Docs 13776, IWM.
16. Docs 16636, IWM.
17. Ibid.
18. Docs 6898, IWM.
19. Ibid.
20. Ibid.
21. Ibid.
22. Ibid.
23. Docs 7309, IWM.
24. Docs 4312, 28 October 1919, IWM.
25. Ibid.
26. Diary 28 May, WLLS 3/1, CAC.
27. Docs 8535, IWM.
28. Diary 24 May, WLLS 3/1, CAC.
29. 11 December 1918, docs 5609, IWM.
30. Docs 4312, IWM.
31. Hindenburg, quoted in Lee, *The Warlords*, pp 375–6.
32. Diary 19 June, WLLS 3/1, CAC.
33. Ibid.
34. Diary 17 June, WLLS 3/1, CAC.
35. Docs 8535, IWM.
36. Roskill, *Hankey*, vol 2, p 95.
37. Docs 5609, IWM.
38. Ibid.
39. Diary 6 June, WLLS 3/1, CAC.
40. Diary 17 June, WLLS 3/1, CAC.
41. Docs 13776, IWM.
42. 6 December 1918, docs 5609, IWM.
43. Docs 11909, IWM.
44. Docs 7433, IWM.
45. Liddle /WW1/RNMN/276, LC.
46. ADM 137/1664, NA.
47. Ibid.
48. Docs 7433, IWM.
49. Docs 6898, IWM.
50. Ibid.
51. September 1919, docs 4632, IWM.
52. October 1919, ibid.
53. Ibid.
54. Docs 7433, IWM.
55. Docs 12746, IWM.
56. Docs 7309, IWM.
57. Ibid.
58. Ibid.
59. Ibid.
60. Ibid.
61. Docs 16636, IWM.
62. Ibid.

Chapter 17

1. Wemyss, *Letters*, p 413.
2. Hansard, HC Deb 12 March 1919 vol 113 cc1324-431.
3. Fremantle, *My Naval Career*, p 261.

4. Wemyss, *Letters*, p 427.

5. Docs 16636, IWM.

6. WMYSS 5/3, CAC.

7. ADM 156/94, NA.

8. Ibid.

9. Ibid.

10. Liddle/WW1/RNMN/050, LC.

11. Ibid.

12. Ibid.

13. ADM 156/94, NA.

14. Ibid.

15. Hansard, HC Deb 29 October 1919 vol 120 cc641-2.

16. ADM 156/50, NA.

17. IWM docs 4312.

18. ADM 156/50, NA.

19. Ibid.

20. Docs 16636, IWM.

21. Bennett, *Cowan's War*, p 202.

22. Docs 16636, IWM.

23. Ibid.

24. Docs 6898, IWM.

25. Hansard HC Deb 03 December 1919 vol 122 cc373-4.

26. Docs 7309, IWM.

27. Diary 10 July, WLLS 3/1, CAC.

Chapter 18

1. Diary 25 August 1919, Roskill, *Hankey*, vol 2, p 107.

2. LG/F/9/1/20 Parliamentary Archives.

3. Kinvig, *Churchill's Crusade*, p xii.

4. CAB 24/90, NA.

5. CAB 23/18/2, NA.

6. Ibid.

7. Ibid.

8. Ibid.

9. CAB/24/92.

10. Webb, *1919*, p 141.

11. HC Deb 20 November 1919 vol 121 cc1106.

12. Ibid.

13. CAB 24/94/19, NA.

14. i/v 22 November, Cowan 25 November, ADM 137/1668, NA.

15. US State Department, Office of the Historian 861.00/5770.

16. Hansard HC Deb 20 November 1919 vol 121 cc1108-9.

Chapter 19

1. Docs 16636, IWM.

2. 25 November, ADM 137/1668, NA.

3. Docs 8535, IWM.

4. Diary 12 November, WLLS 3/1, CAC.

5. Docs 16636, IWM.

6. Dawson, *Sound of the Guns*, p 176.

7. Diary 13 December, WLLS 3/1, CAC.

8. Liddle/WW1/RNMN/050, LC.

9. Docs 4312, IWM.

10. Ibid.

11. Docs 6898, IWM.

12. ADM 196/146/639, NA.

13. WO 106/627, NA.

14. Ibid.

15. CAB 24/106, NA.

Chapter 20

1. *Baltic Times*, 15 December 2004.

2. Smele, *The Russian Civil Wars*, p 23.

3. HC Deb 09 December 1919 vol 122 cc1099-101.

4. HC Deb 10 December 1919 vol 122 cc1368-478.
5. HC Deb 18 December 1919 vol 123 cc647-8.
6. HC Deb 12 February 1920 vol 125 cc199-200.
7. Hansard 03 December 1919 vol 122 cc373-4.

Chapter 21

1. Twiss, CAB 24/95, NA.
2. Ludendorff, *Own Story*, vol II, p 376.
3. Dawson, *Sound of the Guns*, p 252.
4. Ibid, p 253.
5. Churchill, *Churchill in His Own Words*, p 148.
6. Niall Ferguson, *Sunday Times*, 12 November 2017.
7. Ibid.
8. Ibid.
9. *Spectator*, 1 June 1918.
10. Orwell, *Road to Wigan Pier*, p 167.
11. Somervell, *British Politics since the War*, p 124.
12. Liddle/WW1/RNMN/029, LC.
13. Murray, *Herring Tales*, pp 92–3
14. Somervell, *British Politics since the War*, pp 135–6.
15. MKN 9/16, CAC.
16. Bennett, *Cowan's War*, p 137.
17. Diary 6 June, WLLS 3/1, CAC.
18. Hansard HC Deb 19 November 1919 vol 121 cc892-3.
19. Docs 16636, 5 November 1919, IWM.
20. 21 October 1919, ADM 156/94, NA.
21. Liddle/WW1/RNMN/287, LC.
22. Quoted in Massie, *Dreadnought*, p 431.
23. Fisher, *Memories*, p 274.

Chapter 22

1. Taylor, *End of Glory*, p 78.
2. *London Gazette*, 36687, 1 September 1944.
3. WMYS 5/3, CAC.
4. *London Gazette* 31856, 6 April 1920.
5. Liddle/WW1/RNMN/287, LC.
6. 2 December, ADM 137/1668, NA.

Appendix 5

1. CHAR 2/106/142, CAC.
2. Ibid.
3. Hansard HC Deb 15 December 1919 vol 123 cc22-4.

Author's Notes

1. Smith, *Into the Minefields*, p 98.

Bibliography

Primary Sources

Papers of Captain R P Selby, documents 5609, Imperial War Museum, London.

Papers of CPO ERA J F Foster, documents 23738, Imperial War Museum.

Papers of PO Stoker F W Smith, documents 11909, Imperial War Museum.

Papers of Commander A G D Bagot, documents 4632, Imperial War Museum.

Papers of Surgeon Lieutenant W O Lodge, documents 4865, Imperial War Museum.

Papers of A T Wilkinson, documents 6898, Imperial War Museum.

Papers of Captain E R Conder, documents 16636, Imperial War Museum.

Papers of Lieutenant Commander P L Puxley, documents 17490, Imperial War Museum.

Papers of H B Boyd, documents 13776, Imperial War Museum.

Papers of R F Rose, documents 7433, Imperial War Museum.

Papers of W J Robinson, documents 12746, Imperial War Museum.

Papers of Commander J E P Brass, documents 7309, Imperial War Museum.

Papers of Captain R Gotto, documents 4312, Imperial War Museum.

Papers of Squadron Leader E Bremerton, documents 8535, Imperial War Museum.

Many and various documents in the ADM, CAB, FO, WO and RECO series, individually cited, The National Archives, Kew.

Papers of Captain R W Blacklock, Liddle/WW1/RNMN 029,

University of Leeds Library Special Collections, Leeds.

Papers of Captain S F Stapleton, Liddle/WW1/RNMN 276, University of Leeds Library Special Collections.

Papers of Commander C F H Churchill, Liddle/WW1/RNMN 050, University of Leeds Library Special Collections.

Private Papers of D Taylor, Liddle/WW1/RNMN 287, University of Leeds Library Special Collections.

The Diary of Ove Rode, Minister of the Interior, 1914–1918, Universitetsforlaget (Aarhus, 1972).

Papers of Sir Reginald McKenna, MKN 9/16, Churchill Archive Centre, Cambridge.

Papers of Sir Winston S Churchill, CHAR 2 and CHAR 13, Churchill Archive Centre.

Papers of Admiral Sir Algernon Willis, WLLS 3/1, Churchill Archive Centre.

Papers of Admiral Sir Rosslyn Wemyss, WMYS 5/3, Churchill Archive Centre.

Papers of Air Commodore Francis Banks, FROB 2/1, Churchill Archive Centre.

Papers of D Lloyd George, LG/F/9/1/29, Parliamentary Archive, London.

Secondary Sources

The following books and other publications have been cited in the text. The place of publication is London unless otherwise indicated.

Books

Agar, A, *Baltic Episode* (Annapolis: Naval Institute Press, 1983: originally published Hodder and Stoughton, 1963).

_____, *Footprints in the Sea* (Evans Brothers Limited, 1959).

Bennett, G, *Cowan's War* (Collins, 1964).

Cannadine, D, *The Decline and Fall of the British Aristocracy* (Papermac, 1996).

_____, *George V* (Allen Lane, 2004).

Churchill, W, *The Aftermath* (New York: Charles Scribner's and Sons 1929).

_____, ed Langworth, R, *Churchill in His Own Words* (Ebury, 2012).

Crawford, J, *Fallen Glory* (Old St Publishing, 2016).

Cunningham, A, *A Sailor's Odyssey* (Hutchinson, 1951).

Dawson, L, *Sound of the Guns* (Oxford: Pen-in-Hand Publishing, 1949)

De Courcy-Ireland S, *A Naval Life* (Englang Publishing, 1990).

Dukes, P, *Red Dusk and the Morrow* (Biteback Publishing, 2012: originally published 1922).

Dunn, S, *Securing the Narrow Sea* (Barnsley: Seaforth Publishing, 2017).

Evans, E, *Keeping the Seas* (Sampson, Low, Marston and Co, 1920).

Figes, O, *A People's Tragedy* (Pimlico, 1997).

Fisher, J, *Memories* (Hodder and Stoughton, 1919).

Fremantle, S, *My Naval Career* (Hutchinson and Co, 1949).

Gerwarth, R, *The Vanquished* (Penguin Books, 2017).

Gilbert, M, *Winston S. Churchill, Vol IV The Stricken World 1916-1922* (Heinemann, 1975).

Hattersley, R, *David Lloyd George* (Abacus, 2012).

Hiden, J, and Salmon, P, *The Baltic Nations and Europe* (Longman, 1994).

Hopkirk, P, *Setting the East Ablaze* (John Murray, 2006).

Kasekamp, A, *A History of the Baltic States* (Palgrave, 2010).

Keyes, R, *Adventures Ashore and Afloat* (George G Harrap and Co, 1939).

Kinvig, C, *Churchill's Crusade* (Hambledon Continuum, 2006).

Lake, D, *The Zeebrugge and Ostend Raids 1918* (Barnsley: Pen and Sword Military, 2015).

Lee, J, *The Warlords* (Weidenfeld and Nicholson, 1919).

Lieven, D, *Towards The Flame* (Penguin, 2016).

Ludendorff, E, *Ludendorff's Own Story* vol II (Harper and Bros, 1919).

Marder, A, *From the Dreadnought to Scapa Flow*, vol II (Oxford: Oxford University Press, 1965).

_____, *Fear God and Dread Nought*, vol III (Jonathan Cape, 1959).

Massie, R, *Dreadnought; Britain, Germany and the Coming of the Great War* (Jonathan Cape, 1991).

Murray, D, *Herring Tales* (Bloomsbury, 2016).

Norwich, J, *France* (John Murray, 2018).

Oglander-Aspinall, C, *Roger Keyes* (The Hogarth Press, 1951).

Orwell, G, *The Road to Wigan Pier* (Penguin, 1989: first published 1937).

Roskill, S, *Naval Policy Between the Wars* (Barnsley: Seaforth Publishing, 2016: originally published 1968).

_____, *Hankey, Man of Secrets* vol 1 (Collins, 1970) and vol 2 (Collins, 1972).

_____, *Earl Beatty* (Collins, 1980).

Smele, J, *The 'Russian' Civil Wars* (C Hurst & Co, 2016).

Smith, H, *A Yellow Admiral Remembers* (Edward Arnold, 1932).

Smith, P, *Into the Minefields* (Barnsley: Pen and Sword Maritime, 2005).

Somervell, D, *British Politics Since 1900* (Andrew Dakers Limited, 1953).

Spinney, L, *Pale Rider* (Jonathan Cape, 2017).

Taffrail, *Endless Story*, Hodder and Stoughton (1938).

Taylor, B, *End of Glory* (Barnsley: Seaforth Publishing 2012).

Tuchman, B, *The Guns of August* (New York: Macmillan, 1962).

Ullman, R, *Britain and the Russian Civil War* (Princeton, New Jersey: Princeton University Press 1968).

Webb, S, *1919; Britain's Year of Revolution* (Barnsley: Pen and Sword, 2016).

Wemyss, V, *The Life and Letters of Lord Wester Wemyss* (Eyre and Spottiswoode, 1935).

Wilson, B, *Empire of the Deep* (W&N, 2013).

Newspapers and Magazines

Baltic Times.
Daily Mail.
Daily Telegraph.
Hull Daily Mail.
Manchester Guardian.
New York Times.
Sunday Times.
The Spectator.
The Times.

Other Sources

The Office of the Historian, US State Department.
Annual Report of the Torpedo School, 1917–18.

Index

Latvian Riflemen 32

Law, (Andrew) Bonar 43, 65, 66, 86, 87, 88, 210

League of Nations 70, 169, 254

Lees, Charles Cunningham Dumville 163

Lembit 62, 101

Lenin, Vladimir 11, 12, 23, 24, 28–9, 31n, 34, 35, 36, 240n, 241, 252, 267, 268

Lennuk 62, 96

Libau (Liepāja) 31, 35, 41, 46–7, 52, 54, 57, 63, 69, 76, 77–80, 81, 84, 86, 91–2, 93, 96, 124, 128, 135, 172, 181, 191–5, 232, 233, 238

Liebknecht, Karl 83

Lieven, Anatol von, Prince 128

Lieven, Dominic 20

Light Cruiser Squadrons: 1st 79; 2nd 91, 106; 4th 201; 6th 39–40, 44, 47, 48–53

Lilac, HMS 133, 134

Lingfield, HMS 232

Lithuania 17, 26, 30, 32, 83, 168–9, 179, 191

Little, Charles 92

Litvinov, Maxim 231, 272–3

Liven, Anatolii Pavlovich 176

Liverpool 219

Livonia 21, 35

Lloyd George, David 12nn, 26, 38, 65, 66, 68, 69, 70, 89–90, 123, 179, 210, 222, 223, 230, 247–8, 254, 255, 272–3; and Churchill 66, 71, 72, 222–3, 224–5, 227–8, 252; and withdrawal of Baltic force 227–9

Lodge, Henry Cabot 254n

Lodge, William Oliver 99

London mutinies 208

Long, Henry John 51

Long, Walter Hume 66, 70, 86, 87, 89, 121, 123, 141–2, 210, 213–14, 218, 227, 248, 251, 257

Lowe, George W 186

Ludendorff, Erich 22, 26, 29, 83, 250

Lupin, HMS 133, 134

Lvov, Georgy 23

MacBean, Russell 149, 171, 271

Macdonald, Henry Crawford 134

MacDonald, Ramsey 241n

Macdonogh, Sir George Mark Watson 31

Mackay, HMS 170

Mackworth, Sir Arthur William, 6th Bt 129

Mackworth, Geoffrey 57, 90, 98–9, 129, 215, 216, 236, 260

Maclean, Colin Kenneth 164–5

MacLean, Hector Forbes 151

MacMechan, Edith 263

Macnamara, Thomas James 121

Madden, Sir Charles 154, 164, 185, 201, 251

Maidment, Henry David 203

Maidstone, HMS 235

mail 201

Majestic, HMS 106

Manchester Guardian 219

Mander, A E 212

Mannerheim, Carl Gustaf Emil, Baron 99, 104, 153, 173

Mao Zedong 252

Marder, Arthur 74

Marne 180

Marshall, Richard Nigel Onslow 115, 119, 150, 156, 157

Marten, Arthur 185, 186, 187–8, 189, 205

Marx, Karl 253

Maud of Norway 90

McCowen, Gerald R 187

McCutcheon, James 165

McKenna, Reginal 255–6

Mécanicien Principal Lestin 106–7, 181

Miles, Arthur 161

Milner, Alfred, 1st Viscount 26, 37, 38

Milner-White, Eric 56

minelayers: RN 44–5, 52, 129–30, 161–2, 171; Russian minelaying destroyers 170

mines 44, 102, 110, 116, 128–34, 141, 159, 160, 166, 170, 171, 174, 196–7; in Baltic Sea entrance and exit points 22, 42; and *Cassandra*'s sinking 48–50; in Danish waters 40; German minefields 22, 40, 42; Great Belt fields 42; Little Belt fields 42; in North Sea 44; and *Verulam*'s sinking 163–4

minesweepers 44, 46, 130–4, 159–60, 166, 199–200, 217, 232, 235, 249

Mitau (Jelgava) 82, 86, 183, 191; Nikolai cemetery 242–3

Mixol, RFA 193

Molotov-Ribbentrop Pact (1939) 240

Montcalm 179

Moore, Henry Charles Makeum 215–16

Moreton, John Alfred 171, 193

Morgan, Charles 144

Morley, Norman Eyre 156n, 271

Moscow 31, 239

Motor Launches (MLs) 107–8, 159, 217, 232, 235; *ML-98* 235; *ML-124* 235; *ML-125* 235; *ML-156* 233

Mukden, Battle of 19

Murmansk 12, 38n, 171

Murray, Donald 255

mutinies in British armed forces 207–10; in Baltic campaign 12, 211–19, 258

Myrtle, HMS 133–4